School's Choice

How Charter Schools Control Access and Shape Enrollment

Wagma Mommandi
Kevin Welner

TEACHERS COLLEGE PRESS

TEACHERS COLLEGE | COLUMBIA UNIVERSITY
NEW YORK AND LONDON

Published by Teachers College Press,® 1234 Amsterdam Avenue, New York, NY 10027

Library of Congress Cataloging-in-Publication Data

Names: Mommandi, Wagma, author. | Welner, Kevin Grant, 1963– author.
Title: School's choice : how charter schools control access and shape enrollment / Wagma Mommandi, Kevin Welner.
Description: New York, NY : Teachers College Press, 2021. | Includes bibliographical references and index.
Identifiers: LCCN 2021012553 (print) | LCCN 2021012554 (ebook) | ISBN 9780807765821 (hardcover) | ISBN 9780807765814 (paperback) | ISBN 9780807779804 (ebook)
Subjects: LCSH: Charter school enrollment—United States. | Charter schools—United States—Admission. | Discrimination in education—United States. | School discipline—United States. | Student expulsion—United States.
Classification: LCC LB2806.36 .M66 2021 (print) | LCC LB2806.36 (ebook) | DDC 371.050973—dc23
LC record available at https://lccn.loc.gov/2021012553
LC ebook record available at https://lccn.loc.gov/2021012554

ISBN 978-0-8077-6581-4 (paper)
ISBN 978-0-8077-6582-1 (hardcover)
ISBN 978-0-8077-7980-4 (ebook)

Printed on acid-free paper
Manufactured in the United States of America

Contents

Contents

CHAPTER 1

Introduction

For over 25 years, starting in the early 1990s, charter schools garnered wide support from influential policymakers of both major political parties and from a variety of powerful private funders. The remarkable growth of charter schools benefited enormously from the policy's bipartisan appeal, and broad support among policymakers largely insulated charters from tough questions about issues like access. Yet, as explored in this book, student enrollment processes in large school districts throughout the United States have undergone a seismic shift, with corresponding implications for access to learning opportunities, and it is past time that those access issues received serious consideration.

Beginning with Minnesota in 1991, states began to enact laws to allow for the establishment of charter schools. Today, such enabling legislation has passed in 45 states plus the District of Columbia. In 2020 there were 7,500 charter schools serving 3.3 million children across the country—about 6% of all elementary and secondary students in the United States (National Alliance for Public Charter Schools, 2020). Charters are publicly funded, but operate privately, independent of the local school boards and superintendents who govern traditional public schools (National Charter School Resource Center, n.d.).

Originally conceived to be small, teacher-run laboratories of innovation, charter schools were often seen by early advocates as having strong potential to experiment with new ways of reaching those students that large comprehensive public schools were not serving well (Kolderie, 1990; Nathan, 1996a; Pedroni, 2007). Additionally, many early advocates argued that giving control over schools to local stakeholders would restore the democratic function of schools (Lubienski & Weitzel, 2010).

From the start, promises of accessibility and equity were a common refrain within the charter movement. Supporters of expanded school choice policies have long argued that the policies would help families whose incomes are below poverty thresholds, particularly families of color with lower incomes, who face daunting barriers to accessing the best opportunities to learn (Nathan, 1996b). Because of unjust linkages between community wealth and school resources, poorer families rarely have meaningful access to well-resourced neighborhood schools or to elite private schools

(Hiatt, 2017). Charter schools were touted by many policymakers in large part because of their promise to give lower income communities of color greater access to rich opportunities to learn within a redefined and expanded public school sector.

Yet since their inception charter schools have been mired in a debate about their actual publicness (e.g., Lubienski, 2001; Miron, 2008; Miron & Nelson, 2002). Like conventional public schools, charter schools are publicly funded through a combination of local, state, and federal tax dollars, and, like conventional public schools, charters are subject to various federal regulations (Baker, 2012a). For example, charters must adhere to regulations regarding the education of students with disabilities, including the Individuals with Disabilities Education Act (IDEA) and the Americans with Disabilities Act (ADA) (U.S. Department of Education, 2016). Although the specific provisions of legislation creating the legal structure for charter schools vary from state to state, charters are never exempted from all of a state's laws and regulations; antidiscrimination and safety provisions, for example, generally remain in place (Wixom, 2018). However, when it comes to authorization, governance, management, employment, transparency, accountability, and accessibility, charters in many states operate more like private entities (Miron et al., 2015). For example, depending on a given state's laws, charter schools can be authorized, governed, and managed by private groups and organizations (Baker, 2012a).

The success or failure of charter school policies has been measured in a variety of different ways. Most often, we hear of achievement comparisons between charter school students and traditional public school students (e.g., Betts & Tang, 2014; Center for Research on Education Outcomes [CREDO], 2013; Clark et al., 2015), or we hear of the enrollment growth of the sector (e.g., Ladd et al., 2017; National Alliance for Public Charter Schools, 2017; Stein, 2018). We may also hear of good-governance issues such as transparency, accountability, and corruption (e.g., Colton, 2017; Green et al., 2015; Noguera, 2015). Other issues include competition effects on other schools (e.g., Imberman, 2011; Winters, 2012), fiscal impact on public budgets (e.g., Bifulco & Reback, 2014; Ladd & Singleton, 2018; Lafer, 2018), and innovation (e.g., Preston et al., 2012).

Perhaps most importantly, charters have been plagued by issues of segregation and sorting. A long line of research, across many contexts, describes an increase in various forms of school-level stratification associated with charter school proliferation (Roda & Wells, 2012). (For example, see Bifulco et al., 2009 [racial segregation in North Carolina]; Booker et al., 2005 [peer composition in California and Texas]; Cobb & Glass, 1999 [ethnic segregation in Arizona]; Ertas & Roch, 2014 [education management organizations and enrollment of students in poverty]; Frankenberg et al., 2011 [segregation by race and class]; Lacireno-Paquet et al., 2002 [stratification of high-need populations, particularly students with language or special education needs]; Mickelson et al., 2008 [segregation by race, class, and achievement]; and Miron et al., 2011 [low enrollment of students with more severe disabilities].)

A 2021 study documents a strong pattern of increasing racial and ethnic segregation in charter schools. Danielle Jarvie (2021) used the NCES Common Core of Data's State Nonfiscal Public Elementary/Secondary Education Survey to compare data from 2010 and 2019, looking across the five states with the most students enrolled in charter schools: California, Texas, Florida, New York, and Illinois. She separately grouped schools that enrolled at least 50% non-White, 90% non-White, and 99% non-White, and she found—with very few exceptions—that charters were more segregated than district-run public schools and that these segregation patterns were worsening. Most starkly, in Texas, 57.2% of charters are "apartheid charter schools," meaning that they are at least 99% non-White—up from 14.3% 9 years earlier.

In part, these patterns of segregation are explained by self-sorting (Brewer & Lubienski, 2017; Hatfield & Malkus, 2017). Research exploring the so-called demand side of school choice examines how parents and families choose schools, to understand why choice policies may be leading to increased segregation (e.g., Goldring & Phillips, 2008; Schneider & Bulkley, 2002; Schneider et al., 2000; Sinkkink & Emerson, 2007; Weiher & Tedin, 2002). Yet the choices parents make take place within a context that is also shaped by so-called supply-side structures that create and deny opportunities. And decisions and pressures attached to supply and demand interact with one another.

While our focus is primarily on the supply side of school choice, we also highlight these interactions. For example, although studies documenting patterns of segregation and focusing on parental choice do not directly address the motives, mechanisms, or reasons for various types of segregation in charter schools, they do indirectly help raise questions about the potential roadblocks particular families face to *accessing* certain schools of choice. In addition, they inform questions and answers about why some students may be more sought after by charter schools.

THE ISSUE OF ACCESS

The initial hope that the growth of charter schools would result overall in higher quality options for families of color, particularly those whose incomes are near or below poverty thresholds, has never been fulfilled. To the extent that we can accurately measure such things, charter schools have not, on average, shown meaningfully better results than the subset of presumably problematic public schools that charter school families have left behind. Charter schools, like public schools and private schools, show a range of outcomes. Some charters do indeed have the resources and practices to narrow opportunity gaps. These are places that benefit students—they are schools that families wisely attempt to access. Other charter schools appear to provide very limited opportunities to learn, and the choice to attend such schools appears to result in academic harm. Yet, while issues of quality and access are interlinked, in the sense that some may not see access to a poor-quality charter school as an issue of equity, there is also a broader principle at stake: As publicly funded schools, charters should not impede or deny access to any subsections of their communities.

In this book, we largely set aside the issues of quality that have long dominated the charter school research domain, and we focus instead on issues of access. We define equitable access as having equal opportunity to attend a given school. This incorporates two factors: knowledge and barriers. It means that families know what charter school options exist and have the reasonable ability to enroll and attend if they want to, regardless of where the student lives, the student's socioeconomic status, language abilities, special education needs, and so forth. (Note here that residency requirements have long erected access barriers to public schools in a nonchoice context, as discussed in Chapter 2.)

Importantly, as also discussed in Chapter 2, access issues have implications for most or all of the researched factors mentioned earlier: achievement, enrollment growth, transparency, accountability, corruption, competition effects, fiscal impact, innovation, and stratification and segregation. Whether a student can choose to enroll in a charter school fundamentally depends on access. We cannot fully understand issues like achievement comparisons or enrollment growth or stratification without first understanding access. Access issues also lie at the heart of the much-contested debate about the "publicness" of charter schools. In short, access is the cornerstone of understanding charter schools and of determining their value within the U.S. schooling system.

Today, charter schools exist within choice ecosystems shaped in part by incentives and disincentives that, in turn, shape schools' approaches to access. Given that different students come with different financial costs, test scores and behavior, they are differentially attractive as potential enrollees. To survive and to thrive, charter schools must compete; they are successful when they enroll a sufficient number of students and when those students' outcomes and resource needs allow the school to attract a new group of students each year. Success for a charter school depends on an ongoing public perception of success within a test-based accountability system. This creates strong incentives to attract and enroll students with high test scores, fluency in English, no special needs, and behaviors that align with school philosophy. It is within this context of incentives and disincentives that a subset of charter schools has emerged with practices that limit their accessibility (Lubienski & Weitzel, 2010; Mommandi & Welner, 2018).

Because charter schools are state-level statutory creations, and because each state's charter school statute is unique, the rules governing charter schools vary from state to state. This impacts key factors such as who authorizes charter schools, who holds charters (and authorizers) accountable—and to what degree—for various outcomes, and whether charters face any constraints around the access-limiting practices described in this book. In fact, many of the access patterns that we cover in upcoming chapters arise in part because of differing and often inadequate charter laws across the 46 different sets of governing statutes. In the final chapter of this book, we revisit this issue in the context of considering how states and authorizers can address access-related inequities that arise in the charter sector.

A FRAMEWORK FOR UNDERSTANDING ACCESS

The practices described in this book arose in the context of a consequential ecosystem within which charter schools are created and within which they seek to survive and eventually thrive. The forces that shape this ecosystem are often nuanced and sometimes even contradictory. But one set of features is particularly important for those of us trying to understand charter school access issues: features related to differential power, privilege, and efficaciousness of children and their guardians, as well as the perceived value and desirability of those children as potential enrollees.

Distinct stratification marks almost every relevant element of the ecosystem. Individuals and their families have different levels and types of income, wealth, and formal education. Families, often along the lines of race and class, have differently valued forms of cultural capital and are a part of different social networks (Horvat et al., 2003; Lareau, 1987). These differences translate into differential opportunities for students and in different schools in different communities (Berliner, 2009; Darling-Hammond, 2013; 2015; Reardon, 2011). The consequence of differential opportunities and treatment is felt early, when children begin kindergarten and first grade (Ferrer et al., 2015). As we will see, another important difference involves the fiscal price tag for educating students who need more support in school.

In the following sections, we introduce the three main concepts that make up our framework for understanding access issues within this consequential ecosystem or stratified context—a framework that we return to in Chapter 16. This framework helps build an understanding of the incentives and disincentives of choice systems that facilitate opportunity hoarding by an area's most efficacious parents, thereby contributing to a system of effectively maintained inequality. In doing so, the framework helps contextualize and make sense of the charter school practices described in the chapters ahead.

Incentives

Consider the set of incentives and disincentives that typically surrounds a team of people planning a new charter school. By incentives, we do not simply mean the desire to create a good school—which would have plenty of direct and indirect benefits. Rather, we mean the specific market incentives that free market theorists suppose will drive the behavior of people as rational beings (Landsburg, 1995). As a rule, success for a charter school operator in a competitive market will depend on enrolling students who are lower cost and higher achieving.

Yet as a society we want those collective incentives to encourage, if not demand, that this new school strive to use best practices to serve either (1) a cross-section of the community or (2) the most vulnerable and otherwise poorly served students within the community. The evidence in this book suggests that some charter schools do exactly this—but that many others do quite the opposite, detrimentally responding to the incentives to enroll students who do not require additional services and students who are high achieving on standardized tests. In fact, when we look at the incentives facing people planning a new charter school, we can easily see how the movement has become distorted to prioritize growth (and frequently profit) and to become a tool for more elite parents to gain further advantages.

In Chapter 16, we elaborate on the issue of incentives, building on ideas and theory that Professor Chris Lubienski and his colleagues have developed in a series of articles (Lubienski, 2005, 2007; Lubienski et al., 2009). In particular, we examine the practices described throughout this book to tease out the ways charter school operators are placing their thumb on the scale in order to secure not just students, but also the *right* students.

Opportunity Hoarding

The distortion of the charter school ideal that arises because of supply-side incentives is further exacerbated by inequalities on the demand side. Opportunities to learn in the United States are overwhelmingly determined by children's parents or guardians (Carter & Welner, 2013). The United States has failed to provide all families with meaningful economic and educational opportunities. Because of a sociopolitical history driven largely by racism and White supremacy, that failure has been disproportionately felt by families who are Black and Brown. Because of this, Black and Brown families have been undermined in their attempts to thrive in an American system of education that requires a significant level of wealth and social and cultural capital to succeed in K–12 public schools. If parents face job, food, and housing insecurity, then their children face these same issues. If parents cannot afford educational materials in their homes or cannot afford to live in a community with rich opportunities after school and over the summer, then children are denied those resources and opportunities. Wealthier parents with more social capital are able to use their wealth and social capital to procure learning opportunities and manipulate the educational system on behalf of their children. These advantages and disadvantages are passed along from parents to children. Poverty and affluence are very sticky from generation to generation in the United States (Chetty et al., 2014).

Sociologist Amy Stuart Wells and her colleagues (Wells & Serna, 1996; Yonezawa et al., 2002) have documented how the choice elements of ability grouping systems, where students are assigned to classes based on perceived ability or achievement, reinforce existing distributions of power and resources (see also Lewis & Diamond, 2015). They show how parents with high levels of social capital see higher track courses as scarce resources and block de-tracking reforms in order to maintain their privilege and advantage. This is part of a phenomenon that Charles Tilly (1998) describes as *opportunity hoarding*—the effort of some to monopolize access to valuable resources, precluding others from the benefits of resource access and accrual. Just as with ability grouping systems, school choice systems are seen by parents as offering a limited capacity for enrollment, with some of those enrollment opportunities seen as more valuable. Within that stratified marketplace, more elite parents are able to exercise their influence and hoard opportunities for their own children.

Because the United States is not a strong welfare state, policymakers and others look to schools to play the role that Horace Mann (1848) described as the "great equalizer" or the "balance wheel" of our society. To do so, schools must provide opportunities to learn and corresponding educational supports that somehow compensate for the larger societal inequalities. This means, among other things, that the educational system needs to target extraordinary opportunities toward children whose outside-school opportunities are structurally circumscribed. That is, formal schooling opportunities must act as a counter force to inequalities imposed by society on marginalized subgroups of parents and guardians.

This insight highlights a major potential drawback of systems that assign students to schools based on "parental choice." An unregulated system that allocates the most desirable formal schooling opportunities to children with the strongest and most efficacious parental advocates unavoidably creates a rich-get-richer, poor-get-poorer dynamic. The examples in this book concretely illustrate the many ways that this opportunity hoarding has happened through charter schools. We return to this discussion in Chapter 16, drawing in particular on Charles Tilly's (1998) idea of opportunity hoarding, as well as Samuel Lucas's related idea of effectively maintained inequality (introduced in the following subsection). These theorists help us understand how those with advantage create systems that protect their advantages and pass those advantages along to their children—correspondingly walling off others from making gains.

Effectively Maintained Inequality

According to Lucas (2001), "[S]ocioeconomically advantaged actors secure for themselves and their children some degree of advantage wherever advantages are commonly possible" (p. 1652). If policymakers successfully close off one avenue of maintaining advantage, these actors (e.g., parents) will seek out another avenue. The charter school access practices described in this book easily fit within Lucas's framework, which explains how resource differences and behavioral patterns allow inequality to emerge and continue. Charter schools, and the access issues we focus on in this book, are best understood as part of a larger inequitable system. If we hope to improve access to educational opportunities—in charter schools and elsewhere in the system—we will have to deliberately create mechanisms that challenge existing inequalities; reliance on market distribution of opportunities will do the opposite.

As authors, we have tried not to be naïve about the challenges of reforming this system. While we include counter examples in each chapter that highlight charter schools that have recognized and addressed access issues, we know that these counter examples emerged in spite of perverse incentives and that these schools may very well pay a high price for those equity-oriented decisions. We also know that policymakers in most states have shown little appetite for legislatively addressing access limitations concerning charter schools. Many policymakers of both political parties have strong connections to charter school advocacy groups that vehemently push back against regulatory proposals (Blume, 2015; Pelto, 2015; Warner, 2016). Reform will require political will that has thus far been lacking.

We also understand that parents seek opportunities for their children, and we are not here to offer moral judgment on parental behavior. We do, however, see parental behavior as a part of the ecosystem we described earlier—a part that must be understood and accounted for in any workable system. While some extraordinary parents will step back from this sort of opportunity seeking, as Nikole Hannah-Jones describes in *The New York Times Magazine*, we see no signs that this is a widespread phenomenon (Hannah-Jones, 2016). The more marketized our system, the more stratification we can expect.

METHODS

In an ideal research world, we would have designed a somewhat different study to examine the access-related practices charter schools use to shape their enrollment. We might, for example, have surveyed the leaders of a random sample or randomized, stratified sample of charter schools. The survey would ask the leaders to report their use of practices we are aware of, about any other access-restricting practices they have used, and about steps they have taken to avoid the access-restricting practices (or other steps to increase access). There is, of course, every reason to believe that such a survey—even if we somehow generated a strong response rate—would yield less-than-candid answers as well as a biased sample (with the worst offenders declining to respond).

Consequently, we designed a real-world study that would accomplish the important goal of identifying the types of access-shaping practices used in at least some charter schools, even if it could not support generalizable conclusions about the frequency of any given practice. To document how charter schools have shaped access, we combined expert interviews with a review of scholarly literature and a review of media coverage and key documents such as governmental reports, school websites, and parent handbooks. Each of these approaches is described next.

Interviews

We conducted a total of 40 phone interviews with charter school experts, using a semi-structured protocol. An initial round of purposeful sampling was followed by a round of snowball sampling (Maxwell, 2012). Our informants were primarily researchers (17), along with policy analysts and attorneys (11), parents (3), and officials and teachers in schools and districts (9). Six of the nine interviews with officials and teachers in schools and districts were charter school educators or administrators.

To help us identify information-rich examples and cases, the purposeful sampling primarily targeted education and law researchers who have a track record of publishing high-quality, peer-reviewed, and widely cited research on charter schools. During this initial round of interviews, we asked for recommendations of other people to talk with regarding charter school access policies and practices. The resulting second round of interviews brought in more perspectives of charter and district school educators and officials, policy analysts, and parents.

The semi-structured interview protocol asked interviewees about each of the three periods of charter school access that are covered in this book: (1) pre-enrollment, (2) the enrollment process itself, and (3) after enrollment. We probed for examples of access restrictions, then for examples of practices that were remedial or broadening. We also sought documentation of policies and practices (e.g., charter legislation, contracts, applications, parent and/or student handbooks, and reports), which helped us clarify statements and corroborate interviewees' claims.

Documents

We gathered online news articles on issues of charter access, using targeted searches in two full-text news databases: Newspaper Source Plus and ProQuest Newsstand (U.S. Newsstream). Each of these databases provides access to major and regional U.S. newspapers as well as television and radio transcripts. We supplemented these database searches with periodic searches of Google News.

Table 1.1. Search Terms for Database Inquiries

Dirty Dozen Category (Welner, 2013)	Examples of derived search terms
#1: Description and Design: Which Niche?	"niche," "mission," "description," "ethnocentric"
#2: Location, Location, Location	"location," "suburban," "transportation," "bus"
#3: Mad Men: The Power of Marketing and Advertising	"advertising," "marketing," "targeted advertising"
#4: Hooping It Up: Conditions Placed on Applications	"long applications," "application deadline," "common application," "application essay," "application requirements"
#5: As Long as You Don't Get Caught: Illegal and Dicey Practices	"volunteer hours," "illegal," "discipline records," "Social Security number," "birth certificate"
#6: Send Us Your Best: Conditions Placed on Enrollment	"admissions preference," "admission test," "discipline record"
#7: The Bum Steer	"steering"
#8: Not in Service	"special education," "English language learner," "low incidence," "high incidence"
#9: The Fitness Test: Counseling Out	"counsel out," "fit"
#10: Flunk or Leave: Grade Retention	"promotion," "retention," "summer school"
#11: Discipline and Punish	"expulsion," "suspension," "no excuses," "discipline"
#12: Going Mobile (or Not)	"backfill," "attrition"

The search terms we used (see Table 1.1) were derived from the taxonomy set forth in "The Dirty Dozen: How Charter Schools Influence Student Enrollment" (Welner, 2013). Search queries followed the same general format: "charter schools" AND "search term," covering the period between the years 2010 and 2019.

Throughout the book, we generally cite published (publicly available) reports, news articles, and other forms of documentation (e.g., school handbooks) supporting the information provided to us, or pointed out to us, by our interviewees, rather than referencing the interview itself or by itself.

Data Analysis

Before beginning data analysis, we culled the number of news articles significantly by skimming them and removing those that did not include specific access concerns or were duplicating coverage. After this process we had a final dataset consisting of 40 interviews, 216 news articles, 68 published reports, and 59 school- or district-authored documents.

We analyzed the body of data with a coding scheme primarily derived from charter practices outlined in "The Dirty Dozen" (Welner, 2013), following Altheide and Schnieder's (2012) approach to qualitative media analysis. These codes were as follows: location of the charter school, marketing/advertising practices, the description/design of the charter in written materials, conditions placed on applications, illegal practices, conditions placed on enrollment, steering away applicants, lacking services, counseling out students, grade retention, discipline, and student mobility. Two subcodes were added to each parent code to account for whether the practice was exclusionary (has the potential to reduce access) or nonexclusionary (increases access or addresses reduced access). This coding is illustrated by Table 1.2.

A Note on Methods

Our purposive/snowball sampling approach was necessitated by the reality that it would not be productive to ask a random sample of charter school leaders to tell us candidly about the ways they shape (and generally constrain) access. The resulting data set had both strengths and limitations. It allowed us to provide a rich picture of how access issues are playing out in charter schools around the country. Also, when certain practices appear to be more or less prevalent, as described by our interviewees, we included this information. However, our data do not allow for quantification or for a determination of how many charter schools use a given approach.

Table 1.2. Excerpt of Codebook with Examples

Code	Subcodes	Examples
Location	Exclusionary practice	Charter does not provide any transportation services
	Non-exclusionary/ corrective practice	Charter provides own transportation
		Charter partners with local school districts to provide transportation
Description/ design	Exclusionary practice	Charter school is designed for "gifted" students
	Non-exclusionary/ corrective practice	Charter school is intentionally diverse by design

As noted, we asked our informants about steps that they and others have taken to recognize and address access issues so that other schools and policymakers can learn from their experiences and ideas. Because charter school policies are best used as a tool that can further larger societal education objectives, the rules matter (Arsen et al., 1999). Some rules do a better job driving those larger objectives than others. Our research is designed to inform future ruling-making so that the charter school tool can be consistent with larger goals of expanding opportunities to learn.

CONCLUSION

This book[1] describes the pressures felt by charter schools to shape access and how they have responded—sometimes by resisting the pressures and sometimes by surrendering to them. To examine similar issues, Welner (2013) set forth "a taxonomy, a classification of the evidence into twelve different approaches that charter schools use to structure their student enrollment" (p. 2). He included practices that shaped "the likelihood of students enrolling with a given set of characteristics, be it higher (or lower) test scores, students with 'expensive' disabilities, English learners, students of color, or students in poverty" (p. 2). We use that same framework in this book, adding two additional approaches that we identified during the course of our research, but merging the contents of one of Welner's earlier categories ("Illegal and Dicey Practices") into the others.

Accordingly, after a brief discussion of the important role played by access issues in any meaningful understanding of charter schools (Chapter 2), the next 13 chapters present findings from our study of charter schools' access practices. This is followed by three final chapters, the first of which examines this evidence using our conceptual framework and the second of which highlights the examples set forth throughout the book of counter practices that increase access. The final chapter offers a set of policy recommendations. The 13 chapters in the main body of the book follow the chronological order of access—beginning with charter school decisions (such as location and advertising) that precede student applications, continuing to the initial interactions schools have with families during the application process, and ending with practices that can winnow or push out students who are already enrolled. As noted, we used this same sequential approach when discussing access issues with our interviewees.

The resulting 13 categories have considerable overlap. Students with special needs, for example, can face repeated obstacles. School design and marketing may exclude; conditions may be placed on enrollment applications that signal exclusion; parents may be steered away during enrollment, in part by explaining that the school has few resources or services the child needs; after enrollment, students may be counseled out or told that if they remain they will be retained in grade; and discipline may be extreme and burdensome. Practices such as application conditions can impact access during the pre-enrollment stage (by signaling and discouraging) and during enrollment (by directly excluding). In recognition of these overlaps, we include and discuss any given example in the category we think it best fits, but we acknowledge that others may see the example as better illustrating a different practice (or multiple practices).

We also acknowledge that school choice and access-related practices incentivized by choice are not limited to charter schools. Public school choice in America also exists in the form of district magnet schools and intra-/inter-district choice policies. Some of the access-related concerns we bring up in this book directly apply to these choice mechanisms as well. School choice also includes various schemes that funnel public funds into private hands, including voucher programs, education savings accounts (ESAs), tax credit scholarship programs (which Welner [2008] refers to as "neovouchers"), as well as individual tax credits and deductions. Again, some of the access-related concerns we bring up in this book directly apply to these private school choice mechanisms.

These additional types of school choice have significant and troubling access-related implications, but we choose to focus this book on charter schools' access-restricting practices (and their implications) for several reasons. First, access issues around private school choice are complicated by the private ownership and (usually) religious freedom interests of the schools' operators. Second, because of their autonomy charter schools have greater ability to engage in many of the access-constraining behaviors described in this book, as compared to magnets and other public schools operating in choice systems. Charter schools have also rapidly grown, in terms of number of schools and number of enrolled students, over the past 3 decades. And charters are more impacted by, and vulnerable to, the incentives and disincentives that we describe. As a result of their autonomy, their growth, and the competitive pressures that they feel, charter schools appear to be exacerbating many existing access-constraining practices—as well as adding new ones.

One final note: We give relatively little attention to full-time virtual schools, which enroll about 8% of all charter school students. These schools present their own set of access challenges, primarily around internet connectivity and assistance to often needed learning resources beyond those provided by the cyber charter (e.g., tutors and other helpful adults). Researchers have also noted a Matthew effect—the rich get richer, and the poor get poorer (Dynarski, 2017). Students who are academically prepared and successful, with strong supports and/or strong executive functioning, do fine, while those who are academically behind fall further behind. But more importantly, the overall outcomes for cyber charters are horrendous, with very low graduation rates and test scores (Molnar et al., 2019), which complicates access arguments. How does one argue for greater access to harm? For that reason, and because these schools make up a relatively small and unique niche of the charter sector, our discussion of cyber charter access is minimal.

CHAPTER 2

The Centrality of Access

Policy debates about charter schools have been heated in recent years, inflamed by disputes around everything from whether charter schools are public to whether they advance civil rights, to whether they outperform or underperform neighborhood schools, to whether they impose fiscal harms on nearby school districts. These confrontations often implicate issues of access. In fact, virtually every major charter school issue is connected to the issue of access and cannot be fully understood or studied without accounting for access (see Figure 2.1). Yet access issues are rarely brought into these other debates. Next, we illustrate the centrality of access by briefly considering four of these elements: publicness, funding and finance, segregation and stratification, and measured outcomes.

PUBLICNESS

Advocates for charter schools insist that the schools are part of the public school system, and they consistently add the word *public* as a modifier.

Figure 2.1. Charter school issues and access.

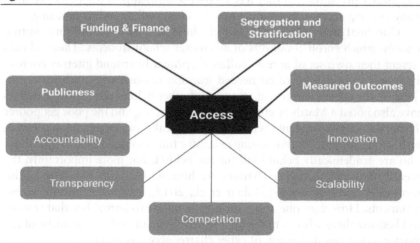

Accordingly, the most prominent charter school organization is called the National Alliance for Public Charter Schools, and the enabling legislation adopted by states to allow for the creation of charter schools invariably includes wording to the effect that the charters are, for example, "part of the public school system of this state" (Texas Education Code, Sec. 12.105). Meanwhile, critics of charter schools insist that "[c]harter schools are in reality, privately run academies funded by the taxpayer" (Network for Public Education, 2017, p. 37).

The actual legal status of charter schools straddles public and private. Courts, usually at the request of charter schools themselves, often apply the legal rules and constructs governing private, not public, entities to charters (Biegel et al., 2019; Miron et al., 2015). Beyond legalities, we find additional evidence of the dual nature of charters. On the public side, we note that they are publicly funded, and they provide a no-tuition education. They also remain subject to many public safety laws as well as laws designed to protect students from discrimination. Decisions to authorize and renew charter schools are primarily—although far from exclusively—made by publicly elected school boards.

On the nonpublic side, the day-to-day and long-term operating decisions are made by private actors who are accountable to their private boards. Private corporations provide services, often own the school building and land, and hire teachers and other employees. Deliberations are generally not conducted pursuant to the same transparency requirements that school districts are held to. Salaries and profit-taking decisions are generally made behind these closed doors.

Consider the role of access in this publicness debate. Private schools, with few limitations, can decide which students to enroll and which to disenroll. In fact, most of the troubling access practices discussed throughout this book are presumptively fine when used in private schools. In short, parents have no right to expect that their children be given access to a private school. (This assertion is admittedly complicated by situations where private schools accept public funding through voucher and voucher-like systems, since taxpayers might reasonably expect that access follows such funding.)

Public schools, on the other hand, bring with them a mixed history of access and denied access. Racism and racial discrimination has resulted in exclusion from opportunities throughout most of the country's history (Carter & Welner, 2013). Even today, a student living outside a school's catchment area typically has no right to access that school—absent open-enrollment policies, which often raise their own access issues (Rowe & Lubienski, 2017). Further, a small number of public schools, including some magnet schools, still erect academic and other barriers to admission (Orfield, 2018; Phillippo, 2019). Most public schools, at the secondary level at least, erect academic barriers to higher-level classes (Oakes, 2005; Welner, 2001). And many public schools still use exclusionary discipline and other push-out policies (Losen & Gillespie, 2012). These are ongoing access issues that supporters of public schools should never gloss over.

Within this flawed context, however, we expect that public schools today embrace the basic promise that every child will be enrolled in one of the district's schools. As a rule, a family can enroll its children in the neighborhood public school, with no questions asked and no access barriers to clear. It is that context against which we must consider the charter school practices described in this book. Charters are relatively accessible when compared to private schools, and they are relatively inaccessible when compared with district-run public schools. More to the point, when charters deny access, they are playing by the rules of private schools; when they open access, they embrace the ideal we expect from public schools.

FUNDING AND FINANCE

Proponents of charter school expansion have claimed that these schools are a bargain, generating better outcomes while receiving less funding (DeAngelis et al., 2018). These claims are problematic for a wide range of reasons, including the basic outcome claims (Vasquez Heilig, 2018). But one key element of any solid analysis of the funding claims concerns access. Consider in particular students with special needs—a group denied access by many of the practices described in this book. Most obviously, a charter school should receive less funding if it enrolls fewer students with special needs. But just as importantly, a charter school should receive relatively less funding if it enrolls lower cost students with special needs—for instance, fewer children with autism and more with speech and language disabilities and specific learning disabilities. (See Baker and Weber [2017] for concrete examples in Newark, New Jersey.) When the state's finance formula does not account for such differences, it can greatly advantage charter schools that game the system by limiting access, while greatly disadvantaging local public school districts, as has been the case in Pennsylvania (Baker, 2012b).

Similar issues arise with regard to the other access-shaping practices we document throughout the book. If a charter school enrolls fewer students who are emergent bilinguals[1] (not yet proficient in English), staffing needs will likely be less than in the surrounding public school district. If a charter school disproportionately serves students who are more academically prepared, with richer opportunities to learn outside of school, it will have a decreased need for intensive intervention resources. Moreover, the nuances again are important; in a disinvested community with a high concentration of residents living in poverty, a charter school is relatively advantaged if it serves students at 130% of the poverty level but largely avoids students below the poverty level or who are dealing with homelessness. Funding needs are implicated by the access issues that drive any of these types of bias in enrollment.

SEGREGATION AND STRATIFICATION

A key demand-side rationale for school choice policies is that families with different approaches to schooling can find their niche. A charter school with a Montessori approach will appeal to different families than a charter adopting a strict discipline approach. In theory, this is a beneficial type of sorting that results in more students learning in environments that personally appeal and resonate—and we do not doubt that this advantageous matching of family to school is occurring.

But the marketplace is unequal, and charter schools themselves often shape their own student bodies. As documented throughout this book, charter schools exercise control over access at every stage of the enrollment (and post-enrollment) process. Accordingly, sorting decisions stray far from seemingly neutral, "I love aviation and my neighbor loves architecture," matching of interests. Instead, the enrollment decisions made within our current choice system are inextricably tied to larger societal inequalities linked to wealth and poverty, to race and ethnicity, to parental education, to first language, and to special education. The resulting differential access yields well-documented segregation and stratification, and notwithstanding the contentions of choice advocates like Michael Petrilli (2014), this sorting is not benign. It is part of a harmful cycle that amplifies inequalities facing the least advantaged in any given community.

MEASURED OUTCOMES

Researchers face daunting threats to validity when they attempt to measure the student outcomes of school choice policies. There are two main types of charter school outcome studies: those using lotteries that separate students offered admission to charters from those denied such admission, and those using panel data of student records over multiple years, with student-level identifiers linked to outcomes, demographics, and other fields.[2] Each of these two approaches comes with strengths and weaknesses.

Studies that take advantage of overenrollment lotteries yield results with stronger internal validity but questionable external validity. For example, most charter schools in the Boston area are in unusually high demand, so schools use lotteries to determine who is offered admission. This generates a random assignment of students in the "intent to treat" and "control" categories. While these categories become muddied or lose some policy relevance because of students who either (1) decline the offer, (2) later leave the charter school, or (3) respond to losing the lottery by enrolling in a different charter school (or a private or homeschool or public school outside the area of the specified counterfactual), such studies generally allow for well-grounded causal inferences about the outcomes of those particular overenrolled charter schools (Tuttle et al., 2012). These studies, however, are not generalizable to charter schools (in Boston and elsewhere) that are not overenrolled, which are presumably of lesser quality. In fact, these studies may also not tell us much about how well these schools would do with the population of students whose families did not participate in the choice process (i.e., did not apply for admission in the first place).

On the other hand, studies using longitudinal data sets to measure charter school outcomes have stronger claims to external validity but are undermined by internal validity problems. These studies use ordinary least squares regression or matching (propensity score or "virtual twin") approaches to generate models that compare charter school students to a group of students enrolled in local public schools. The models use panel data with fields such as prior test scores, race and ethnicity, and eligibility for free or reduced-price lunch. By controlling for these measured differences, the studies attempt to isolate the impact of the charter school "treatment." While this approach is more generalizable to the broader population, it is particularly susceptible to omitted variables linked to the core reality that students are not randomly assigned to charters and noncharters. The parent or guardian of a student enrolled in a charter school has, by definition, actively opted into the choice process. In contrast, we can think of the group of comparison students as including two subgroups: (1) all of those students with parents or guardians who did not engage with the choice process because they lack the time, resources, or social capital to engage; and (2) students with parents or guardians who have the time, resources, or social capital yet have nonetheless eschewed the charter school option because they actively decided against it. This second subgroup houses the most appropriate (yet imperfect) comparison students, but they cannot be separated from the first. And researchers cannot fully account for the differences by merely controlling for factors like prior test scores, race and ethnicity, and eligibility for free or reduced-price lunch.

Access issues amplify these problems of nonrandom assignment because they can introduce systematic enrollment bias. This is most obvious for some "elite" charter management organizations (CMOs) that make no secret of their disinterest in students who lack the right "fit." But even subtler enrollment-shaping choices like location and advertising can result in systematic yet unmeasured differences between those families that apply for enrollment and those that do not.

Consider, then, the reporting about charter school studies, which often give readers definitive-sounding statements to the effect that charter school students are "faring worse" or are making "greater academic progress" than their public school counterparts (Hanna, 2019; Marbella, 2019). Typically, reporters make sweeping statements like this one from *The New York Times*: "Nationally, the schools perform about the same as traditional neighborhood schools. But charter schools that serve mostly low-income children of color in large cities tend to excel academically" (Green & Shapiro, 2019). While both parts of this statement do find support in the research, most readers could not know, for example, that the main support for the claim about charters serving "mostly low-income children of color in large cities" is found in those lottery-based studies with low external validity.

The most prevalent outcome studies are conducted by CREDO, which released seven state-level reports in 2019. For charter schools in South Carolina, Pennsylvania, and Ohio, the researchers found that the reading outcomes were indistinguishable from those of a group of matched noncharter students, but they found that the charter school results in math are slightly lower than those of noncharter students (Center for Research on Education Outcomes [CREDO], 2019a, 2019b, 2019c). For New Mexico and Washington state, the results of charters and noncharters were indistinguishable for both reading and math (CREDO, 2019d, 2019e). For Idaho, the researchers found similar gains in math but slightly strongly charter school gains in reading (CREDO, 2019f). Finally, in Maryland, the charter school results were slightly stronger for both reading and math (CREDO, 2019g).

In short, the seven 2019 CREDO studies yielded results very much in line with the overall body of charter school research: The test score outcomes for the two sectors are uncannily similar. But the CREDO researchers cannot control for unmeasured, omitted variables—the systematic enrollment biases linked to choice. Nor can they fully account for attrition and backfill-related biases. Therefore, we, as consumers of this research, cannot know, for any given study, the extent to which these data limitations are impacting the bottom-line findings. Small differences, the discussion of which is confused and amplified by CREDO's "days of learning" reporting metric (Maul, 2015), can emerge as a result of this omitted-variable bias or can be hidden by these same systematic biases. Such limitations become particularly salient when reading these studies with a full understanding of the charter school access issues discussed in the following chapters.

CHAPTER 3

Description and Design
Which Niche?

> The designers of a new charter school face a variety of decisions. Will the
> school portray itself as focused on rigorous academics? Or perhaps the
> design will cater to children with autism? Will it have the facilities to provide
> free or reduced-price lunch? Will it have teachers for English learners and
> for students with special needs? In short, which niche will it be designed to
> fill? (Welner, 2013, p. 2)

The description and design of a charter school send a strong message about
who is desired at that school. In a competitive market, charter schools survive and thrive by distinguishing themselves from other schools (for examples beyond those found in this chapter, see Mommandi & Welner, 2018).
Early decisions about the mission of a school can shape enrollment long
before a school opens its doors.

BACKGROUND BRIEFING

Charter schools' description and design may tailor applicant pools by specifying the students they seek to serve, with the potential effect of "choosing" prospective populations. Garcia (2008) analyzed the racial segregation
levels of what he called themed charter schools (e.g., Montessori or charter
schools designed for at-risk students) in Arizona. He found that students in
specialized or themed charter schools experienced more racial integration
than students in traditional public schools and that students in college preparatory elementary-level charter schools experienced more racial segregation than those in traditional public schools.

Eckes (2015) examined the legal and policy complexities involved
with students who self-select into "haven" charter schools. These charter
schools are generally grouped into three categories: (1) ability-focused charter schools (e.g., specials needs or highly gifted); (2) language- or culture-
focused charter schools (e.g., Hebrew or Afrocentric); and (3) gender- or

sexual-orientation-based charter schools (e.g., single-sex schools and schools designed to serve LGBTQ+ students).

Several articles note the growing number of charter schools that focus on serving a specific culture (Buchanan & Fox, 2003; Eckes & Carr, 2014; Fox et al., 2012; Minow, 2010). Relatedly, researchers have documented the growing number of Catholic schools across the country that closed down and then reopened as charter schools (Brinson, 2011; Decker & Carr, 2015; Horning, 2013). Other researchers have examined charter schools specifically designed to serve children with disabilities (Drame & Frattura, 2011; Mead, 2008; Miron et al. 2010) and gifted and talented students (Decker et al., 2010).

Charters with progressive education foci can also lead to an overrepresentation of advantaged groups (Carpenter, 2006; Wamba & Ascher, 2003). Brown and Makris (2018) described these progressive niche schools as "prestige schools," with a disproportionate number of advantaged families and an enrollment that is demographically distinct from local public schools.

FURTHER RESEARCH

As with most of the access issues discussed in this book, some design choices seem intended to push away undesirable students (e.g., schools designed for high-achieving students), while others seem intended merely to serve unique interests (e.g., military academies and language-immersion schools). While the latter design choices strike us as much less problematic—and arguably sometimes even beneficial—we include them for two reasons. First, our goal is to present a comprehensive picture, and these designs do indeed shape enrollment. Second, even they can take steps to broaden and increase access.

Academically Rigorous Schools

Charter schools that portray themselves as focused on rigorous academics or as catering to gifted students tend to enroll a more affluent—and more White—student body. BASIS schools in Arizona, which are all managed by a for-profit company, are consistently ranked in *Newsweek*'s "America's Most Challenging High Schools" list and on the Best High Schools list of *U.S. News & World Report*. BASIS schools are elite and college preparatory. They emphasize a very rigorous curriculum. BASIS uses "elite and international" messaging (Wilson & Carlsen, 2016), and students and parents who are not highly confident academically understand that these schools are not designed for them. In the 2019–2020 school year, BASIS enrolled 15,667 students in 22 schools; only 2.8% were students with disabilities and 1.7% of students were English learners (emergent bilinguals) (Arizona Department of Education, 2021). In 2013, a spokesperson for BASIS explained, "The schools are academically rigorous. Any kid can go, but these schools aren't going to be for every kid, just as Harvard or Princeton isn't for every kid" (Smith, 2013).

In 2017–2018, 57% of all Arizona public school students were eligible for free or reduced-price lunch (Arizona Department of Education, 2018); BASIS reported none. In fact, BASIS refuses to participate in a subsidized lunch program. BASIS also provides no transportation for students. Students who face food security concerns or who have no reliable transportation to the school site are very unlikely to opt into these charters.

Great Hearts Academies, another network of charter schools operating in Arizona, is also highly acclaimed for its students' test scores. But, as with BASIS, these outcomes appear to be the result of access barriers. In 2012, the Nashville school district denied a charter application from Great Hearts because of what one official described as "serious and persistent questions about their definitions of excellence, and reliance on selectivity and mission fit for success" (Smith, 2013).

Consider also the Academy for Advanced and Creative Learning charter school in Colorado Springs, which is designed and presented as a school for the gifted. The school's website tells prospective applicants that there are no entrance requirements; parents are asked to use their own judgment about whether the school is right for their children. But the website and the application materials stress repeatedly the unique qualities of gifted children and how "heartbreaking" it is for them to see their students "feel overwhelmed because they were in classrooms with content well above their needs" (Academy for Advanced and Creative Learning, 2018). These materials expressly send a dual message: We're a school that is open to our entire community, but please don't enroll here unless you are gifted.

The Academy for Advanced and Creative Learning appears to be a great deal more supportive and welcoming than the BASIS charters, but it too appears to provide no transportation or subsidized lunch for lower-income students (Great Schools, 2018). Elite messaging, as well as availability of transportation and free meals programs, send a powerful message about who is welcome, and who is not, at such schools. The resulting demographics are not surprising: In 2018 The Academy for Advanced and Creative Learning enrolled a student body that was 79% White and only 18% from families with low incomes.

Unlike BASIS, Great Hearts, and the Academy for Advanced and Creative Learning, some charter schools are designed specifically to serve students who have historically academically struggled in the current system. In New York City, Reinventing Options for Adolescents Deserving Success (ROADS) is a network of charter high schools with a mission to ensure that overage, under-credited students graduate from high school. ROADS has an admission priority for students who are involved in the juvenile or criminal justice system, who are homeless or in transitional housing, or who are involved in foster care or child protective services (ROADS Charter High Schools, n.d.).

Another charter school designed to enroll underserved populations is Washington DC's Monument Academy, a weekday boarding school with a mission to "provide students, particularly those who have had or might have contact with the foster care system, with the requisite academic, social, emotional, and life skills to be successful in college, career, and community" (Monument Academy, n.d.).

Language Immersion Schools

Several interviewees pointed to the messages sent by certain language-immersion or ethnocentric charter schools. One researcher pointed to the Francophone Charter School of Oakland; in 2018 this French immersion charter school had a student body that consisted of 12.3% English language learners (ELLs) and 22.8% free/reduced-price lunch recipients. Meanwhile, 31.4% of Oakland Unified School District students were ELLs, and 72.3% of students qualified for free/reduced-price lunch (Ed-Data, 2018). A different researcher pointed out the Mandarin-immersion Washington Yu Ying charter school in Washington, DC. In 2014, the population of Ward 5, home to Washington Yu Ying, was 72% African American but during the 2016–2017 school year only 35.9% of Washington Yu Ying's enrolled students were African American (DC Public Charter School Board, 2017; U.S. Census Bureau, 2014).

Enrollment in Kansas City Public Schools is nearly 90% students of color, yet in 2018 the Academie Lafayette French language immersion charter school in Kansas City enrolled a student body that was nearly 70% White (Williams, 2018b). Academie Lafayette has no neighborhood boundaries; to be eligible to send a child to the school, a family must simply live within the Kansas City district. This was not always the case. When Academie Lafayette opened in 1999, the first year that charter schools were allowed in Missouri, almost 60% of the school's students were African American. School leaders point to a number of likely reasons for the student body drift toward White enrollment, including new enrollees coming over from private schools after the 2008 recession. But whatever the reasons, these leaders have now responded, beginning what they expect to be a multiyear recruitment effort seeking more balance. Interestingly, they point out that the school's sibling preference will considerably slow down their progress (Williams, 2018b).

Language-immersion schools, because of the nature of their niches, often must take such extra steps if they hope to reach a representative group of their larger communities. An example is Yu Ming Charter School, a

Mandarin immersion charter in Oakland that took steps in 2017 to become more accessible. Yu Ming originally had a dual language immersion model. In this model, the incoming students were evenly divided as native speakers of English and Mandarin. An interviewee familiar with Yu Ming shared that a student's odds of getting in were higher if they were in the Mandarin lottery, but the English side of the lottery is where the school could access low-income Black and Latinx students. Yu Ming had a goal of serving a student population that was more closely reflective of the surrounding demographics, both ethnically and socioeconomically, and had set annual goals to increasingly diversify the student population but was not meeting those goals. So the board decided to do away with the requirement of incoming language proficiency and added a low-income categorical preference in the lottery, which helped even out the odds of getting in regardless of incoming language proficiency (Yu Ming Charter School, 2017).

Schools with Religious Messaging

These design influences are perhaps even clearer with a separate group of schools, where religion and language are tightly correlated. Ben Gamla School in Florida is the country's first English Hebrew charter school, and it is run by a rabbi. When it opened, many students left private Jewish day schools to attend Ben Gamla (Goodnough, 2007). This school was marketed to the Jewish community in ways that built an understanding that it would be similar to a yeshiva, a traditional religious school where Judaism's authoritative texts are studied. In this case, language combined with marketing and location to shape an ethnically nondiverse charter. Similarly, after opening in 2009, Brooklyn's Hebrew Language Academy Charter School became the founding school in the Hebrew Public network of charter schools, a group of 10 charter schools. The curriculum in this network of charter schools emphasizes the Hebrew language and the culture and history of Israel (Medina, 2010).

According to Justice and MacLeod (2017), in the last decade, religious organizations have flocked to charter schools as a way to benefit from public tax dollars. Sometimes, religious schools simply close at the end of the school year and reopen in the fall as public charter schools, hiring many of the same teachers and taking on most of the same students (see Daley [2018] for one example). According to a 2014 analysis of 18 Catholic schools that converted to charter schools, most schools kept many of the same employees but replaced religious aspects such as Bible lessons with lessons on the school's core values (Kebede, 2018; McShane & Kelly, 2014). Consider also Ohio's Patriot Preparatory Academy, which arose from the private Liberty Christian Academy in 2010. The charter school sets forth its "creed" as "Today I will act in wisdom, cooperation and faith" (Patriot Preparatory Academy, 2020). When it converted from the private Christian school, it kept the same building, many of the same teachers, the same founder, and half of the same students (Richards, 2010). A community development organization in South Memphis, Tennessee, created by St. Andrew's AME Church operates the Circles of Success Learning Academy charter school, and the organization is itself housed inside the church building (Kebede, 2018). These sorts of church connections to charter schools can be structured in ways that largely avoid legal (establishment clause) concerns but that still raise policy concerns about access and how the schools shape their enrollment.

Consider New York based Seton Education Partners, which was established to revitalize urban Catholic schools after years of enrollment declines. Their mission is to expand opportunities to underserved children by "supporting academically excellent and vibrantly Catholic education," and they describe themselves "an instrument of the Church" (Hess, 2018). One of their primary initiatives is launching and managing "virtues based" charter schools that offer optional, privately funded Catholic after-school programs. Seton operates three K–6 charter schools in the South Bronx. According to co-founder Stephanie Saroki, the charter initiative was launched as a result of the 2011 decision of the archdiocese of New York to close nearly 60 Catholic schools due to declining enrollment and financial instability. As she explains,

> In response to these closings, and at the request of Cardinal Dolan, who did not want to abandon his most underserved communities, Seton set out to pioneer a new charter school of virtue—Brilla. Our hope was that, when paired with a vibrant after-school faith-formation program—one that is voluntary for children and that does not use government funds—Brilla would achieve the goals of Catholic education for the underserved and would do so in a financially sustainable way that complies with charter school laws in both word and spirit. (Hess, 2018)

Similarly, New Day Schools, a new charter organization led by the president of Christian Brothers University, submitted nine charter school applications in 2018 to Shelby County (Tennessee) schools. New Day Schools sought to take over nine private Memphis Catholic schools slated for closure and turn them into charter schools. The district denied all nine applications and sent them back to New Day for revisions. Chalkbeat reported that Brad Leon, the district's chief of strategy and performance management, claimed New Day did not clearly strip all the religious components in its new vision and mission for the schools (Kebede, 2018). Also in 2018, the *Northwest Arkansas Democrat Gazette* reported that the Arkansas charter authorizing body rejected an application for Seven Arts Lyceum, a statewide virtual charter school. State education department officials were concerned, in part, by the religious elements in the curriculum of the proposed charter, including proposed standalone Bible courses (Howell, 2018).

Another phenomenon that should be noted here is the conversion of charter schools into private religious schools. In Indiana, some failing charter schools, in danger of having their authorizers end their charters, have converted into religious private schools. These conversions enable the schools to remain open and to take advantage of the state's voucher laws. After 2 consecutive years of failing ratings, Indianapolis charter school The Padua Academy avoided being shut down by becoming St. Anthony's Catholic school. The school retained the same principal (Burris, 2018). One can imagine a cycle, where a school shifts back and forth, between charter and voucher status, retaining essentially the same student population, but seeking out the most advantageous status for any given period of time.

Those machinations may, however, not be necessary in the future. Pursuant to the Supreme Court's decision in *Espinoza v. Montana Department of Revenue* (2020), barring an institution from receiving public benefits due to its religious nature or church affiliation amounts to anti-religious discrimination, in violation of the U.S. Constitution's Free Exercise Clause. In fact, even before that decision, the U.S. Department of Justice's Office of Legal Counsel issued a memorandum concluding that the federal Charter Schools Program must place religiously affiliated charter schools on equal footing (Whitaker, 2020). The memorandum focused on the religious affiliation status of the grant recipient, as opposed to the question of whether the grant money could be used for religious purposes (e.g., religious teaching).

This leaves at least four questions open. First, during the Biden presidency will this conclusion be reversed? (Answer: Probably yes.) Second, notwithstanding any Justice Department opinion, is this a conclusion that the current U.S. Supreme Court would agree with? (Answer: Probably yes.) Third, given the *Espinoza* decision and the likely direction of the Court, might this decision be extended beyond religious affiliation status, to prohibit laws that restrict the use of public funding for religious teaching? (Answer: This seems possible, perhaps even likely.) Finally, might otherwise charter-friendly "blue" states like California and New York, faced with this new legal reality, decide that they would rather eliminate charter schools altogether than be forced to have their charter school laws used as a mechanism to create a stream of public funding for privately operated religious schools—essentially transforming a charter school system into a voucher system? (Answer: This seems possible.) These issues are explored in Black (2021).

Classical Academy Charter Schools

Another growing niche is the classical charter school. Generally speaking, these schools tend to advertise an elite, academically rigorous liberal arts curriculum coupled with character education and an emphasis on Western civilization as well as the study of classical languages (see Golden View Classical Academy, 2018). In addition, many classical charter schools emphasize a "back to basics" approach to learning, guided by the Core Knowledge curriculum (Hirsch, 1995). Many of these classical charter schools also have gender-normative policies about grooming and uniforms. Addressing such issues, a judge ruled in 2019 that North Carolina's Charter Day School could no longer mandate that girls wear skirts. That policy had prohibited girls from wearing pants or shorts, as part of Charter Day School's overall approach emphasizing "traditional values" in education, all as summarized in the judge's ruling (Mervosh, 2019).

In appearance and practice, classical charter schools have been described as schools similar to parochial schools that offer a classical Christian education but without an explicitly faith-based curriculum (Bailey & Cooper, 2009). This can become problematic, even for people one might expect to be supportive. In a 2016 *World Post* article, David Goodwin, president of the Association for Classical Christian Schools, and LouAnn Webber, director of admissions at Memorial Lutheran School and vice president of Houston Area Independent Schools, both voiced concerns about classical charter schools (Jones, 2016). Specifically, they worried that these schools were attracting parents because of their use of a curriculum and language similar to private Christian schools, but without the important religious teachings.

It is not unusual for these schools to also project political or ideological messaging that can shape enrollment. In 2015 the Brighton (Colorado) Public Schools Board voted against issuing a charter to American Classical Academy. One issue was founder Pascual Battaglia's blatant racism, religious bigotry, and Tea Party rhetoric on social media (Up North Progressive, 2014). Relatedly, two interviewees flagged the politically and religiously conservative Hillsdale College in Michigan, which offers the Barney Charter School Initiative as an "outreach project" to open charter schools based on the Hillsdale College model (Hillsdale College, 2016). Schools that are part of this initiative also tend to adopt policies and practices that differentially appeal to politically conservative parents—sometimes in extreme ways. Hillsdale-affiliated Seven Oaks Classical Academy in Bloomington, Indiana, was designed to emphasize "America's founding principles" and to focus on traditional teaching methods and Latin. After its charter was denied twice through the Indiana Charter Board, Seven Oaks was granted its charter by Grace College and Seminary, a private evangelical institution (Colombo, 2016).

Classical Academy charter school, in Escondido, California, uses a text entitled *The Story of the World: History for the Classical Child*, which presents Bible stories and creationism as factual history, in sixth-grade history courses. Classical Academy also does not provide free or reduced-price lunch (Mercurio, 2016). In 2016, the *Alianza North County*, a bilingual newspaper serving Northern San Diego, questioned whether this and other local charter schools were catering to Christian families. At the time, *Alianza* reported that Escondido's public elementary district had 74% Hispanic students, while Classical Academy had 18% (Mercurio, 2016).

Also in California, American Heritage Charter Schools have been accused of including Christian curricular content and other Christian messaging, such as a teacher giving a prayer in the name of Jesus at the school's commencement ceremony (Eakins, 2006). Similarly, in 2016, Heritage Academy in Arizona (which runs three charter schools) was sued for Establishment Clause violations related to textbooks and other teachings that were allegedly overtly religious (Fisher, H., 2016).

Military Education

Charter schools have also become a small but growing area of K–12 military education. There are about 40 military-themed charter schools around the country, according to Ray Rottman, the president of the Association of Military Colleges and Schools of the United States. At North Valley Military Institute outside of Los Angeles, students are grouped in military units, wear uniforms, and earn commendations (Phenice, 2016). Grizzly Youth Academy in San Luis Obispo, California, is a charter boarding school run by the National Guard. At Grizzly, "[b]oys and girls are separated. Students ask permission to speak. They all dress the same. Police officers are replaced by sergeants, who control almost every aspect of the schools' operation" (Godsey, 2015). At Maritime Charter School in Buffalo, New York, students wear $500 uniforms courtesy of the U.S. Navy. In 2015, Maritime had the highest attrition rate of all of Buffalo's charter schools, and in 2014 a quarter of the school's students were either expelled, suspended, or withdrawn. The charter school's leaders openly acknowledge the school's strict approach to discipline, which emphasizes that students must follow the rules, succeed academically, and commit to physical fitness (Tan, 2015).

As noted, this book includes a discussion of designs like military education as part of its goal of presenting a comprehensive picture of how charter schools shape their enrollment. To understand why this is important—even if readers see only benefits in such niche schools—consider the ongoing debates about studies that attempt to determine whether charter schools increase test scores. These studies control for variables like eligibility for free and reduced-price lunch, attempting to isolate the test-score variations attributable to the sector (charter versus traditional public school). But a family that opts for a military academy or the charter mentioned earlier serving overage, under-credited students is likely different in unmeasured ways from a family that stays in the neighborhood public school. When we understand how these sorts of differences are driven by factors like design, we can understand how measured differences between sectors, which are generally very small, can emerge for reasons unrelated to school quality.

CONCLUSION

One of the goals of the charter school movement is to have different models of schooling that match families' varied educational preferences. These different models are usually evident in how a school is designed or describes itself. From one perspective, fitting new schools into these niches is benign and even beneficial—helping students and schools match each other's interests and styles. But in the process, schools inevitably shape the students who apply and attend. As discussed throughout this book, this has implications for research, since regression models cannot include covariates to adequately control for the resulting unmeasured differences. It also has implications in terms of stratified schooling experiences. In this chapter we touched on schools that, for instance, portray themselves as rigorous or that cater to gifted students. We also note the rise of classical charter schools, language immersion schools, and ethnocentric schools. While some of these school designs are, in our view, more problematic than others, they all likely result in differences between the student compositions in charters and district-run schools.

In the next chapter we turn to location as a determinant of access.

CHAPTER 4

Location, Location, Location

Decisions About Site and Transportation

> As has long been recognized by the courts, the siting of a school is an
> effective way to influence student demographics.... A school that intends
> to serve students who live in an urban area will locate in that neighborhood,
> while a school with an intent to serve a suburban population will make a
> different decision. Because families with less wealth tend to have fewer
> transportation options, this is particularly important when thinking about
> disadvantaged groups. (Welner, 2013, p. 2)

Location decisions cannot be helped; all charter schools (except, to some
extent, cyber schools) must locate somewhere. But decisions about location are sometimes highly strategic. As a charter school researcher told us,
"[T]here is geographic selection going on in how they [charters] identify
themselves and where they are located."

BACKGROUND BRIEFING

Parents choose schools that are geographically convenient in terms of the
distance between (and the time it takes to commute between) the school
and their homes, jobs, or other children's schools (Andre-Bechely, 2007;
Bell, 2007; Hamilton & Guinn, 2005; Hastings et al., 2005; Henig &
MacDonald, 2002; Kleitz et al., 2000; Schneider & Bulkley, 2002). For all
demographic groups, issues of distance and transportation are among the
most important factors considered by school choosers (see Altenhofen et al.,
2016 and Jacobs, 2011). For these reasons, where schools decide to locate
is likely to have a significant impact on access.

   In making school location decisions, schools may be responding to competitive incentives to avoid certain students (Lubienski & Gulosino, 2007;
Lubienski et al., 2009). Bifulco and Buerger (2015) argue that in the absence
of offsetting revenues, the high costs of serving students living in poverty or
emergent bilingual students might discourage charter schools from locating
in areas that are likely to attract concentrations of these subpopulations of

students. Henig and MacDonald (2002) contend that market-oriented charter schools (charters with links to enterprises seeking to make a profit) are more responsive to cost considerations in choosing a location, and as a result are more likely to avoid locations that will attract high concentrations of students from low-income families. In a study of metropolitan Detroit, Lubienski and Gulosino (2007) also found that profit-oriented charter schools are less likely to locate in high-need areas than are mission-oriented charters. Similarly, in their spatial analysis of school openings and closures in Detroit, Gulosino and Lubienski (2011) described how profit-oriented charter schools appear to be willing to pay higher real estate costs in exchange for the ability to "cherry-pick" students from more affluent neighborhoods. Another study in Detroit investigated whether distance and district boundaries were constraints to accessing high-quality and effective schools, as measured by academic performance. Edwards (2011) found that students living in neighborhoods where families had lower incomes and did not have access to a car were less likely to participate in choice, particularly with schools located outside city limits.

LaFleur (2016) found that although many charter schools locate in Chicago's higher-needs census tracts, they avoid locating directly within those that are highest need. LaFleur reasoned that charters may be strategically leveraging location to help shape student enrollment. Lubienski and Gulosino (2007) concluded that all new entrants into an increasingly competitive education marketplace, including mission-oriented charters that historically have served high-need populations, make decisions about location that provide access to more affluent students. In metropolitan New York, Lee and Lubienski (2021) found differential access to charter schools based on demographic and socioeconomic attributes, concluding that charter schools use location strategies to exclude students who may be considered less desirable.

FURTHER RESEARCH

As the examples that follow illustrate, the location of certain schools can remove those schools from parents' choice sets. In deciding where to locate, charter schools effectively choose the groups of parents who will consider enrollment.

Transportation Costs

Intertwined with issues of location are issues of transportation. If parents have time and ready access to affordable transportation to a school, then distance becomes less important. In such cases, it is not uncommon for students to attend charter schools located relatively far away from the neighborhoods in which they live. But the usual situation is that transportation options are limited and, thus, limiting. In a 2014 report about enrollment and choice in Detroit, a local expert explained, "Transportation acts as passive selection criteria in Detroit. If your school doesn't offer transportation, you are selecting for certain people" (Institute for Innovation in Public School Choice, 2014, p. 13). In the same report, the chief external relations officer of a charter school operator attributed a 24 percentage-point drop in the school's free and reduced lunch population to the school not providing transportation. Similarly, a 2015 Institute for Innovation in Public School Choice report about Indianapolis concluded,

> In most instances, families must appear in person at the school in order to apply to that school. This is burdensome to families, particularly those who do not own a car. Public transportation in Indianapolis is not exhaustive in its coverage of neighborhoods and service is intermittent, at best. This issue inconveniences all Indianapolis families, but it has an outsized impact on some of Indianapolis' most vulnerable children and has led to a system where socio-economic status has an outsized impact on a family's ability to participate in school choice. (p. 14)

The process of converting to an all-charter district in New Orleans has left families facing ongoing transportation woes despite a requirement to provide transportation. New Orleans charter schools are supposed to offer children up to the sixth grade who live more than a mile away from school free yellow-bus transportation (Clark, 2017). During a 2017 town hall meeting hosted by Orleans Parish School Board, the mother of two students at Einstein Charter School at Sherwood Forest reported that the school was not providing busing for her children. Instead, the school offered to give her children tokens to take public transit as a means for getting to and from school (Clark, 2017). In an interview with WWNO New Orleans Public Radio, the mother said she has been driving her children (who are 5 and 10 years old) to school, rather than allowing them to use the public transit tokens. She's quoted as saying, "Anyone can grab them or do something to them. . . . And besides that, there are many sexual predators there. It can't be done. You can't. It's illogical" (Clark, 2017). Similarly, a parent profiled by the *Times-Picayune* described spending $90 a month for a private van service to take her children to and from a charter school. The parent noted that the already burdensome transportation costs she was facing would worsen when her younger children reached school age (Nobles, 2018b).

New Orleans Crocker College Prep (2021) does provide transportation to students but with a condition: "Crocker College Prep provides transportation for any scholar living more than one mile from school through A&S Transportation. However the right to free transportation is dependent upon the scholar's behavior while waiting for and/or riding the school bus" (p. 2).

Although the New Orleans experience shows that realities can overcome legal requirements, other districts, cities, and states are also attempting to arrive at rules that will address transportation barriers to charter schools. The large, countywide district in Jacksonville, Florida, offers transportation for all students, including charter students, who live 1.5 miles or further from the school they attend (as cited in Marshall, 2017). The School District of Philadelphia allocates $92 million annually to provide universal transportation to students in the city (Pennington, 2014). All students, regardless of whether they attend TPS, schools of choice operated by the School District of Philadelphia (i.e., open enrollment schools and magnet schools), Philadelphia charter schools, or Archdiocese of Philadelphia schools, have access to free transportation to and from school (as cited in Marshall, 2017).

According to a 2016 review by the Education Commission of the States, 15 of the 43 states with charter school laws at the time specified who must provide transportation to charter school students. Among those 15, some provide clear assistance (e.g., charter schools in Delaware, Missouri, Minnesota, and Wisconsin have access to state transportation aid) (Education Commission of the States, 2016). The resulting patchwork of access to transportation helps perpetuate the corresponding patchwork of transportation-related barriers to charter school access.

Locating in Affluent Suburbs

When charter schools choose to locate in affluent suburbs, they are more accessible to economically privileged families. In fact, the large and, in some states, growing number of charter schools in affluent suburbs is potentially at odds with the original goals of the charter movement (Chi & Welner, 2008; Hu, 2011). As of 2011, one out of five of the country's 5,200 charter schools was in a suburb, according to the National Alliance for Public Charter Schools (Hechinger, 2011). Anderson Creek Club, outside of Fayetteville, North Carolina, is a luxury, gated golf community that offers "resort-like amenities," including a charter school. Anderson Creek charter is located right outside of Anderson Creek Club. A local paper described it as "the first of its kind where a developer has created a charter in such close proximity to their development" (Harnett Dispatch, 2014). The developer made tactical use of the state's charter school law to create a publicly funded school for the private, gated community.

Bullis charter, a suburban school located in Los Altos, California, had a hierarchy of enrollment preferences that included reserving half of all open seats for students residing in the wealthiest part of the Los Altos School District (Hechinger, 2011; Madhaus, 2012). In 2014 Bullis signed a 5-year facilities agreement with the Los Altos School District that included a stipulation that this enrollment preference would be decreased by 10 percentage points each year for incoming kindergarten classes until it reached zero in 2019–2020 (Morgan, 2019). But in a surprise to the Los Altos School District, Bullis school officials said enrollment preferences would go back into effect in 2020–2021, once the 5-year agreement's restriction expired (Morgan, 2019).

In 2018, there were 115 charters around the country where the percentage of White students was at least 20 points higher than the traditional public schools in their home districts (Felton, 2018). Lake Oconee Academy in Green County, Georgia, was one of the 115 schools. In its 2007 charter application, Lake Oconee Academy established a priority attendance zone for the gated communities that surround it, which ended up ensuring that the school would serve a Whiter and more affluent student body than the county in which it was located (Felton, 2018). While that enrollment zone is no longer in place, the school remains disproportionately White.

Rocklin, an affluent suburb outside of Sacramento, is home to Rocklyn Academy schools. This group of charter schools serves mostly White and Asian students who are children of college-educated parents, mirroring the demographics of the well-regarded public schools located nearby (Whitmire, 2015).

The segregation resulting from such location decisions reflects larger patterns of segregation in housing and schooling. But charter location decisions can exacerbate those patterns if they create segregated enclaves within communities that have diverse public schools.

In a 2013 study of charter schools in the Minnesota Twin Cities area, researchers found that an increasing number of predominantly White suburban charter schools were located near racially diverse traditional schools. They found that 44% of suburban traditional schools were predominantly White compared to 67% of suburban charter schools, noting that the percentage of majority White suburban charter schools had increased threefold in 5 years. The researchers concluded that suburban charter schools were fueling White flight from increasingly diverse suburban traditional schools in the outskirts of Minneapolis and St. Paul (Orfield & Luce, 2013).

> In St. Paul, for instance, Nova Classical Academy, which is located in the predominantly white Groveland-Highland neighborhood of St. Paul, effectively siphons off white middle-class students from the racially diverse traditional public schools in the area. Similarly, some suburban school districts, where individual schools are beginning to show signs of racial and economic transition, have seen predominantly white charters spring up near those schools. Examples of such schools include Beacon Academy and Beacon Preparatory School in Plymouth, Paideia Academy in Apple Valley, and Seven Hills Classical Academy in Bloomington. All of these schools have admission interviews, parental involvement requirements, and strict disciplinary policies that can be used to selectively admit students. The result in many cases is an increase in the rate of transition in surrounding traditional schools. (Orfield & Luce, 2013, pp. 409–410, internal citations omitted)

Similarly, charter schools have been widely used in North Carolina as a way for affluent White families to opt out of traditional public schools. In 2018, the state legislature passed legislation (HB 514) that allowed Cornelius, Huntersville, Matthews, and Mint Hill, which are majority White suburbs of Charlotte, to create their own charter schools. Although traditional charter schools in North Carolina cannot limit admission to students based on their zip code, these newly proposed municipal charter schools give enrollment priority to students who reside in these towns (Schlemmer, n.d.).

Locating in Wealthier Parts of Cities

Likewise, charters located in wealthier parts of diverse cities also risk limiting accessibility to low-income families. If a school locates itself in an affluent part of a city and does not offer transportation, it can largely, or altogether, avoid lower-wealth students. Our interviewees named Old Arsenal and MaST charters in northeast Philadelphia as examples of such schools. Looking at MaST, we see that it is located in Somerton, a White, upper-middle class neighborhood in northeast Philadelphia. In 2016, 8,000 applicants applied for 99 openings at the school (Rocco, 2016). Over 70% of MaST students are White and only 1.7% are emergent bilinguals (EBs) (Great Philly Schools, 2016b). In contrast, only 14% of students in the School District of Philadelphia are White, while 10% are emergent bilinguals (School District of Philadelphia, 2021). Similarly, in Washington, DC, BASIS D.C. is located in Ward 2, a commercial part of the city near the National Portrait Gallery, with relatively few schoolchildren. BASIS, unlike many DC charter schools, draws kids from Ward 3, the more affluent Northwest Washington (as well as Georgetown and Foggy Bottom, affluent areas in Ward 2). BASIS is the only charter school located in Ward 2 (DC Public Charter School Board, 2016).

Rather than intentionally locating in affluent suburbs or neighborhoods within cities, a small group for charter schools are intentional about locating in areas that make them geographically accessible to diverse populations. In Tennessee, Valor Collegiate Academies located two middle school campuses in southeast Nashville, which is home to a large population of recent immigrants and refugees. While lower-income and immigrant families comprise most of the families that live in the school's immediate neighborhood, there are more affluent neighborhoods within a few miles of the school. Valor Collegiate Academies CEO Todd Dickson explained, "One of the key things if you want to get socioeconomic diversity is locating the school in a lower-income area. This is really smart and important because it's easier for your families from disadvantaged backgrounds to get to the school if it's closer to them." Dickson adds that "[i]f you could pick the perfect spot, you'd also want to be close to multiple different communities so that they all have access to the school. Southeast Nashville was a perfect spot for us for that reason" (Kern, 2016).

Locating in High Poverty Areas

Strategic location decisions are, of course, not always designed to avoid students who live in underresourced communities; a charter with a mission to serve high poverty, urban areas would likely locate there, and a charter that defined itself as a diverse charter might locate itself in a gentrifying neighborhood. As one interviewee who studies Latinx parents explained to us,

> A lot of time when we read charter literature, charters make a concerted effort to locate where there are more advantaged students, serving kids that aren't as needy [and] will do better on academic achievement metrics. But at the same time there is this flip side: a number of charter schools that are highly mission oriented and mission driven [and] tend to be not-for-profit charter schools; they are interested in locating in communities where there is a great need.

Building on this latter point, another interviewee noted that private philanthropic funders support charter schools that serve low-income and minoritized youth, thereby pressuring schools to locate in these more impoverished areas. The interviewee noted this as a potential benefit but also as exacerbating patterns of segregation. Several interviewees described how "no-excuses" charter schools are almost exclusively located in low-income, segregated neighborhoods of color. These schools combine intensive interventions and extended school time (which likely have broad appeal to parents) with strict behavioral and discipline policies as well as a test-focused data and accountability approach (which likely are harder sells in more affluent areas) (Thernstrom & Thernstrom, 2003; Whitman, 2008).

CONCLUSION

Location decisions are far from neutral. As described in prior research and in our research outlined in this chapter, transportation costs undergird most challenges with access and location. When charter schools locate in affluent suburbs, they cater to affluent suburbs; likewise, when charter schools locate in wealthier enclaves of diverse cities, they cater to wealthier families. When combined with the description and design decisions outlined in Chapter 3, location decisions can powerfully shape student enrollment.

Strategic location decisions are, of course, not always designed to screen more low-income students; a charter with a mission to serve high-poverty, urban areas would likely locate there, and a charter that defined itself as a diverse charter might locate itself in an area that can serve a cross section of the larger community. The latter schools definitely exist, but, as discussed in the next chapter, they are relatively small in number.

CHAPTER 5

Narrow-Casting

The Power of Marketing and Advertising

> Charter schools are not allowed to directly select students based on those students' demographic characteristics. But if a school wants to enroll English learners, it will produce and distribute materials in the first language of those families. If it does not, it will produce and distribute materials overwhelmingly in English. Similar decisions can be made regarding special needs populations and lower-income populations. And if it wants students with higher incoming test scores and a drive to excel academically, it can advertise as "college prep" and highlight the rigor of its curriculum. Even the visual images used in marketing materials can send distinct messages about who is welcome and who is not. (Welner, 2013, p. 2)

Related to school design decisions are the marketing choices made by various schools. When a school makes deliberate decisions about how and where to market, it exercises influence over who applies. Moreover, in areas with substantial competition among schools, marketing becomes increasingly necessary, particularly (as is typically the case with charter schools) for schools without catchment areas or other means of enrollment of some students by default.

BACKGROUND BRIEFING

DiMartino and Jessen (2018) argue that the expansion of market-based policies in education has incentivized the emergence of marketing and branding policies in public education. Such "edvertising"—the marketing, branding, and advertising of education—has been spearheaded by charter management organizations such as KIPP and Success Academy (DiMartino & Jessen, 2018). One consequence of such "edvertisting" may be that the charter movement makes a quality public education—once recognized as a universal guarantee—contingent on the education consumer's ability to navigate a marketplace (Eastman et al., 2016).

Cucchiara (2016) notes how "educational organizations use marketing to develop and promote a particular identity, recruit or exclude students, and navigate new systems of competition and accountability" (p. 121). Because charter schools must attract prospective students and retain current students, or risk loss of funding or even closure, they have reasons to employ effective and innovative ways of marketing or otherwise distinguishing themselves for consumers (Lubienski, 2005, 2007).

In her work in New Orleans, Jabbar (2016) explored how school leaders used different marketing strategies based on positions in a market hierarchy to recruit or not recruit students. She describes how some schools found ways to avoid enrolling certain groups of students, often by avoiding public marketing altogether. She documented invite-only school information nights where current school parents were asked to bring like-minded friends. She also interviewed principals who stopped attending citywide school fairs because the demand for their schools made it unnecessary (Jabbar, 2015). By not participating in school fairs, however, schools were even more difficult to access for noninsider interested parents.

Examining schools in Minnesota's Twin Cities, Wilson and Carlsen (2016) outlined a typology of schools based on charter school websites. They argue that websites act as a mechanism that contributes to the segmentation and differentiation of the emerging local marketplace of school options. Other research shows that the visual over- or underrepresentation of populations of students on school websites reflects specific strategic decisions on the part of schools (Bifulco et al., 2009; Charles, 2003; Scott, 2008).

Mission statements may also indicate marketing strategies. Looking at charter schools in the Detroit metropolitan area, Lubienski and Lee (2016) identified charter schools with mission statements targeting more academically skilled applicants.

Increased competition and associated marketing are not limited to the charter sector. Some public school districts have increased their emphasis on image management and have begun using district funds to advertise their schools (Basco, 2016). In their study of several choice-based schools (both district and charter) in New York City, DiMartino and Jessen (2014) found that schools sought out "high performing" students, as well as "well-behaved and focused students who 'understand the culture of the school'" (p. 22). Similarly, DiMartino and Jessen (2014) documented how small schools in New York City used marketing to create boutique or niche identities within an educational system, in ways that exacerbated segregation. Here, the literature points to connections between school-based marketing and the segregation of schools within an educational market.

Researchers have also suggested that families of emergent bilinguals (EBs) may not have accurate and consistent information about charter schools, may not be aware that charter schools are a tuition-free option for their children, or may not know how to navigate the application pro-cesses (Bulkley & Sattin-Bajaj, 2011; Frankenberg et al., 2011; Garcia & Morales, 2016; Villavicencio, 2013). Garcia and Morales (2016) found that the charter schools that were most successful in attracting and retain-ing EBs often used strategic "boots on the ground campaigns" in which school leaders intentionally reached out to the families, connected with community organizations, and provided information about their school in multiple languages. Conversely, charter schools tended to be less success-ful if EBs were not intentionally recruited, if the cultural backgrounds and linguistic skills of the charter school's staff did not reflect those of com-munities in which EBs were concentrated, or if the charter school staff's lack of EB-specific expertise and capacity discouraged them from actively recruiting EBs (Garcia & Morales, 2016).

FURTHER RESEARCH

The foundational lesson from this research is that marketing is not sim-ply used to broadcast the purportedly wonderful opportunities at a given school. As the following examples illustrate, marketing can and is used to "narrow-cast"—to shape a school's enrollment by reaching and appealing to preferred audiences while avoiding and discouraging undesirable audi-ences. Charter schools wishing to avoid this market segmentation make deliberate efforts to craft marketing to reach and appeal to their entire com-munity. Further, some cities have taken steps to publish comprehensive and accessible enrollment guides for all schools, a step that serves to increase accessibility to schools.

Choosing Not to Advertise

In some cases, established charters make deliberate decisions not to formally advertise or market. These schools are in high demand and rely on social networks of current families to fill the few vacant seats that do open up. One researcher interviewee explained how a particular New Jersey charter school did not advertise at all; rather "it was a word [of] mouth kind of thing. . . . It wasn't well known by everyone in the community." Another interviewee explained, "[W]ord of mouth is one of the biggest ways parents find out about schools." He added that schools often encourage applicants by ask-ing parents and teachers to informally market for them, which becomes an important recruiting tool. This has the predictable effect of benefiting those with the most social capital and, more generally, of reproducing existing enrollment patterns and demographics. A third interviewee explained, "On the pre-enrollment side of things, certainly we in Oakland have this kind of choice system where we don't fully know how parents get information and make decisions about where to send their kids. We do know the White well educated affluent parent in Oakland Hills has [a] different set of info than many immigrant [parents who don't] speak English."

By not participating in school fairs, schools become even more difficult to access for noninsider interested parents. One of our interviewees described attending school recruitment fairs in Minneapolis and Denver and noticing the schools that did not show up were those that were known to be exclusive by reputation. An interesting twist on this approach comes from Detroit Prep, the city's first intentionally diverse charter school. The school's leaders made a strategic decision to hold open enrollment during a short 2-week period in November to increase their ability to maintain the desired diverse enrollment. Michigan's rules require a lottery if open enrollment yields more applicants than seats, but if there are more seats than applicants the remaining seats are filled on a first-come, first-served basis. "By holding [the open] enrollment early in the year, [the school] hoped the process would stay largely under the radar, drawing few applications and enabling [the school] to spend the rest of the year doing targeted recruitment," focused on yielding a diverse student body (Einhorn, 2016). This strategy did not work, as word of the school reached affluent circles, and the school was flooded with applications during open enrollment from wealthier and Whiter families. The school plans to have a "speakeasy" enrollment system for 2018, which means there will only be targeted outreach with no advertising at all (Einhorn, 2016).

In other cases, charters make the deliberate decision not to advertise open seats, specifically to avoid enrolling students they deem undesirable. In her study interviewing New Orleans school leaders, Jabbar (2016) describes leaders who preferred underenrollment to broadly advertising open spaces, which allowed a greater degree of control over who enrolls. Jabbar also describes a school that did not advertise open seats, even though the school needed more students. If the school did advertise, the seats would be automatically filled by the Recovery School District—thus taking control away from the school with regard to the types of students they would receive.

Selective Advertising

Testing also plays into these issues. To stay competitive in districts marked by the pressures of high-stakes accountability, charter schools advertise selectively. An interviewee who worked on Philadelphia's School Reform Commission described how some schools would hold meetings to learn about their programs:

[T]he meetings to learn about [the] school were located in areas which were inconvenient for groups that the charters [were] not anxious to enroll. That's how it would appear to a parent. If a meeting were scheduled during [the] day, a working parent could not get to them, if it was located in a horticultural park in the far end of the city, not near public transport, same thing. [We] saw those kinds of things.

Jabbar's (2016) work in New Orleans illustrates how the pressures of high-stakes accountability can be so intense that, as a matter of perceived survival, a school's marketing will target higher-scoring students. Lagniappe Academies in New Orleans maintained a "Do Not Call" list "of families whose children they did not want back and instructed staff to skip them when phoning families with key information about registration and summer session" (Dreilinger, 2015b). Another interviewee explained that students with "low buying power" in these competitive markets are seldom the targets of recruitment. She illustrated this point by describing foster families, who tend to be overrepresented in urban district schools but rarely marketed to. LISA Academy, a charter school in Little Rock, Arkansas, offers a compelling example of this phenomenon. The charter was cleared for expansion, so in 2016 it sent out targeted mailers to recruit students in central Arkansas. The mailers went to area neighborhoods, except for the three zip codes for the heavily Black and Latinx parts of town, with the highest concentration of low-income housing (Petrimoulx, 2016). Similarly, in California, a charter school founder told us that many Oakland charter schools were not actively targeting the Black community in outreach efforts.

Even well-intentioned initiatives can veer into selective outreach. An interviewee who previously served on the Philadelphia School Reform Commission worked closely with the Philadelphia Charter Schools Office when the city launched the Renaissance Initiative in 2010. Under this initiative, district schools with "long-term academic and climate challenges" were turned over to various charter operators. In the 2017–2018 school year there were 21 Renaissance Charter Schools in the city (School District of Philadelphia, 2017). According to the interviewee, the intention of the initiative was to have Renaissance Charter Schools continue to serve the same students the former district schools did. This "catchment area" mission is unusual for charters, which generally do not formally prioritize students in the immediate neighborhood. Early on, however, some Renaissance charters started to stray from the neighborhood directive. They began drawing students from elsewhere, outside of the former district schools' catchment areas. This trend concerned the School Reform Commission. So, according to the interviewee, "[The School Reform Commission] incorporated into the terms under which we granted Renaissance charters the idea that they would recruit in a particular catchment area. Some of the charter [operators] had to agree [to] serve the catchment areas [the schools] served when they were district schools."

Students who speak a language other than English at home are also, as "customers," often a less favored group with lower "buying power" within the charter marketplace. This is reflected by English-only advertising in linguistically diverse urban settings. For example, an interviewee explained that there are no laws or regulations in Minneapolis about charter schools translating materials into different languages and, as a consequence, many do not do so—although the number of emergent bilinguals in Minnesota has tripled in the past 20 years (Raghavendran, 2016).

One effort to address this concern is in New York City, where a pro-charter group called the Charter School Center launched a multimedia, multilingual campaign to alert non–English speaking families and students with learning disabilities about charter schools (NYC Charter School Center, 2014). Another effort is found in Massachusetts, which has seen a growing number of charter school students with disabilities or who are learning English. In 2010 the legislature passed "An Act Relative to the Achievement Gap," amending the state's charter law. The act required charter schools to create recruitment and retention plans to attract special needs students and emergent bilinguals. In addition, but much more problematically, the law gave charter schools access, through an independent third party, to comprehensive lists of district students, which the schools could use for marketing (Schoenberg, 2019). School districts are required to share such lists. A charter school wanting to broaden its enrollment could use these lists for good purposes. Alternatively, a charter wanting to skew enrollment could use some of the marketing and targeting approaches noted.

A Chicago-based interviewee shared how the city's large charter networks have reputations for marketing to students along the lines of race, ethnicity and class, which indirectly excludes kids who do not fall into the targeted group. The interviewee shared that the Acero network (formerly called Uno), targets Latinx students. The name Acero (steel), according to the network, "evokes strength [and] resilience" and "honors the network's roots within the Latino community" (Rice, 2017).

Marketing Rigor

Finally, as noted earlier, a key way that charter schools can use marketing to shape their student population is by prominently emphasizing the intellectual rigor of the school. This has the effect of prescreening for higher-achieving students. Wilson and Carlsen (2016) identified a group of charter schools as "elite and international," which generally enrolled more White and economically advantaged students. Studying official websites, the researchers found these schools present themselves "as institutions that will prepare students for success in an increasingly competitive globalized world" and appeal to a sense of academic excellence—in terms of intellectual rigor or international norms.

Of course, sometimes the messaging is more explicit. A 2016 report by Public Impact and the ACLU of Southern California called *Unequal Access* highlights the mission statement of Mueller Charter in San Diego County, which reads as follows:

> Mueller Charter Leadership Academy (MCLA) is an academically rigorous, accelerated program that reflects the curriculum standards and expectation of a high achieving middle school honors program. All eligible students are welcome to apply. However, it should be noted that because this is a highly advanced, demanding program, it may not be appropriate for everyone. (Leung et al., 2016)

In contrast, rather than marketing in a way that might make schools seem exclusive, High Tech High in California advertises strategically by using student zip code data; they blanket zip codes where there was a relative shortfall of applications. This charter is a member of the National Coalition of Diverse Charter Schools, a group of approximately 35 charter schools or charter networks that holds, among other beliefs, that "[a]chieving diversity often requires deliberate efforts through recruitment, admissions policies and school design."

Enrollment Guides

The school-improvement theory underlying choice and competition depends on parents making fully informed decisions (Lubienski, 2007). Without access to information about available schools and how they can apply, parents cannot exercise school choice, at least in any meaningful way. One small step taken by several choice-intensive cities (Denver, Washington, DC, New Orleans, and New York City) is the establishment of common enrollment guides to help parents navigate the multitude of choices (district and charter) by effectively gathering and presenting information about public schools in a city.

For example, Denver Public Schools (2021) publishes a "School Choice Enrollment Guide" that explains the school choice process, offers advice on selecting schools, and lists and briefly describes every public school. Similarly, in Washington, DC, MySchoolDC.org publishes an online guide to the public schools that participate in the common enrollment process. The guide explains, in great detail, the application and choice process, the enrollment process, and the mechanisms by which applicants are prioritized for admission to schools. It also briefly describes all participating public schools, including statistics on school quality and data that is updated weekly on seat availability at each grade level. MySchoolDC.org also includes links to DC schools that do not participate in the common enrollment process.

CONCLUSION

When marketing is used to appeal to preferred audiences—or avoid dis-favored ones—it puts families that are deemed undesirable at a significant disadvantage. This marketing is a logical response to competitive pressures that create an environment that incentivizes schools to attract better per-forming students through their advertising campaigns. Policymakers who hope to design fairer school choice plans for the future must address this issue, improving the quality of information available to all families, as well as the inclusiveness of messaging.

In this chapter, we reviewed the access- and equity-related implications of charter school advertising—particularly practices that target advertising to select audiences. Along with decisions about description and design and location, marketing decisions round out the three key ways charter schools shape enrollment by shaping the potential pool of applicants—before the application process even begins.

The book now shifts to issues related to access that come up during that application process. We begin with the practice of putting conditions on applications.

CHAPTER 6

Hoop Schemes

Conditions Placed on Applications

> For years, parents have had to jump through astonishing hoops to apply to
> the popular Green Woods Charter School in Northwest Philadelphia.
>
> Interested families couldn't find Green Woods' application online. They
> couldn't request a copy in the mail. In fact, they couldn't even pick up a copy
> at the school.
>
> Instead, Green Woods made its application available only one day each
> year. Even then, the application was only given to families who attended the
> school's open house—which most recently has been held at a private golf
> club in the Philadelphia suburbs. (Herold, 2012)

Charter schools are usually in charge of their own application processes and
are therefore able to impose a daunting array of conditions. Those hoops
can effectively shape the pipeline that leads to enrolled students. Policies
and practices include lengthy application forms, mandatory references, and
requirements of parental visits before applying. These obstacles discourage
parents, especially those who lack the time and resources, and they can
sometimes even directly turn away families.

BACKGROUND BRIEFING

A key finding from the research is that application requirements can be
differentially burdensome for particular students and families (Dynarski
et al., 2018; Gross et al., 2015; Lacireno-Paquet, 2006; Weiler & Vogel,
2015; Wells et al., 1998). In an early study of California charter schools, researchers noted that admissions requirements and processes exemplify how
charter schools are better able to shape who they enroll than other public
schools (Wells et al., 1998). Many of the charter schools in the study had
admissions preferences or priorities for certain students including students
whose parents worked at the school, who attended before the school converted to charter, and those who had siblings at the school. In addition,
some schools required a parent to visit with school officials—meetings that

were used to "ensure there is a fit between the charter school and the family" (Wells et al., 1998, p. 44).

In their study of Colorado charter schools, Weiler and Vogel (2015) identified 22 schools that required a visit from parents prior to registration. Using the 1999–2000 Schools and Staffing Survey Public Charter School Questionnaire, Lacireno-Paquet (2006) found that 255 (26.1%) of 980 charter schools had at least one admissions requirement, 19.3% required a personal interview, and 10.8% required recommendations.

Susan Dynarski and her colleagues (2018) leveraged randomized admission lotteries to assess the impacts of attending Michigan-based National Heritage Academies (NHA), the fourth largest for-profit charter operator in the country. They noted how the timing of enrollment periods seemed to influence whether a school will have a lottery:

> Over the course of our year-long fieldwork, we took note of the significant role the open enrollment period appeared to play in whether a school had a lottery or not. . . . The timing of a school's open enrollment period could directly impact the likelihood of a lottery. For example, schools that had an earlier open enrollment period for only two weeks could usually accept all the eager and savvy applicants that applied and keep a first-come first-serve waitlist after the open enrollment period. Schools that had a longer and later open enrollment period (when parents were more likely to be thinking about the next school year) were more likely to need a lottery, since more students could apply during this time. And with a lottery came the inability to just accept all the students, presumably with the savviest parents, who applied first. And since each school set its own open enrollment period, parents had to be exceptionally organized if applying to multiple schools with multiple deadlines. (p. 72)

The researchers further noted how this process influenced the behavior of schools: "We also noticed schools getting into open enrollment bidding wars, setting their open enrollment periods to be earlier than competing schools so as to not miss out on prime students" (p. 72).

The school choice system in Boston engenders a similar set of concerns. Parents new to the district are required to go in person to registration centers and rank order their school preferences. Assignments and, if needed, lotteries are then held, with parents given their preferences as much as possible. If parents register late, their chances of gaining entry to a preferred school are decreased. Drawing on surveys, administrative data, and interviews with 33 parents in Boston, Fong and Faude (2018) found that nearly half of Black kindergarteners missed the first registration deadline for schools. This rate was almost three times higher than their White peers, and confined Black kindergarteners to their least preferred schools. The authors concluded that inequality in school choice outcomes and experiences results from a misalignment of district bureaucratic processes with family situations (Fong & Faude, 2018).

   Trying to understand how enrollment processes played out at the parental level, Gross et al. (2015) studied parents negotiating "common enrollment" programs (centralized enrollment rather than systems that require a different application for each school). These parents indicated that streamlined processes made navigating the application process easier. But misunderstandings about the process led some parents to complete the applications in ways that were disadvantageous for their children. Also, parents in both locations studied felt a lack of high-quality options from which to choose. The common enrollment processes did manage to level the playing field in one regard. Parents with more social and political capital would have previously been able to work around the system to enroll their children in schools they deemed desirable; the common application process substantially reduced that. Moreover, although most schools in both locations participated in the common application programs, a few did not, thereby leaving in place increased barriers for parents to enroll their children in nonparticipating schools.

FURTHER RESEARCH

Five notable approaches for limiting access during the application process include long and burdensome applications, required documentation related to disability and/or citizenship, required in-person visits, entrance assessments, and application deadlines. Each one of these could deter a family from applying by itself, but when used in concert, they are particularly onerous and effective. To some extent, however, none of this is new or unique to charter schools; other types of school choice pioneered restrictive application practices. A 2017 report by the Institute for Innovation for Public School Choice found that the act of applying to selective enrollment choice schools and programs in Chicago is cumbersome and complicated:

> Separate applications must be completed in Chicago for selective enrollment schools, magnet schools, military schools, IB programs, neighborhood high schools (if living outside of the neighborhood), and for charter schools. Each of these application processes works on its own timeline and requires its own operations. In some cases, parents must appear in person as part of the application process. This is a labor-intensive process that requires a degree of organization and planning that can be confusing and unduly challenging for a large portion of the population. (p. 12)

This broader scope of the "hoop" problem is useful to keep in mind while considering the charter school practices described in this chapter.

Long and Burdensome Applications

Applications for charters are sometimes straightforward and even uniform within a school district. But some charter schools have long and burdensome applications, making them inaccessible for many families.

These are obstacles that some states have tried to head off, but with only limited success. According to the Oklahoma Charter Schools Act (Section 42.22(D)), charter schools in the state are not allowed to base enrollment on past academic performance, income level, or the abilities of parents. Yet an analysis of the state's 29 charter schools by *The Oklahoman* found a number of burdensome application requirements that seem to violate at least the spirit of the law (Felder, 2017). Some applications required recommendation letters from teachers; others asked for details of students' discipline histories and asked if students receive special education services (Felder, 2017). The ASTEC Charter School in Oklahoma City required that prospective students and parents fill out a 14-page application with over 80 questions. Among these are questions demanding short essay responses about, for example, why a student is applying and a student's greatest strengths. The application also asked questions that can be used for screening, for example, if a student has ever received special education services, for a student's discipline history, and whether they can write in cursive (Felder, 2017).

These sorts of applications are found throughout the country. According to a 2016 report by the ACLU, at least 92 California charter schools maintained mandatory essay or interview requirements (Leung et al., 2016). A 2016 *Los Angeles Times* editorial highlighted the intimidating application form of Roseland Accelerated Middle School in Santa Rosa, California. The form, which was several dozen pages long, was required to be completed prior to acceptance. A "Getting to Know You" section required students to write five short essays in addition to six short response questions; parents were also required to write several essays of their own. To top it off, the application required a three-page minimum autobiography from the potential student that was "well-constructed with varied structure" (Times Editorial Board, 2016).

An Oakland-based interviewee who works in the charter sector told us that, "with the exception of a few cities, every charter [in California] has its own enrollment process and timeline." This means, she said, that each charter is "on its own in terms of marketing and outreach, [and] it takes parents' time, work, and resources to navigate such a complicated system."

Requiring Documentation

One of our interviewees zeroed in on the unclear legality of requiring applicants who receive special education services to document their disabilities during the application process. Such practices are clearly contrary to the intent and spirit of the Individuals With Disabilities Education Act (IDEA), because they have the effect of discouraging these students. In some states, such as Pennsylvania, charter schools are legally forbidden from requiring parents to provide their children's individualized education plans (IEPs) prior to enrollment and forbidden from denying admission based on special needs status (Pennsylvania Department of Education, 2009). The latter prohibition is also written into federal law (Section 504 of the Rehabilitation Act, as well as the IDEA). Yet this clearly happens. Windle (2018) reports from Philadelphia on Franklin Towne Charter High School's apparently illegal decision to deny a student admission because of her special education status. The student's grandmother (guardian) had been informed of admission, via winning a lottery, but had then provided the school with the student's relatively expensive IEP, which included emotional support needs. The school then told the grandmother that the student could not attend Franklin Towne, because the emotional disturbance class she needed was "full."[1]

Across Ohio, there are 12 charter schools that are part of Performance Academies, (2021a), and, as the network's website proclaims they "do not discriminate based on race, color, national origin, sex, disability, or age in its programs." However, upon completion of an online registration form, parents are asked to fill out a separate application for enrollment, which asks students to bring in a number of items, including a copy of a birth certificate, special education paperwork (IEPs), current proof of residency, and a copy of a parent or guardian's license or state ID. Additionally the "student history section" of the enrollment application asks students to document and explain any previous suspensions or expulsions, asks if students have ever received counseling or psychological testing, and if parents describe "any special need that your student may require including medical conditions, physical limitations, or other special needs of which you would like the school to be aware." Additionally, the "parent agreement" portion of the application asks parents, among other things, to commit to a minimum of 20 volunteer hours a year (The Academies, 2021b). As noted, Cleveland's Believe to Achieve charter had a similar requirement, as did many others we learned about during the course of this study.

In Philadelphia, Global Leadership and Khepera charter schools were cited in 2017 for requiring special education information on their applications for admission (School District of Philadelphia, 2018). This was in violation of Pennsylvania and Philadelphia law; special education information or documentation may not be required at any time during application and admission. Furthermore, it cannot be optionally requested during the pre-lottery stage. Special education documentation for enrollment may only be requested after acceptance (School District of Philadelphia, 2018).

Several interviewees additionally explained that the relatively common practice of asking for information such as Social Security numbers and birth certificates before enrollment strongly discourages undocumented students, or documented students with undocumented parents or guardians, from attending a school. One person we interviewed with experience in Cleveland shared practices of several schools that are problematic. For example, Horizon Science Academy, a Cleveland charter school, requests that students submit "a birth certificate, proof of residency, shot records, report cards from the previous schools, release forms, IEP documents if they exist, emergency contact information, a home language survey, and lunch application along with other forms" as part of their enrollment process (Horizon Science Academy, 2021). Related to practices documented elsewhere, Horizon Science Academy (2021) also requests in-person interviews with parents and has students take diagnostic tests in math and reading during the enrollment process. Yet according to a 2014 guidance that was jointly issued by the U.S. Departments of Justice and Education, among the documents that schools should not require prior to enrolling students are Social Security number or card of student or parent, proof of citizenship or immigration status, and birth certificates (U.S. Department of Education, Office of Civil Rights, 2014).

Notwithstanding this guidance, Public Impact and the ACLU of Southern California identified 132 charter schools that required students or guardians to provide a birth certificate or Social Security number without clarifying that alternative forms of documentation can be provided and without explicitly stating that noncitizens are eligible for enrollment (Leung et al., 2016). Examples of these schools include Morris E. Daily Charter school in Fresno County, which asked for birth certificates and Social Security cards as kindergarten enrollment requirements, and Juan Bautista de Anza Charter in San Diego, which asked a series of questions about citizenship status (e.g., "Check here if foreign student temporarily schooling in the U.S."). Importantly, these sorts of practices are not limited to charter schools. In New Jersey, the ACLU filed a lawsuit in 2016 that included the Jersey City Global Charter School, as well as four school districts, alleging discrimination against the children of undocumented immigrants by requiring certain paperwork (Hubbard, 2016). Although the charter school website says documents that reveal immigration status are not required for registration, as of 2021 it still asks for a copy of a child's birth certificate (Jersey City Global Charter School, 2021a). Jersey City Global Charter (2021b) also asks students to provide a range of applicable special education documentation (speech, 504, IEP, occupational therapy) and whether or not students receive English language services and when those services began).

In 2017, West Philadelphia Achievement Elementary Charter School was cited by the School District of Philadelphia, Charter Schools Office (2018) for requiring a number of items that are not on the list of fields permitted by Pennsylvania state law, including a Social Security number, ethnicity, place of birth, and primary language. Requesting a Social Security number is specifically prohibited.

Even routine interactions can erect barriers. An advocate for parents in charter schools told us how schools would make parents wait for hours in the middle of the day, thus risking loss of jobs with little security. She noted that these meetings would sometimes take place in buildings that required IDs that undocumented immigrants simply did not have: "A school wouldn't let me into a building. I didn't have ID. [This] was a school with [a] Parent Center, [where parents go] to find other schools. I gave them my passport, [but] they said we can't use this—this is a passport, [and] they had [only] an ID scanner. Undocumented parents, they have passports but don't have IDs."

Requiring In-Person Visits

Another practice that limits access during the application phase involves requiring or rewarding visits from interested families. A parent we interviewed described calling Edward Brooke Mattapan, a Boston-based charter school, after not finding an application on its website—only to be told that the only way she could get an application was to first show up for a meeting at the school. Another interviewee asserted that the Conservatory of Vocal and Instrumental Arts, an Oakland charter school that was closed in 2017 (see Sernoffsky, 2017), insisted on a one-on-one interview with every elementary school applicant as part of the application process—what she described as "a clear sign of a bad actor deliberately trying to cream."

In a 2015 report on public school enrollment in Indianapolis, the Institute for Innovation in Public School Choice found that in most instances, families must appear in person at the school in order to apply to that school. Brandon Brown, director of charter schools for the mayor's Office of Education Innovation, quoted in the report, reflected on the challenge this practice presents for families:

> The fact that you physically have to go to a charter school to enroll, particularly if you don't have access to the Internet, makes it hard on families. The forms to fill out look different, the process looks different, and the documentation they require might be different. (p. 15)

Justin Ohlemiller, executive director of Stand for Children Indiana, echoed Brown's concern:

> You've got parents that are middle to lower income that are working jobs that literally don't allow the flexibility to visit schools. The insinuation that if a parent just cared about their kid they would make an informed choice, that just doesn't take into account the fact that some families literally don't have that opportunity. (Institute for Innovation in Public School Choice, 2015, p. 15)

In Loveland, Colorado, New Vision K–8 charter school has a policy where parents who are interested in entering a lottery for the school are required to attend a student enrollment parent information Meeting (New

Vision, 2021). There is no online availability of the necessary paperwork for application or enrollment.

For several years New York City's "limited unscreened" admissions method gave admissions priority to students who attend an open house or high school fair. In 2018 the city identified this practice as an obstacle for parents who work long hours or have caretaking responsibilities. The district noted that higher need students were less frequently the recipients of "limited unscreened" admissions priority, and it took the positive step of pledging to eliminate the practice as part of its effort to make schools more integrated and accessible (Valant & Lincove, 2018).

Entrance Assessments

Another practice that turns away families during the application process involves the use of an admissions test to determine grade placement or academic level—or even actual eligibility for admission. This role of testing as an access barrier first arose in noncharter contexts, with elite public schools like Lowell in San Francisco and Bronx Science and other specialized schools in New York. In New York City in 2017, only 4.1% of offers at the specialized high schools that require an entry exam went to Black students, while 6.3% went to Hispanic students. In comparison, these two groups of students made up about 70% of city students (Veiga, 2018).

Yet the practice appears to be even more widespread in charter schools. In Delaware an Enrollment Preferences Task Force, formed in 2013 through House Bill 90, examined the situation and developed recommendations about enrollment preferences and practices of charter, magnet, and vocational schools. The Task Force made recommendations about including or excluding each question asked on schools' supplemental and enrollment applications; however, subsequent legislation has not addressed the entrance exam issues raised in the report.

The Task Force found that in 2013–2014, nine of the state's 33 charter schools required, as part of the admissions process, a "content knowledge and ability exam, essay, audition, or portfolio submission" (Enrollment Preferences Task Force, 2015). These nine charters had lower percentages of low-income students and were among those identified as higher performing compared to other charter schools in the state (Wolfman-Arent, 2014). The Charter School of Wilmington, ranked as the 48th best school in the country and the top school in Delaware by U.S. News and World Report in 2017, was identified as one of the nine schools with an entrance exam (Wolfman-Arent, 2014). In a 2008 review of the school, a student wrote, "[A]lmost every student that attends [Charter School of Wilmington] has spectacular academic ability, due to a rigorous entrance exam" (Davidson Institute, n.d.).

In New Orleans, three of the most in-demand charter schools—Lusher, Lake Forest, and Benjamin Franklin—have entrance assessments that help determine eligibility (Jewson, 2015; Juhasz, 2020). West Ridge Academy in Greeley, Colorado, the district with the largest per-capita charter school population in the state, also requires placement tests for students in grades 3–8. West Ridge's website states:

> West Ridge Academy is a smaller school with limited resources for Special Education. Our ultimate goal is to meet the needs of our students and to make sure we give them the best education possible to meet those needs. The assessment test allows us to evaluate their knowledge and make sure they are placed suitably. After the assessment test is taken and evaluated, students will be admitted. At this time there is a $75.00 non-refundable Materials Fee per student that will be paid. . . . Once the Materials Fee is paid in full your student will be officially enrolled at West Ridge Academy. (West Ridge Academy, n.d.)

Stargate charter school in Colorado is more explicit about the students it wants and does not want. It presents itself as serving the gifted and talented; students must pass an IQ test to be accepted. In the 2020–2021 school year, 80% of students were White or Asian. In comparison, in Stargate's home district, Adams 12 Five Star School district, 50% of students were White or Asian (Colorado Department of Education, 2021). In 2017–2018 (the last year FRPL data was available for Stargate), 3% of students qualified for free or reduced-price lunch, while 40% of Adams 12 Give Star students qualified for free or reduced-price lunch (Colorado Department of Education, 2018).

Rhode Island has a policy that requires charter schools to admit students by a blind lottery. Such policies should, in theory, work to prevent charters from requiring admissions tests. However, in 2017, the *Providence Journal* reported that Woonsocket Beacon charter school, a well-regarded high school for the arts, required entering freshmen to pass an eighth-grade English and math assessment. The Rhode Island Department of Education discovered the violation as part of its renewal review, but the consequences of the policy violation were muted: The Department recommended the school only receive a 3- rather than 5-year renewal (Borg, 2017).

Related incentives can lead to charter schools making themselves an unattractive option to families of emergent bilinguals. Apart from English-only advertising and communicating, schools can have enrollment policies that are discriminatory against EBs. As the ACLU and Public Impact report pointed out, to enroll in Forest Charter in California's Nevada County, for instance, students were required to score 80% or higher on a language arts assessment and could not be more than one grade below their enrolled grade level. In addition, students were required to write a letter on their own in front of a teacher, in order to demonstrate their language arts ability (Leung et al., 2016).

Following this 2016 report, dozens of charter schools changed their policies to be more inclusive. In fact, according to the ACLU, more than

100 charter schools reached out to the authors to fix or clarify their policies (ACLU Southern California, 2017).

Application Deadlines

Finally, we note that charter schools are generally able to set their own application deadlines. Interviewees named early application deadlines and short application windows as factors that limit access to certain charter schools. During the 2017–2018 school year, 36 of the 66 non-Renaissance charters in Philadelphia had application deadlines in February or earlier for the following school year. The earliest deadlines belonged to Boys Latin of Philadelphia and Franklin Towne Charter, where applications were due in October and November of the previous year, respectively (Great Philly Schools, 2016a; School District of Philadelphia, 2017).

Similar problems were identified in other cities. In Detroit, a 2014 report revealed the following:

> Even popular [charter] schools that wind up fully enrolled, almost never use lotteries to fill seats. The decentralized structure of the enrollment and choice process in Detroit leads to opaque admissions in general—applying for a seat is a transaction conducted between family and school, without oversight. Beyond the basic structural issues, there are mechanisms that allow, and in fact encourage schools to do their enrollment without any transparency. This, in the end, allows individuals at schools to have essentially complete discretion regarding admissions. Families are in a compromised position—there are no guarantees that admissions decisions are made justly and there is no accountability mechanism for families to access. (Institute for Innovation in Public School Choice, 2014, p. 20)

Common Applications

As noted in Chapter 5, several large cities (such as Denver, New Orleans, Philadelphia, and Washington, DC), make a common application available for some or all charter schools. The application serves as a resource for the schools and as a possible way to avoid the deadline problem as well as the problem of burdensome and improper application demands.

Yet implementation has been uneven. In some of these cities charter schools can opt out of participating in common application processes. New Orleans is the most important and clear example of the progress made as well as its limitations. In 2012, New Orleans launched a centralized application process known as OneApp (Gross et al., 2015; Harris et al., 2015). Parents can complete a single application and rank order their preferences for schools. A number of factors are considered, including proximity and whether siblings are also enrolled at the school, and then an assignment is made (Harris et al., 2015). However, several of the most in-demand schools do not participate in the OneApp, and recently one participating charter was reprimanded for enrolling students outside of the OneApp (Jewson, 2018).

In October of 2018 ApplyLA, a website that allows Los Angeles parents to apply for multiple independent charter schools with a single application, launched (Romero, 2018). During the 2018–2019 school year, only 31 schools, or 10% of the city's charter schools, participated. Accordingly, parents in Los Angeles now have two online enrollment systems to navigate; LA Unified School District launched its own unified enrollment site in 2018, but independent charters were not included in that system (Romero, 2018).

In Philadelphia most charter schools accept a common application called the Charter School Standard Application, developed by Great Philly Schools (which is not affiliated with the district). But charter schools can nonetheless choose their own application deadlines. This means that parents are still called on to turn in a separate copy of the application to each school they are interested in (Great Philly Schools, n.d.). Similar systems are set up through OneMatch in Indianapolis and GoodSchoolsRoc in Rochester (McCoy, 2018; Spectrum News Staff, 2018). Their success over time will largely depend on how well they address manipulation of the timing and content of applications for the most selective of choice schools.

CONCLUSION

Charter schools that require visits and entrance assessments on top of long and complicated forms have a more burdensome application process than many private universities. Add in the varying deadlines, and it's easy to see how the application stage is a time where many charter school policies and practices shape access. Because charter schools are usually in charge of their own application processes, they are often able to impose a daunting array of conditions.

In this chapter, we touched on practices that restrict access such as long and burdensome applications, early application deadlines, required in-person visits, and mandated assessments prior to admission. These conditions, especially when used in concert, clearly shape the pipeline of potential students.

In the next chapter we consider another way charter school officials can steer interested students and families away during the application phase: through conversations that occur early on with parents.

CHAPTER 7

The Steering Wheel
The Art of Dissuading Applications

> I [don't know if] we are not able to help all students . . ., but we recommend highly they look elsewhere if they have so many hours of special ed because of our limited services and we are not able to give as many hours as they need. _This is communicated with parents_. (Charter educator, personal communication, July 6, 2016, emphasis added)

This issue of whether a charter school is a good match for a student—in terms of, for example, pedagogical approach, services offered, and curriculum—arises repeatedly and spans multiple categories of our study. From this perspective of "match," it is reasonable to expect that charter schools routinely meet with parents prior to admission in an effort to ensure appropriate schooling opportunities for a student. However, such counseling sessions can easily cross over into discouraging students with greater need from following through with their charter school applications.

BACKGROUND BRIEFING

An early but particularly important study of special education in charter schools found that parents were successfully enrolling children with "mild disabilities" in charter schools, but only rarely were parents successfully enrolling those with more significant disabilities (Fiore et al., 2000). The exception noted in that early study, and confirmed in later research, involves mission-driven charters created specially to serve a particular type of students with special education needs (e.g., the New York Center for Autism Charter School). This same study, commissioned by the U.S. Department of Education, found that one in four charter schools reported having advised parents the school was not a good fit for a student with a disability (Fiore et al., 2000; see also Miron, 2014). Horn and Miron (2000) also documented that charter schools enrolled disproportionately fewer children with significant disabilities and found that some charter schools advise children with disabilities against enrolling.

Other research has documented mechanisms by which charters steer away students with disabilities (Estes, 2004; Howe & Welner, 2002; Welner & Howe, 2005; Zollers & Ramanathan, 1998). These mechanisms include communicating to parents or caregivers that the school does not have the services the child requires, applying repetitive disciplinary measures to students (e.g., suspensions), and not providing the services required in the student's IEP. Likewise, Casanova (2008) documented a practice of some charter school officials who meet with interested students and their families and counsel them out of attending the school due to perceived negative characteristics of the student.

The resulting enrollment disparities between charter and district schools become more acute for students with more severe disabilities. In Arizona, Anthony Garcy (2011) found that it was less likely for students who had more severe disabilities to attend charter schools in that state. He also found that students receiving special services enrolled in Arizona charter schools were less expensive, on average, than similar traditional public school students receiving special education services. Such enrollment disparities are a national trend. According to the 2015–2016 U.S. Department of Education's Civil Rights Data Collection (CRDC), students with disabilities that typically require fewer supports and services represent 82% of students with disabilities in charter schools versus 77% in traditional public schools (Lancet et al., 2020).

In a 2010 study of New York City schools (district and charter), Jennifer Jennings (2010) examined the role of schools in managing school choice. She found that although district policy did not allow principals to select students based on their performance, two of the three schools in her study circumvented these rules to recruit and retain a population that would meet local accountability targets. One principal, for example, was told by higher-ups in her charter school network to not produce a brochure in Spanish for a school choice fair because it would attract the wrong type of student (Jennings, 2010).

A 2018 study used an "audit" approach to uncover significant differences between charter schools and traditional public schools of choice in terms of the rates at which they responded to application inquiries from parents of students with special needs. Researchers posing as parents sent emails to over 6,000 charter and traditional public schools of choice in 29 states. In the emails, the "parents" inquired about how to apply to the school, and each email disclosed or signaled one of several randomly assigned characteristics of their child, including disability status, high or low prior achievement status, behavioral concerns, or none of these. They also randomly varied the students' implied gender and race. The researchers found that all schools of choice, charter and traditional, were less likely to encourage applications from students who had poor behavior and low prior achievement. But when the researchers signaled that the child had a potentially significant disability, charter schools withheld application information at higher rates—with "no excuses" charters being the prime offenders (Bergman & McFarlin, 2018).

FURTHER RESEARCH

Our research suggests the initial discussions between parents and charter school authorities have very real implications for access. In such preliminary conversations, charter schools can steer potential applicants away from that charter or toward a school that might be argued to better meet the needs of the family. Charter schools can thus signal their interest to parents and families they find most desirable, and they can signal their lack of interest to parents and families they find least desirable. In this way, there is a clear overlap between steering and marketing.

Signaling

There are many times parents have the opportunity to "shop" for charter schools, such as open houses, school enrollment fairs, and school tours. Several of our interviewees indicated these are times schools may signal to parents who they are seeking to enroll. Similarly, one of our interviewees described the hesitation many elite New Orleans charter schools had as the district transitioned to OneApp, the citywide centralized enrollment system, because of fears of losing autonomy. They were concerned that they could no longer rely on the strategy of using interviews to emphasize school expectations to students and parents. A school's established interview process can serve as an important shaping mechanism, and this option did in fact survive the switch over to OneApp, since students could still decide to enroll elsewhere after post-lottery interviews were conducted.

Another interviewee described how these steering conversations can interact with a charter school's location decision. She explained that while attending open house fairs in New York City it was not uncommon to hear charter schools ask parents where they lived; if the parents lived far away, charter officials would follow up with questions asking if students would actually be able to commit to attending school every day, given long subway commutes.

In 2017 The ACLU of California reported that to enroll in Leading Edge Academies, a network of seven charter schools in Arizona, parents and prospective students were required to meet with principals for an interview, which the school framed as helping to determine if the learning environment will benefit the student (Zetino, 2017). Similarly, when space became available at the Flagstaff Arizona's Pine Forest School, parents on the waitlist were contacted for an interview with the executive director and a teacher to ensure the school's specialized curriculum and program are suitable for the student (Zetino, 2017). These pronounced goals of suitability and benefit are not facially problematic, but parents may be differentially discouraged by the interview hurdle, resulting in relatively more student applicants with efficacious parents.

At Success Academy's Bronx 1 Elementary School, parents who win a seat for their child through the lottery must then attend a mandatory pre-enrollment meeting (Pondisco, 2019a). In his book, *How the Other Half Learns*, Robert Pondisco (2019b) describes the "warning" message Shea Reeder, a Success Academy principal, gave to Bronx 1 parents at this meeting:

> Echoing the language students hear daily in their classroom, Reeder tells the parents that she has a "thinking job" for them this evening. "Keep this question in mind during this entire presentation," she says. "Is Success Academy the right fit for me and my child?"
>
> "Although you're going to hear a lot of great and amazing things about us, there are some things you may say, 'Mmm, doesn't work for me,'" [Reeder] warns. "And that's fine too. Success Academy is not for everyone." She hits the word "not" emphatically. Nor is she freelancing or going off-message: As she speaks, a network-designed PowerPoint is projected on a screen above the stage behind her. The words "Is SA right for you?" loom over her. (p. 262)

During the hour-long meeting, Reeder also reminded parents about mandatory early pickups on Fridays and that the school did not provide transportation. Parents had to be able to return teacher calls within 24 hours because, as Reeder explained, "We want to make sure you are making an informed decision about coming to our schools. Because we expect that you accept us 100%" (Pondisco, 2019b).

Steering Away Students with Disabilities

In 2016, the U.S. Department of Education published a short fact sheet called, "Know Your Rights," along with accompanying resources, clearly stating that IDEA and Section 504 of the Rehabilitation Act fully apply to charter schools and their students (U.S. Department of Education, 2016; U.S. Departments of Education, Office of Civil Rights, 2016). However, many interviewees shared examples of schools steering away students with disabilities. The schools' expressed and implied concerns range from cost to disruption to test scores.

At Cambridge Lakes Learning Center in Illinois, the school board of the authorizing school district has heard complaints about special education services, including concerns that parents were being coached to modify their child's IEP in order to attend and that families were steered away because the school stated it could not serve their child's IEP needs (Community Unit District 300, 2016). Circle of Seasons charter school, a Waldorf school located in the suburbs of Allentown, Pennsylvania, required that a parent or guardian attend a public enrollment event to make a decision if the school is the right fit for their child (Of the Morning Call, 2016). The Northwestern Lehigh School District started the process of shutting down Circle of Seasons in 2016 after a comprehensive review found that the school failed, among other responsibilities, to comply with state and federal guidelines pertaining to children with disabilities, specifically, "failing to perform evaluations to comply with its Child Find obligations and discouraging the enrollment of special education students in the Charter School" (Northwestern Lehigh School District, 2016; Of the Morning Call, 2016).

An interviewee familiar with Child Find efforts in a major urban school district told us that parents inquiring with charter schools during the summer months about possible special needs identification were regularly told to instead seek evaluation with the school district. This redirection is particularly important because the district offers automatic placement if a child is identified as having special education needs upon evaluation. Consequently, when a child whose family was directed by a charter school to seek evaluation over the summer was identified by the district as having special needs, the charter schools were often able to avoid enrolling them.

Another interviewee, a researcher and practicing attorney, explained that he occasionally sees what he called "subtle gentle steering" of kids with severe emotional and behavioral disabilities. In these situations, a charter school tells parents that the school may not be the best fit. He shared that parent clients tended to describe these experiences as "I wanted to go to that charter school, but after talking with them it seemed like a bad fit."

The Southern Poverty Law Center and the Lawyers' Committee for Civil Rights Under Law sued the Louisiana Department of Education in 2010, alleging that post-Katrina New Orleans schools violated the Individuals with Disabilities Education Act (IDEA) (Mock, 2010). The basic contention of the lawsuit was that, "[a]s a result of the unique structure of public education in New Orleans, students with disabilities face insurmountable challenges when attempting to access educational services" (Dreilinger, 2015a). The founder of the Recovery School District and school choice supporter, Leslie Jacobs, admitted that the city failed students with disabilities after Hurricane Katrina and that many schools were simply not knowledgeable about or equipped to handle the needs of these children (Dreilinger, 2015a). The parties reached a settlement in December of 2014, requiring monitoring, training, and technical assistance for New Orleans schools. The settlement also dictated changes to the charter renewal process focused on properly serving students with disabilities (Southern Poverty Law Center, 2014).

A similar issue was identified in a recent report by the National Council on Disability (2018). The report describes how parents were questioned, after their children were "accepted" to a charter school but before they were enrolled, about whether their children had IEPs and about the level and types of services required. The parents said that these questions "adversely affect their child's enrollment at the school" (p. 60). We can think of this as early-stage counseling out, which is discussed in more depth later in this book.

But this underserving is not found everywhere. Washington in 2012 became the 42nd state in the nation to adopt a charter law, following a long and well-funded campaign by charter advocates. The rollout of charters in the state has been far from smooth, with several schools having to close soon after opening, due to low enrollment and other problems (Morton, 2019). But the story regarding access for students with special needs is more positive (Tuchman et al., 2018):

- Charter schools in Washington are serving students with disabilities, and almost all of them are doing so at rates higher than averages in Washington state and in the district in which they are located. (p. 1)
- Looking at the 10 then-existing Washington charter schools as a whole compared to the state average, these charter schools are serving a wide range of disabilities, both low-incidence disabilities such as visual impairments, or multiple disabilities and high-incidence disabilities like specific learning disabilities and communication disorders. (p. 3)

The Center on Reinventing Public Education, which published the analysis, did not explore the question of why Washington's initial patterns vary from national patterns. But if Washington is able to maintain those exemplary results, they should be studied in greater detail.

One other state, Maine, is also exemplary in this regard, and we do have a good idea of its beneficial practices. In Maine, charter schools enroll twice as many students with disabilities as the national average. The Maine Charter School Commission has been able to avoid the controversies that plague many other jurisdictions. This is, in part, due to an exhaustive review process prior to approving a new charter school and periodic site visits once a school is in operation. In response to accusations of charters in other states discouraging students from applying, the executive director of the Maine Association of Charter Schools told the Portland Press Herald, "Our law is very prescriptive about taking every child. We're serious about that" (Gallagher, 2015).

CONCLUSION

Closely related to description and to marketing is the steering process, when school staff signal their interest or disinterest to certain students. All of these approaches are about communicating "fit." The steering process often takes place right before or during the application process, when parents are seeking and considering schools for their children.

Discussions prior to admission between school representatives and prospective parents can be useful and healthy. But under the pressure of high-stakes accountability and competition, these discussions often morph from genuine conversations about addressing needs and matching interests to steering mechanisms that shape access.

In this chapter we considered the access implications of these early conversations between parents and schools that emphasized school rules and expectations for students and parents, often making the conversation much more about what the school wants as opposed to answering questions that parents may have.

We also reviewed the evidence concerning the steering away of students with disabilities. While generally not firmly refusing to admit these students with special needs, these charter schools push parents toward other schools or emphasize that they do not offer the students' needed program or resources. At times, these conversations go beyond problematic and stray into violations of the IDEA, which charter schools are not exempted from and which requires the schools enrolling students with special needs to provide them with a "free appropriate public education" via a uniquely tailored IEP.

In the next chapter we turn to another set of questionable practices—those that restrict and shape access during enrollment, usually immediately following the application process. Conditions placed on enrollment, like conditions placed on applications, serve to discourage families that charter operators may decide are less desirable.

CHAPTER 8

Send Us Your Best

Conditions Placed on Enrollment

> OCR [the U.S. Department of Education's Office of Civil Rights] is concerned
> . . . that the exclusion from admission and enrollment in [Harmony Public
> Schools] charter schools of students with a documented history of a
> criminal offense, juvenile court adjudication or discipline problems may
> improperly contribute to the lower enrollment of students with disabilities
> or ELL students in the HPS charter schools. (U.S. Department of Education,
> 2014, p. 20)

After completing the initial application process, students and families are tasked with navigating the remainder of the enrollment process to gain entry into a charter school. During this acceptance stage, charter schools can make enrollment decisions that shape their student population. As with conditions placed on applications, these conditions can shape enrollment by directly turning away families as well as by discouraging families that are perceived as less desirable.

BACKGROUND BRIEFING

When charter schools place conditions on enrollment, these conditions often overlap with a broader set of exclusionary policies and practices. Accordingly, several studies discussed earlier also directly address the findings we present in this chapter (e.g., Weiler & Vogel, 2015). A school that discourages enrollment by students with more severe disabilities, for example, might communicate this message through online program descriptions and through their applications, and then through expressly stated enrollment requirements. Looking at for-profit charter schools in Massachusetts, Zollers (2000) found that (1) some students who gained admission by lottery may have been barred once their disabilities were discovered, and (2) some students may have been rejected after admission because the school claimed it could not adequately serve them. Zollers and Ramanathan (1998) argued that these charter schools "engaged in a pattern of disregard and often blatant hostility toward students with more complicated behavioral and cognitive disabilities" (p. 299; see also Bulman & Kirp, 2000).

Jennings (2010) examined practices that appeared to impact a broader set of prospective students. She described New York City's system at the time, which allowed a charter school to give priority in admissions to students or families whose preference of that school was "informed":

> At the time of the study, schools were told to identify two groups of students: students who made an informed choice, and students who did not make an informed choice but whom the school was willing to accept. Students in the informed choice group were given first preference in the lottery, and if seats remained, students in the second group were then admitted. . . . [W]hat constitutes an informed choice was left to the discretion of individual schools. In an effort to ensure a strong incoming class, some schools used this discretion to raise the bar for admission. (Jennings, 2010, p. 231)

FURTHER RESEARCH

As explained by a researcher we interviewed, the in-house nature of enrollment practices makes it difficult to capture the specific nature of these enrollment barriers: "[W]hat is happening at that level no one knows. . . . A decentralized system with no oversight or regulations is so problematic on so many levels. We don't have good data or research on what's happening [at] that stage or how people are being pushed aside or out or in." Nonetheless, we were able to document several examples of how charter schools are limiting access during the enrollment phase, including avoiding students who schools might classify as disciplinary burdens and using enrollment preferences to strategically shape the student population.

Extended Days and Years

Many high-profile operators of charter schools have extended school days and years. KIPP schools, for example, routinely add 3–4 hours to the day and a few weeks to the year (e.g., via mandatory Saturdays and/or summer school) (Di Carlo, 2014). Although such extended days and more time in school are well intended and often beneficial and welcomed features of charter schools, they can effectively reduce access and become burdensome requirements for parents.

In a 2016 op-ed, parent Deborah Bennett identified these increased hours as a reason she chose to take her child out of Massachusetts's Conservatory Lab Charter School. She explained, "Our children put in marathon days, with only one break for recess in the middle. This kind of structure is not only harmful to students' physical and emotional well-being, it also runs contrary to recent research, which suggests that learners need physical breaks to promote academic achievement" (Bennett, 2016).

Sometimes, this extended time is evident across a district's entire charter sector. In 2008, for instance, the New York City charter school sector as a whole offered an average of 30% more school time than the city's regular public schools (Di Carlo, 2014). But these practices place a burden on students, their families, and even their educators. In 2016 Success Academy shortened school days because the network struggled to retain teachers and because of feedback from some parents who hesitated to enroll their children in the network's schools because the longer day meant they were unable to take part in activities outside of school (Taylor, 2015).

Dissuading Students with a Disciplinary History

An interviewee told us about two charter schools in Cleveland that screen out students who they see as potential disciplinary burdens. A 2015 report from the Delaware General Assembly corroborated that the Ohio Virtual Academy has an enrollment procedure that asks for information, including psychological reports, custody documentation, disciplinary records, and any weapons violations (Enrollment Preferences Task Force, 2015). Meanwhile, Stockyard Community Elementary will not enroll any student who is currently under suspension or expulsion from any other school or district. Further, Stockyard asks parents about IEPs and behavior modification plans. (The application also requests a birth certificate.) Five states (Arizona, Illinois, New Hampshire, New York, and Texas) have charter laws with specific language that allows charter schools to deny admission to students who have been expelled or are in the process of being expelled or who have a criminal offense (Enrollment Preferences Task Force, 2015). But just asking in applications about disciplinary history—rather than outright denial of admissions—can have the intended effect. As stressed by one of our attorney interviewees, this practice of asking students for a disciplinary or criminal record as part of the enrollment process has a large influence over who decides to enroll in a charter school.

Interestingly, even in those five states with permissive language about denial of admission, charter schools may be overreaching. In 2014, Harmony Public Schools, a Texas-based charter management organization with 54 campuses, was subject to a compliance review by the U.S. Department of Education's Office for Civil Rights (OCR) that found students with disabilities and emergent bilinguals (EBs) were significantly underrepresented. As set forth in the letter from OCR to Harmony quoted at the outset of this chapter, the OCR explained that although Texas state law provides that charter schools may exclude such students, OCR remained concerned that these practices may illegally have the effect of discriminating against students with disabilities and emergent bilingual students (U.S. Department of Education, 2014).

In Arizona, the law is slightly different. Charter schools may refuse to enroll students who are in the process of or have been expelled from another school, but they cannot deny students who have been or are in the process of being suspended. Yet, in 2017, the ACLU of Arizona found that 39 of the state's charter schools either refused to admit students with prior suspensions or implied that prior suspensions could affect admissions. In addition, the ACLU found that charters requesting disciplinary records often did not make it clear that the documentation would not affect a student's enrollment eligibility. This practice, the ACLU concluded, may suppress the enrollment of some students and send them a message that they are not welcome (Zetino, 2017).

Enrollment Preferences and Screening for High Achievers

Charter schools sometimes deny enrollment to students who fail to demonstrate high enough academic performance or who do not have high grades and test scores from previous years.

Simon (2013) noted a charter high school in California that "will not consider applicants with less than a 2.0 grade point average. Another will only admit students who passed Algebra I in middle school with a grade of B or better." She also pointed to states that allow charter schools to give admissions preferences to students who express interest in a school's theme or focus: "Some schools use that leeway to screen for students who are ready for advanced math classes or have stellar standardized test scores."

One of our interviewees shared that in addition to requiring that applications include copies of students' IEPs and birth certificates, Benjamin Franklin High School in New Orleans requires students to take an admissions test in reading, language, and math to avoid students whose test scores (combined with prior GPAs) are insufficient (Benjamin Franklin Charter School, 2016).

According to a 2015 report, this practice of explicitly screening applicants by academic performance is allowed in Florida, Louisiana, New Hampshire, Ohio, and Texas (Shapiro & Wysong, 2015). A second 2015 report identifies seven states that appear to allow charter schools to include a preference for demonstrated interest or academic performance: again Florida, Louisiana, New Hampshire, and Texas, as well as Delaware, Pennsylvania, and Wyoming (Enrollment Preferences Task Force, 2015).

These sorts of preferences allow charter schools to select their desired students during the enrollment phase, by prioritizing seats for students with high academic potential. Some approaches include an academic preference in a lottery, some use prior academic achievement as a condition of enrollment, some require a demonstration as part of the application process, and some require students to have a demonstrated interest in the focus of the school. Supporters of these strategies contend that it is important for schools and students to match interests. This can ensure, for example, that a school focused on the arts identifies students with the talent and passion for art. The resulting barriers to entry, however, create elite schools that systematically exclude students who are less advantaged.

A report by the ACLU Southern California and Public Advocates identifies 22 California charter schools that discriminate based on academic performance. For example, to apply as a sophomore to Western Center Academy in Riverside County, "Students must be earning an 'A' or 'B' in both Geometry and Biology," and "students must have an overall 3.0 or higher GPA with no failing grades." The school further "[r]equires 3.0 minimum G.P.A. without failing grades for 9th grade applicants, and 'A' or 'B' grades in Geometry (along with the 3.0 G.P.A. without failing grades) for 10–12th grade applicants" (Leung et al., 2016).

Similarly, the ACLU of Arizona found that although most charter schools in Arizona appear to accept all students, many schools still signaled that students with lower scores and grades might not be welcome. Close to half of charter schools analyzed in the report request academic records as part of the enrollment process and do not make it clear that those records will only be used for post-enrollment placement (Zetino, 2017). The report also notes how a placement exam required by Heritage Academy Gateway was apparently used in order to effectively deny admission:

> A parent filed a complaint with the Arizona State Board for Charter Schools in June 2016. The parent tried to enroll her daughter, who was entering 7th grade, for the 2016–17 school year. The school required her to take a placement test as part of the enrollment process. A few days after her daughter completed the placement test, the parent said she received a call from the school's registrar. "She called to let me know that the school wouldn't be a good fit for [my daughter] because she didn't score high enough," the parent wrote in her complaint. She said she asked if her daughter could participate in an organization and leadership class that the school offered to help students with the need for additional instruction. She said the registrar told her the class was only for students with an Individualized Education Program (IEP). The parent then asked if she could set up a meeting with the school to create an IEP for her daughter. The registrar, however, declined "and again said that she didn't think the school was going to be a good fit," according to the complaint.

Founder, Staff, Sibling, and Corporate Enrollment Preferences

Among the most common admissions preferences given by charter schools are those for siblings of current students, plus children of staff members and of the schools' founders. But this can be problematic, particularly for smaller, in-demand charters. In an interview with the *Washington Post*, Karyn Schwartz, a mother of 3-year-old twins, explained that after sibling preferences are considered, a very limited number of seats sometimes become available to new families hoping to enroll their children into some of the most in-demand charter schools in Washington, DC. She explained that by adding a preference for school employees, which was under consideration at the time by the DC Charter Board, "the greater community would be shut out of [those] schools" (Chandler, 2014a). The board did adopt a sibling, founder, and staff preference policy (DC Public Charter School Board, 2015), which was in part aimed at helping DC charters recruit and retain employees.

Several of our interviewees made the same point as Ms. Schwartz—that after these preferred applicants are admitted, schools can become virtually inaccessible to other families. Yet these preferences are very common. Consider Environmental Charter School in Pittsburgh, a school that was identified to us by an interviewee as "exclusive by design," because of its emphasis on ecological literacy. In addition to its unique mission, this charter school gives preference to siblings of already enrolled students. In 2014, after awarding seats to siblings of current students, only 28 seats were available for the more than 500 families who applied (Conti, 2014), making it nearly impossible to access for families not already in the school.

In Philadelphia, a 2015 audit of Infinity Charter School in Penbrook revealed a policy that gave preferential enrollment to children and grandchildren of its employees and board members. Infinity, a consistently top-performing charter school in the state, focuses on teaching gifted students and has had a waiting list of students wanting to gain admission since the school opened in 2003 (Murphy, 2015). The Pennsylvania auditor general concluded that this grandchildren policy created an unfair advantage to those students, which violated the intent of the state's charter school law.

In contrast, Arizona's charter school law clearly allows this, as well as plenty of other preferences.

> [Arizona's law permits] charter schools to give preference to children, grandchildren, or legal wards of employees of the school; employees of the charter holder; members of the governing body of the school; or directors, officers, partners, or board members of the charter holder and to a pupil who attended another charter school or to the siblings of that pupil if the charter school previously attended by the pupil has the identical charter holder, board, and governing board membership as the enrolling charter school or is managed by the same educational management organization, charter management organization, or educational service provider as determined by the charter authorizer. However, this preference does not address the children of a school's founders, and there is no limit on the percentage of a school's total student population that may be admitted via these preferences. (National Alliance for Public Charter Schools, 2018)

While preferences for siblings and children of staff and founders is grounded in a sound logic, it also has a predictable effect of eluding outsiders. As explained by an Idaho teacher discussing preferences in that state, when a charter school's parents, board members, teachers, and existing student body are already affluent and White, preferences will ensure that the newest groups of students will continue to be so as well (Trillhaase, 2015). Responding to this and other concerns, the Center for Community and Justice filed a 2015 federal civil rights complaint against the state of Idaho and all of its public charter schools. The charter school system, they argued, evolved into "a separate but unequal public school system" where students from low-income families, racially minoritized students, students with limited English skills, and students with disabilities were vastly underrepresented. The complaint named enrollment preferences given to children of school founders, employees, and siblings prior to a lottery as a process that "more often than not . . . leaves very few spaces available for those students who must participate in the lottery," which results in a system that favors well-connected students (Russell, 2015). One result of these preferences is that the vast majority of Idaho's charter schools are less racially diverse than the overall school population; they also enroll fewer non-English proficient students, fewer special education students, and fewer students eligible for free and reduced-price lunch than the state average (Idaho Public Charter School Commission, 2015).

In 2017, North Carolina legislators passed a flurry of bills related to charter schools. House Bill 800[1] originally included a unique provision effectively creating a corporate enrollment preference. The provision allowed charter schools to give enrollment priorities, for up to 50% of the school's total enrollment, to the children of charter school business partners who contribute land or other items valued at $50,000 or more (Hinchcliffe, 2017). The bill was, however, amended in the Senate, and this provision was removed.

In Georgia, charter enrollment guidelines allow a school to give priority to a group of students who are matriculating from another school. Taking advantage of that provision, Savannah Classical Academy gave priority to middle school graduates of another charter (Oglethorpe), effectively squeezing out the many other applicants for high school slots on the charter's long wait list (Meyer, 2019).

While these preferences tend to result in lessened diversity, charter schools can also act to use preferences in the opposite way. Recognizing this, the U.S. Department of Education issued new guidance in 2014 pertaining to the weighted lotteries used by charter schools receiving federal funding. These charter schools may now use weighted lotteries to give better chances for admission to all or a subset of educationally underserved students if state law also permits the use of such weighted lotteries.

While some states do not permit weighted lotteries for public charter schools (Baum, 2015), we found some examples of charter schools using such weighted lotteries and enrollment preferences to increase accessibility for students with higher levels of need. For instance, K–8 Carbondale

(Illinois) Community School initiated a new policy in 2016 designed to attract and increase Latinx enrollment. The policy gave an enrollment preference, during the school's annual admissions lottery, to applicants whose primary home language was not English (Stroud, 2016). Similarly, in New York, Brooklyn Prospect Charter and Community Roots Charter School, both located in gentrifying Brooklyn, adopted pro–diversity weighted lotteries by giving preference to applicants based on income status or whether they were emergent bilinguals (Potter & Tegeler, 2016).

Trinket Economy

Finally, consider the practice of charter schools encouraging enrollment by engaging in what is called the "trinket economy"—promising sneakers, laptops, iPads, and other gifts to enrollees and recruiters (Institute for Innovation in Public School Choice, 2014). For the most part, these practices are used to increase, rather than to shape, enrollment. But the decision about whether to offer gifts—and, if yes, what type of gift—can attract or even deter different segments of the student population. As explained in *The Intercept*, "In recent years, some charter schools have discreetly turned to a controversial recruitment strategy: offering low-income families cash stipends or other prizes in exchange for drawing new students into their schools. . . . Critics say these incentives amount to unethical bribes targeting primarily low-income families, though defenders say they're just shrewd marketing techniques" (Cohen, 2018). The article notes that at least one state (Colorado) has banned the practice, but that examples of financial incentives for recruiting—from gift cards for groceries to straight-up cash rewards—have been reported throughout the United States, including a post-ban example in Colorado.

The practice appears to be disproportionately used by for-profit charter companies, which tend to operate schools that serve relatively few advantaged families. A 2017 ProPublica article highlighted a number of for-profit charter schools that aggressively market to families with lower incomes in an effort to boost enrollment. For example, Edison Learning, the parent company of many for-profit charter schools, hands out Walmart gift cards for student referrals at its Bridgescape schools in Illinois and Ohio, claiming the gift cards enable students from low-income families to buy essentials (Vogell, 2017).

These approaches use parents and students as an appendage to a school's compensated salesforce. In doing so, we see a dynamic of publicly funded schools using those funds to recruit students away from other publicly funded schools. But beyond these ethical issues, these trinket economy practices probably skew enrollments toward families who are more financially strapped.

Continued Enrollment Policies

A given student's continued enrollment in many charter schools is not guaranteed. In fact, we identified an array of policies that determine whether a student remains enrolled in a charter school. In 2018, parents of 30 students enrolled at Marion P. Thomas, a New Jersey–based charter school, found out their children were dropped from the roster over the summer months for failing to provide proof of address as a form of documentation of continued residency. The school dropped students 2 months before the deadline that Newark Public Schools gave families in charter and district schools to submit residency forms, in an apparent violation of state regulations (Wall, 2018a). Another example is found in the GPA requirement policies at some charter schools, as discussed later (in Chapter 12). When students' grades fall below a given threshold, they are formally counseled out or told that they cannot remain at the school.

CONCLUSION

A report by Pennsylvania's Education Law Center (2019) notes that Philadelphia's Russell Byers Charter School presented itself as an open enrollment school while reserving the right to limit the enrollment of "at-risk" students, defined by Pennsylvania's charter school law, as "student[s] at risk of educational failure because of limited English proficiency, poverty, community factors, truancy, academic difficulties or economic disadvantage." This enrollment-limitation provision may sound extreme, but Russell Byers is not really an exception; about 40% of non-Renaissance charter schools in Philadelphia did not adhere to federal and state enrollment standards related to equitable access (Education Law Center, 2019).

For families in neighborhood public schools, enrollment is usually a simple process. But enrollment practices in decentralized, choice-based systems can be byzantine, particularly if the system has only minimal oversight. Enrollment preferences can strategically select high achievers and can deny enrollment to students with disciplinary histories. In schools with extended school days and years, required agreement to those terms can also significantly shape access.

Like most of the practices outlined in this book, conditions placed on enrollment often overlap with a broader set of exclusionary policies and practices. In many cases, for example, parents are required to agree to volunteer at their child's school during the enrollment phase. In the next chapter we consider the oxymoron of such mandatory volunteer commitments that charter schools sometimes require of families.

CHAPTER 9

Putting in the Hours

Requiring Parents to Volunteer

> Each family _must_ complete 30 or more hours per school year; however, 10 of
> that can be given by some form of donation in lieu of fulfilling these hours
> in increments of ½ hour per donation, not per item. All donations must
> be authorized by the principal in advance. [Parents or guardians] shall be
> able to satisfy a portion of their thirty (30) parent service/volunteer hour
> requirement by purchasing up to twenty (20) of these hours as follows:
>
> - The first ten (10) hour may be purchased for $10.00 per hour
> - The second ten (10) hours may be purchased for $20.00 per hour.
>
> (Pembroke Pines Charter School, 2018)

Traditional public schools can and sometimes do ask parents to help out, but it is generally understood that these are public institutions open for children to attend irrespective of such contributions. In contrast, some charter schools, like Pembroke Pines Charter School in Florida, have policies that state or imply that parents are required to commit hours of work as a condition of enrollment. Mandatory work commitments, sometimes called _sweat-equity contracts_, serve to turn away families that cannot afford to, or simply do not want to, make the significant time commitment, with enrollment shaped as a result.

BACKGROUND BRIEFING

A long line of research points to the numerous benefits of parent involvement in education for students, parents, schools, and communities (e.g., Fan & Chen, 2001; Jasis & Ordoñez-Jasis, 2012; Jeynes, 2003, 2007; Lee & Bowen, 2006). However, the level and type of involvement of a family in their child's education is strongly associated with demographic markers; White middle-class parents are typically the most visibly active in public schools (Lee & Bowen, 2006; Waanders et al., 2007). Language barriers, work schedules, and a sense of disenfranchisement have generally resulted in lower levels of (at least visible) involvement among working-class parents of color (Arias & Morillo-Campbell, 2008; Desimone, 1999; Jasis & Ordoñez-Jasis, 2012). Moreover, parental involvement can take on many forms, from community organizing and activism to school maintenance and fundraising to help with their children's studies—and sweat-equity contracts tend to focus on the former. Accordingly, while a solid research base generally finds support for increased parental involvement, the type of involvement demanded by charter schools is (1) less directly tied to student learning and (2) very likely to discourage parents with limited time and resources.

A few key academic studies document volunteer requirements of charter schools. A 1997 study by SRI International reported that 32% of the charter schools in their study had denied families admission to their schools due to parents not fulfilling a parental involvement requirement. This was more likely to have occurred in startup charter schools (37%) versus schools that had converted to charter status but were originally district run (27%).

Using the 1999–2000 Schools and Staffing Survey Public Charter School Questionnaire, researchers found 388 (40.9%) of charter schools in the weighted study sample had parental volunteer requirements (Lacireno-Paquet, 2006).

In a study examining parental involvement in 12 charter schools across six states, researchers found that these schools often reported using contracts specifying between 10 and 72 hours of service from each family annually. Moreover, the types of volunteer activities (e.g., school maintenance or beautification) were not commonly assigned to parents at traditional public schools (Smith et al., 2011).

In one of the first intensive studies of charter school reform in California, researchers conducted case studies of 17 charter schools in 10 school districts across the state. They found charter schools' most common requirement for parents was that they volunteer at the school and participate in school activities, either a certain number of hours or a certain number of events per school year (Wells, 1998). They also found that many of the charters reserved the right to ask families to leave if parents did not meet these requirements and could deny families admission to the school if parents did not agree to fulfill the sweat-equity requirements (Wells, 1998).

In a 1997 study, researchers found that 71% of California charter schools had a parent contract committing those parents to help at school and/or at home, compared to 8% of comparison district schools. The study compared survey responses from 28 charter school administrators with the responses of 39 comparison district school administrators (Becker et al., 1997).

FURTHER RESEARCH

As the examples that follow illustrate, sweat-equity contracts and other demands of parents' time remove certain schools from parents' choice sets. In deciding whether to demand parental involvement, charter schools are effectively choosing the groups of parents who will consider enrollment.

Sweat-Equity Contracts

Charter schools often call mandatory work commitments "volunteer hours," but as a 2014 report by Public Advocates concludes, work is not voluntary when it is required (Hammel, 2014). That report reviewed over 500 charter schools and found that nearly one third explicitly required unpaid parent or family "service hours," while only six had policies clearly stating that working at the school was not required (Hammel, 2014). The report prompted the California Department of Education to issue a guidance statement clarifying that schools cannot legally require parents to volunteer as a condition of student enrollment (Yamamura & Kalb, 2015). Nevertheless, a report a year later found that at least 63 California charter schools still maintained illegal work requirements. Schools were characterized as having an illegal policy when the words "required' or "requirement" appeared or when policies threatened to disenroll or penalize students (Leung et al., 2016).

For instance, the 2014–2015 family participation agreement at the River Charter School in Napa County, California states,

> I AGREE to fulfill my 25 hour volunteer commitment to the River School Community. I UNDERSTAND that my work at River School is valuable because it shows my student what it means to be a responsible member of a community. I UNDERSTAND that my work at River School is important because it helps keep River School's administrative costs low and frees up that money to be [spent] on the students. I UNDERSTAND that failure to complete my volunteer commitment will result in the loss of sibling priority status in the school admissions lottery; AND, it will result in my 8th grade student not being able to attend the 8th grade field trip; AND, it may result in my student's dismissal from River School. (Leung et al., 2016, p. 14)

In 2015, after Public Advocates published the report "Charging for Access," which called into question the parent involvement policies of many charter schools across the state, the California Department of Education (CDE) issued an advisory. The CDE, with the support of the California Charter Schools Association (2015), told charter schools and school districts that the law prohibits them from requiring parents to donate service hours.

However, these practices go far beyond California and are, in fact, not prohibited in most states. In Colorado, Weiler and Vogel (2015) found that most charter schools merely encourage parental involvement, but 39% of charters require a specific time commitment from parents for a student to attend the school. They found nine charter schools that expected between 50–150 hours per year.

According to one of our interviewees, Tennessee's Chattanooga Charter School of Excellence (2019) requires 20 hours each year from parents and guardians. This requirement is confirmed by the school's website which states, "CCSE parents are required to volunteer at least 20 hours each school year. Parents, grandparents and guardians may earn these hours." A *Chattanooga Times Free Press* article about the school explained that parents would be required to contribute assistance like raking the playground, and the article noted that parents must be involved if they wanted to attend the school (Hardy, 2011). At Keys Gate Charter School (2019) in Florida, parents must volunteer 20 hours of service for one child and then 10 more for additional children, and half of the hours must be completed prior to the winter break. Richmond's Patrick Henry Charter School (n.d.), the first charter elementary school in the state of Virginia, asks parents to sign a commitment to contribute 24 hours of time each school year. The school website explains, "Parental involvement is for the benefit of the child even more than it is for the school. That is why we require parental involvement and that is why we do everything we can to see that each parent participates." The website adds that its students "may return each year unless the involvement requirement is not met."

In 2014, a second grader was denied admission to Ben Gamla Charter School in South Florida over a parental volunteer contract. The school's volunteer protocol stated that parents must volunteer 30 hours a year to keep a child enrolled in the school. The mother of the second grader lost her job in March of the previous spring and took care of her younger child at home, preventing her from volunteering the required time at Ben Gamla. So when her son showed up in the fall, he was kicked out. The Department of Education issued a statement to NBC Miami claiming the school was correct in its move, elaborating that failure to fulfill responsibilities under a contract would be sufficient grounds to deny admission for the following year (Jones, 2014).

Paying Your Way Out

Other schools allow parents to buy their way out of mandatory volunteering commitments. Several examples of this practice were documented across California in the ACLU's "Unequal Access" report, including at Santa Ynez Valley Charter in Santa Barbara County, where parents were given the option of giving a financial contribution of $25 per volunteer hour. The school required a minimum of 3 hours per month, which amounts to $900 a calendar year. If a family did not fulfill their work quotas or make the required payments, then the student could lose priority enrollment for the following year (Leung et al., 2016).

In 2018, the Florida *Sun Sentinel* reported that for nearly a decade parents at eight highly rated Pembroke Pines charter schools could pay money to fulfill part of the network's mandatory 30-hour volunteer requirement, as suggested by the quotation at the outset of this chapter. This policy was despite the fact that paying down volunteer hours is forbidden by state law (Ballou, 2018). Although district schools in Palm Beach and Broward counties do not mandate volunteer hours, charters can. Charter schools in these counties can also deny admission to students for the following year if the obligation is not fulfilled. Parents at Pembroke Pines could pay $300 for up to 20 hours of service, and only have to "volunteer" for the remaining 10 hours of required labor. The Broward County School District alerted city officials after noticing the violation during a routine review (Ballou, 2018).

Other Demands on Parents' Time

Finally, we learned of several examples of charter schools that ask for significant time commitments from parents in ways other than mandated work for the school. An interviewee explained that the practice of requiring parents and guardians to visit schools several times prior to admission—a feature of charter schools inspired by Montessori and Waldorf—is a barrier to many families. Even beneficial practices, when mandated, can be highly problematic. For example, in 2013, local media reported that Inlet Grove (charter) High School in Riviera Beach required parents whose children have reading trouble to attend school with their children on Saturdays (Palm Beach Post, 2013). At Sun Ridge Charter in Sonoma County, parents must ensure children receive "wholesome, minimally processed family meals" and "protective layers of natural fibers, including hats for warmth and protection from the sun." Parents must also ensure a media-free experience at home (Leung et al., 2016). Finally, at Community Montessori charter school in San Diego, parents are expected to be enrolled in a program to learn English (Leung et al., 2016). Parents without the luxury of time to carry out these required tasks are discouraged from applying to such schools.

We also explored this work issue with some of our interviewees from the charter sector. One response was to acknowledge the sweat-equity provisions ("We do have schools who require parents to sign contracts where they commit to certain amount of work for the school") and then add, "but the schools can't require that, so they can't expel a kid for not living up to [the] commitment."

Yet, as another interviewee explained, the effect of these contracts can be strong even when they are not enforceable: "[The provisions] amount to non-binding contracts where as a parent you are asked to provide a certain level of support and commitment to a school's volunteer hours. . . . I know that those contracts can have the effect on some parents . . . of feeling like they [contracts] are . . . the trump card if things go south. If they are worded broadly enough, they can be interpreted to include all kinds of things." The "things go south" comment refers to the parents' concern that the school may use failure to comply with the sweat-equity provisions as a push-out lever if the school wants the children to transfer.

More generally, many of our interviewees pointed to these work requirements as daunting barriers for families, with the result that these provisions significantly shaped the population of students who could access the charters. As one interviewee explained, "[I]t is basically a tuition," and schools are effectively "pick[ing] students based on parental involvement."

CONCLUSION

Sweat-equity contracts serve as a steering mechanism. While any school can encourage parent volunteering, choice-based systems add the potential for schools to make enrollment conditional upon such contributions. As seen in this chapter, many charter schools have policies that either openly mandate or strongly infer that volunteering is required. When a school imposes mandatory work requirements for parents or guardians, it sorts potential enrollees between those with and without the capacity to volunteer. Specifically, it becomes near impossible for students to attend the school if their families do not have the time or resources to complete the volunteer requirements. While family engagement in school is important, requiring involvement ultimately serves to exclude certain students.

Another way charter schools are able to steer away students viewed as less desirable is by eschewing services for those students. In Chapter 10 we consider what happens when charter schools do not have services for emergent bilinguals and students with special needs and when they do not provide free or reduced-price lunch.

Not in Service

Emergent Bilinguals, Special Education, and Free and Reduced-Price Lunch

> A charter school may or may not have services designed to meet the needs of a given group of higher-needs children. For instance, teachers with TESOL (Teachers of English to Speakers of Other Languages) training or certification may be unavailable. Similarly, a charter school may not have the resources necessary to meet the special needs of a child with so-called low-incidence disabilities. [E]ven reading specialists . . . may be unavailable. (Welner, 2013, pp. 3–4)

Closely related to the steering issue is the actual availability of services. That is, parents of a student with special needs might be discouraged from enrolling at a charter school because a school official said that other schools could better serve that student (steering), or these parents might be discouraged because the charter school in fact does not have the instructional personnel or other services to serve the student. When, for instance, a charter school lacks services for students with special needs or emergent bilinguals (EBs), it is shaping its student population in a way that generally drives higher test scores and lower costs.

BACKGROUND BRIEFING

An early study of Michigan charter schools found that the schools were creaming the least expensive students to educate (Arsen et al., 1999). In particular, 75% of Michigan's charter schools were found to offer no special education services.

Similarly, a study carried out in Washington, DC, found that market-oriented charter schools, rather than "skimming the cream off the top of the potential student population . . . may be 'cropping off' service to students whose language or special educational needs make them more costly to educate" (Lacireno-Paquet et al., 2002, p. 145). Likewise, in interviews with Texas charter school officials, Estes (2004) found that wheelchairs could not access some charters and that a general lack of expertise and understanding of special education and disability law was common. As noted in Chapter 7, the enrollment disparities resulting from these practices appear to be more severe as the student needs themselves become more severe (see Garcy, 2011).

Drawing on qualitative data collected throughout the 2008–2009 academic year and a range of quantitative data from New York City's public high schools, Jessen (2013) showed that while small schools and choice were intended to expand schooling options for all, selection sets were often narrowed for students with special needs when entering the public high school choice process. Jessen (2013) also found that families of students with special needs did not consider schools to be viable options if they lack adequate special needs resources.

A study of charter school lotteries in Massachusetts found that applicants to charter schools were less likely to require special education services or qualify for free or reduced-price lunch. Charter school applicants also had generally higher baseline tests scores. The data suggested the possibility that some families were less likely to apply to Massachusetts charter schools (Angrist et al., 2013). This is consistent with findings from a 2017 study comparing enrollment trends in special education across disability categories and grade spans for public neighborhood and charter schools in Chicago. Researchers found that neighborhood schools served significantly higher proportions overall of students receiving special education services than charter schools (Waitoller et al., 2017). Importantly, they also found differences at a more granular level. The differences were driven by substantially smaller proportions of charter school students within some disability categories (autism, sensory impairments, and intellectual disabilities), while other categories saw charter schools enrolling equal or occasionally higher proportions of students (learning disabilities, speech and language impairments, other health impairments, and emotional disturbance) (Waitoller et al., 2017).

The same patterns emerge when looking at research concerning EBs. In their 2011 study, Bulkley and Sattin-Bajaj examined the enrollment of EBs in charter schools and traditional public schools in New York City and found that most charter schools enrolled a smaller percentage of EBs than did the district. But they noted that there was also variation in the sample, with some charter schools enrolling a similar percentage of EBs or a greater percentage than the district average. In terms of outreach, Bulkley and Sattin-Bajaj (2011) suggested that some New York City charter schools might deliberately exclude some students, specifically EBs and students with disabilities, in order to increase the school's test scores.

In an analysis of the 40 states, Washington, DC, and metropolitan areas with large enrollments of charter school students, Frankenberg and colleagues (2011), found the percentage of White students in charter schools without the School Lunch Program to be nearly twice that of White students in charter schools that do offer the School Lunch Program. Those charters that offer the School Lunch Program not only have a much higher percentage of students of color—58% are Black and Hispanic—but nearly 60% of students receive free or reduced-price lunch.

FURTHER RESEARCH

We identified three service-provision mechanisms that allowed charters to shape enrollments: (1) lacking special education services, (2) lacking services for emergent bilingual students (those whose primary language is not English), and (3) not offering free and reduced-price lunch. Notably, several of our interviewees explained, as reasons for why these services were not available, that charter schools may not have the expertise to properly interpret federal law, or they have insufficiently trained staff who do not know their obligations.

Lacking Resources for Special Education

An Arizona mother who tried to enroll her sons in the Great Hearts Archway Arete school in August of 2015 described the following:

> I tried enrolling my sons and was placed in the school's lottery system. In January, we were selected from the lottery and were invited to enroll. I called the school and asked to speak to whoever was in charge of special education services. I wanted to make sure my son, who had been diagnosed with autism, would get the services he needed. At the time, he had an Individualized Education Program (IEP), which spelled out his learning needs and the services the school was to provide. The school's response, however, was disappointing. I was told the school could not accommodate my son and that they didn't have the resources to serve my son's needs. At the time, I didn't know much about charter schools. I thought they operated similar to private schools and, therefore, weren't required by state and federal law to provide the same special education services as district schools. (Zetino, 2017, p. 14)

While a charter school cannot generally, under the IDEA, reject students with special education needs or refuse to honor their IEPs, it is often sufficient for the school merely to point out the unavailability of resources and services (Welner & Howe, 2005). As one interviewee told us, some charter schools in New Orleans "present themselves as not having the expertise of serving students with disabilities; we know that happens because we talked to parents." Another interviewee described how she was told on a school tour that services were not readily available for students with IEPs.

A third interviewee explained how it is not always clear whether, when schools do "some dumb stuff" regarding special education, it is because of naivete or negligence. Ultimately the result is the same: Parents of children with special needs often return to district schools because, even if they have the time and resources to advocate for their children, getting services will likely take a lot of time and aggravation. This is precisely the situation described in a 2015 article about a lawsuit against the Achievement Prep network of charter schools in New York City. Dottie Morris, the mother of a child at Achievement Prep Crown Heights, told *The New York Times* that it took more than 2 years to provide a paraprofessional to help her son (Harris, 2015). As rational people, parents of children with special needs will shy away from placing those children in the hands of a school that outwardly professes inexperience, incompetence, hostility, or lack of necessary resources.

The challenges facing these parents can indeed be daunting. In a 2015 report reviewing Illinois charter school admissions practices, the advocacy organization Equip for Equality (EFE) describes an unnamed charter school that explicitly warns parents that admissions and continued enrollment is contingent on the availability of special education services. The report also describes an EFE client with autism who was initially told that there was space in a charter school but when the mother provided the student's IEP, the school case manager told her she could not enroll her son due to his special education needs, so the mother sent him back to a district school (Shapiro & Wysong, 2015).

Beginning in 2014, Stargate Charter School, a Colorado school referenced previously in regard to its entrance assessments, started battling numerous civil rights violations. Between 2014–2018, nine civil rights complaints were filed against Stargate. In a 2018 Westword article, a parent described how despite being sold on the school's focus on twice exceptional students she ended up having to fight to get her son services: "[B]ecause it was a charter school, I thought I didn't have the right to demand the level of support services as [at] a regular school," the parent said (Olabi, 2018). Additionally, although the responsibility for identifying students with disabilities also falls on a school, this same parent had to spend thousands of dollars to bring a diagnosis to Stargate and finally got her child on an IEP for the 2017–2018 school year. However, even with the legally binding plan, she learned that her child hadn't received services until months after the year started (Olabi, 2018). Similarly, an Arizona mother of a child with autism explained to a reporter how San Tan Charter School signaled to her that her son is unwelcome:

> The [San Tan] school told me to send in copies of his IEP and to take a tour. Not one word was mentioned on the tour about special education services, but there sure was a lot of talk about their program for gifted students. I tried to follow up with repeated emails and phone calls but was completely ignored. (Zetino, 2017, p. 14)

Policy steps can be taken to address these exclusion issues. A good example is provided by a 2010 policy adopted in Denver. Charter leaders and Denver public schools (DPS) signed a district charter collaboration compact, which promised equity regarding special education. Approximately 1.9% of DPS students (or nearly 1,400 children) have significant disabilities; these students attend center-based programs within schools across the city that provide specialized education services. Historically, these centers were exclusively in district-operated schools, but this policy has changed as a result of the collaboration compact. In 2016–2017, 25 charter schools offered center or inclusion programs to approximately 175 students, representing 12% of all center students in Denver's public schools. By 2017–2018 the charter sector in Denver was expected to serve a proportional share of students with significant disabilities. Further, all charter contracts now include a provision requiring charter operators to open a center if the need arises in their neighborhood or region (Doyle et al., 2017). In the 2019–2020 school year, 11.8% of students in Denver Public Schools and 11.1% of students in Denver charter schools had IEPs (Colorado Department of Education, 2020).

Similarly, the Thrive network of charter schools in San Diego has put in place a set of best practices designed to address Child Find and service issues for students with special needs (Rhim & Lancet, 2018). After the school's enrollment period ends and students accept their spaces, Thrive requests all related documents and data for those students with IEPs, and school staff work to provide their students with a continuity of support and services. At the beginning of each school year, students who do not yet have an IEP but may qualify for special education services are evaluated for their progress in the general program. If a student demonstrates potential eligibility, additional evaluations are performed to determine an appropriate course of action. Thrive's school leadership also fosters an intentional partnership between general and special education teachers, through 300 hours of annual collaborative planning, data review, and professional development. The Thrive network's curriculum, built on active and personalized learning, is also amenable to a diverse group of students. These cumulative steps increase access: Compared to San Diego and the entire state of California, Thrive enrolls higher percentages of students with disabilities and EBs (Rhim & Lancet, 2018).

Refusing to Screen Students

Charter schools can deny services by simply refusing to screen students for learning disabilities, even though refusing to evaluate and identify students with special needs violates the Child Find requirements of IDEA. An interviewee who works for an early childhood education Child Find center described receiving a large number of requests for evaluation from parents who were enrolled in charter schools when the center first opened. These parents, he said, were unsuccessful at initiating the process at charter schools, and reported that the charters were unwilling to screen their children.

The *Times-Picayune* reported in 2015 that New Orleans' Lagniappe Academies were accused by the state of refusing to screen students for special education services, even when families provided documentation of a diagnosis from a doctor. The charter school also refused to allow a student to come back unless the family produced a note from a doctor proving the student was taking their medication. Finally, the school allegedly "illegally deprived special education students of the teaching they needed—and then faked forms to hide it once the Louisiana Department of Education was on its trail" (Dreilinger, 2015b). As outlined in a 2010 lawsuit (later settled) filed by the Southern Poverty Law Center (2010) on behalf of 10 families in post-Katrina New Orleans, charters in that city also over-relied on Section 504 plans (under the ADA) in an effort to avoid providing special education evaluations.

A few hundred miles to the west, parent Britany Miller described being told by YES Prep, a growing network of Houston charter schools, that charter schools did not have to offer accommodations to students with learning disabilities (Tedesco & Webb, 2019). According to the *Houston Chronicle*, Miller confronted this when she spoke with the school about enrolling her son, who struggled with attention issues. When Miller then inquired at a second Houston charter school, Yellowstone College Prep, the school refused services and refused to screen her son (Tedesco & Webb, 2019). Similarly, Jenn Smith, a BASIS North Central parent, shared that it took her nearly a year to get the school to evaluate her daughter who she suspected had a reading disability (Tedesco & Webb, 2019). In 2018, only 48 of 2,600 students received any type of special education services at BASIS schools in the state of Texas (Tedesco & Webb, 2019).

Low- Versus High-Incidence Disabilities

When asked about charter school access, experts repeatedly mention special education. In particular, they point to fiscal issues regarding students with special needs. The ultimate financial burden incurred by a school depends in part on the state finance system, but in any given state there are very real financial incentives and disincentives involving the enrollment of students with special needs. Moreover, these incentives differ among different students with special needs; it is costlier for schools to serve students with more severe (low-incidence) disabilities—which is why the aforementioned Denver collaboration compact is noteworthy.

An interviewee with experience as an attorney representing students with special needs explained his experience with charter schools resisting the provision of needed services for students with low-incidence disabilities:

> I would say that the biggest issue that I see is kids with low incidence disabilities [such as] Down Syndrome. I have seen some schools,

infrequently, hire one to one aides to make school more accessible, but there is a real resistance with most charters providers I work with to modify what they do too much. They believe their current methods already differentiate. [For] a client with autism, I would never say you should go to that charter school because I know that school would have to change its practices . . . not to say it wouldn't, but it would be a struggle through the IEP process.

Another interviewee, who had experience working in a school district on these special education issues, explained a time where the district was providing special education support to a chain of charter schools in the city:

[F]or any kids that [are] enrolled in those charter schools and who had severe needs, they would be headed our way because [the schools] didn't have a set up to run a self-contained autism classroom, for example. So we [the noncharter schools run by the district] would get a consolidation of the greatest-need kids in [the district], a practical outcome of charter schools not targeting those kids.

A 2012 *Twin Cities Daily* article highlighted Dugsi Academy, where only 4% of students were identified as needing special education (Brown, 2012). This is much lower than the 18% rate in Minneapolis and St. Paul district schools. In an interview with the newspaper, the assistant director of Dugsi explained the school did not have the space to serve students with level 3 special education needs—students who spend at least 60% of the school day away from their regular education peers. Nova Classical Academy, also highlighted in the article, served only a single level 3 student in 2012 and none in the previous school year.

Similarly, Pennsylvania's Education Law Center (2016) found that the charter sector in Philadelphia serves a population of students with disabilities that requires lower cost aids and services. According to the report, students requiring higher cost services are more heavily concentrated in traditional public schools, with a few exceptions. The report also found that *segregation by disability type* results in racial segregation. Black students are overrepresented in the population of students with disabilities that require higher cost aids and services. A later report from the Education Law Center found that although, on average, district and charter schools in Philadelphia serve similar percentages of students with disabilities, the differences in disability populations are significant. Charter schools in Philadelphia serve higher percentages of students with low-cost (or high-incidence) disabilities and very few students with high-cost (or low-incidence) disabilities. For example, only five charter schools serve the same or higher percentages of students with autism than the district average, and 20 charter schools serve no children with autism (Education Law Center, 2019).

This same pattern is documented in a 2019 report by the California Teachers Association, which found higher concentrations of students with less severe disabilities in charter schools compared to district schools in Los Angeles, Oakland, and San Diego:

> Students who generally require greater support and more costly accommodations are systematically under enrolled within privately operated charter schools. This statistically significant disproportionality by severity was identified in nearly half of the IDEA eligibility categories considered most severe. Conversely, students with disabilities considered to be mild to moderate—generally requiring less costly accommodations—made up a greater percentage of the special education enrollment within privately operated charters. When it comes to moderate to severe disability, these students comprised between 23.7 and 28.9 percent of the special education population enrolled within the three cohorts of district schools. Conversely, within privately operated charter schools the concentration of these students ranged between 12.9 and 16.25 percent on average. (California Teachers Association, 2019, p. 18)

These examples illustrate the practices and tensions underlying the consistent finding of lower special needs enrollment in charter schools, as well as the disproportionately low enrollment of students with the most severe needs (Garda, 2011).

Other Special Education–Related Concerns

One interviewee told us that charter schools in New Orleans would routinely deny services that the therapist declared necessary—but that parents have few realistic remedies:

> [T]hey do illegal things here all the time. They count on a large percentage of black people being poor and so they don't have the money to afford an attorney to sue them. Because the schools have no one [single] system—it's a system of systems here—so you would have to go to their board which is often made up of their friends, and then you have to go to court. Most parents cannot afford an attorney, and [even] if they can, lots of attorneys don't know education law.

These concerns arise far beyond New Orleans, however. As mentioned earlier, Cambridge Lakes Charter School in Pingree Grove, Illinois, generated complaints to the authorizing school district that parents were "coached to modify their child's IEP in order to attend CLCS" and that CLCS counseled "families away from the school, . . . stating that they 'cannot serve their child's IEP needs'" (Community Unit School District 300, 2016).

Even though charter schools in Arizona cannot legally limit the number of enrolled students with special needs or turn away these students (citing absence of special education programming or accommodations), in 2017 the ACLU of Arizona reported apparent violations. Examples include Rising School in Tucson, which put all students with an IEP on a waiting list because their special education department was full, and AmeriSchools Academy, where special education placements are limited to a capacity of 10 students for each school site (Zetino, 2017). In addition, close to half of the charter schools in Arizona analyzed by the ACLU asked during the enrollment process if students had a disability and needed special education services (Zetino, 2017).

Emergent Bilinguals

Charter schools must ensure that EB students can participate meaningfully in educational programs, pursuant to the Equal Educational Opportunities Act of 1974 and Title VI of the Civil Rights Act of 1964. However, as with students with special needs, we found many examples of charter schools lacking the resources necessary to support these EBs. This is illustrated by the application form for Manzanita Middle School in Contra Costa, California, which has a single sentence in Spanish that says all instruction is in English and that the school has no bilingual classes (Leung et al., 2016). As another example, two former teachers charged the Oakland Charter Academy with giving no accommodations or differentiated instruction to EBs in core classes, which resulted in many students failing all subjects. They further claimed that EBs were pulled out of English classes by untrained tutors, and that these students were then sorted into separate groups with low-performing students and students with special needs, without any instructional differentiation (Epstein, 2016).

In 2014, two groups, the Vietnamese American Young Leaders Association (VAYLA) of New Orleans and the Asian American Legal Defense and Education Fund, filed a complaint with the United States Education and Justice departments. The complaint alleged that several New Orleans schools violated civil rights law by failing to adequately serve families whose native language was not English. The majority of Asian American and Latinx respondents to a 2011 VAYLA survey said no adults at their schools spoke their native tongue. Three quarters said their families were not provided with interpretation services for important school meetings. Respondents described English as a second language (ESL) classes where "watching movies and sleeping" was the norm. Some respondents thought they were enrolled in ESL classes only due to their last names (Dreilinger, 2013).

Illinois has a law setting minimum standards for teaching EBs. A 2017 audit of Chicago-area public schools found that the majority of worst violators of this law were charter schools, including 15 schools belonging to the UNO Network of charter schools and nine belonging to the Noble Network of charter schools (Belsha, 2017).

Similar audits in Philadelphia use the Charter School Performance Framework to inform Annual Charter Evaluations (ACEs), interim evaluations in between charter approval and renewals. But researchers with the Education Law Center (2019) found an interesting glitch in evaluations as they are applied to English learner students:

> [C]harters are uniquely likely to meet EL compliance standards without actually serving EL students. Many of the schools that score compliant on the EL standards of the ACEs have no EL students at all. Because 2 of the 3 EL standards are dependent on the presence of EL students (EL Timely Evaluation and ESL Access), charters can be deemed successful in serving EL students while enrolling few, if any, of such students. (p. 17)

Further, the ACEs mandate that limited English-proficient students and families receive translation and interpretation services to ensure they understand enrollment processes. Despite this, the Education Law Center found that 15% of traditional (non-Renaissance) charter schools in the city failed to demonstrate compliance with the legal requirements for enrollment language policy. The majority of that 15% did not tell callers posing as interested parents that they would provide them translation or interpretation services (Education Law Center, 2019).

Free and Reduced-Priced Lunch

Several interviewees shared that when charter schools do not participate in the federal free and reduced-priced lunch program they are cutting out low-income students who cannot afford to pay for meals. In fact, a Reuters investigation found that thousands of charter schools are out of reach for children in poverty because they do not provide subsidized lunches (Khrais, 2016). According to a 2010 California state audit of brick-and-mortar charter schools (that is, not including cyber schools), 18% did not offer free and reduced-priced meals, and 39 charter schools in the state did not offer any meal service at all (California State Auditor, 2010). For families that qualify for these subsidized meals, choosing a charter without that service would mean sacrificing an important benefit.

The Arizona- and Texas-based CMO Great Hearts Academies, a network of charter schools enrolling more than 13,000 students at 29 schools, is highly acclaimed for its results. Great Hearts' pass rates on Arizona's statewide achievement tests and the average SAT scores of students have been substantially higher than peer district schools and national averages (Alonzo, 2014). But who is served by these schools? While "more than half of Arizona's public school students qualify for free or reduced-price lunches, ... only two of 19 Great Hearts schools in the Phoenix area participated in the National School Lunch program and received federal Title I funding for at-risk populations" (Malik, 2015).

School meals legislation and funding vary by state. On one end of the spectrum are states like Arizona where there is no legislation requiring schools to participate in the national school lunch/breakfast programs; on the other end are states like Hawaii where breakfast and lunch must be made available in every school (including charter schools) (Food Research and Action Center, 2017). In California, all public schools (excluding charter schools) must offer at least one meal on school days to all free and reduced-price certified students (Food Research and Action Center, 2017). In 2018, this requirement was extended to charter schools, via AB 1871. In 2020–2021 over 690,000 students attended California charter schools, and, based on family income, over 57% of them would qualify for free and reduced-price (FRPL) meals (California Department of Education, 2021). Even though all charter schools are eligible for federal funding that reimburses schools for money spent on meals, as of 2018 more than 81,000 low-income students in the state attended charter schools that do not offer free and reduced-price school meals (Kritz, 2018).

CONCLUSION

Charter schools looking to limit expenses will benefit from enrolling fewer students whose educational needs include costly interventions and resources. If these schools enroll fewer students with special needs, who are poor, and who are not yet fluent in English, then they can also anticipate a boost in average test scores. Accordingly, charter schools often feel incentivized to not provide free and reduced price lunch or lack special education and language services. Whatever the reason—a venal desire to lower costs and raise test scores or merely a lack of knowledge, funding, preparation, or capacity—the result is largely the same: Students who need special education and language services and students who face food insecurity are pushed away from schools that do not offer them these basic accommodations.

In the next chapter we begin to consider access-restricting practices that occur after students have already enrolled in the school. These push-out practices are particularly problematic because they don't just restrict access; they also disrupt students' education.

CHAPTER 11

The Fitness Test

Counseling Out

> Students who are accepted to KIPP [Knowledge is Power Program] and who
> have IEPs do not get the correct services or help to be successful. The school
> would rather make it difficult, leaving the parent frustrated and forcing her
> to remove her child. The principal always invited me to take my child out
> if I did not like the way she was being treated. (Charter parent quoted in
> Haimson, 2012)

Decisions to leave a charter school can be motivated by many factors, some unrelated to the school (e.g., changing neighborhoods because of parental employment). In this chapter, however, we address a school-related practice called *counseling out*, and in the two following chapters we address additional school-related practices: strategic use of grade retention and school discipline.

Parents of students who are not meeting the standards of a particular charter school or those whose enrolled children are viewed as a poor fit may simply be told that they should consider transferring out. This is usually accomplished through ongoing meetings with the charter schools' teachers and administrators (e.g., "Bobby isn't responding well to instruction, getting along well with other students," etc.). A reasonable way to address a disappointing experience in a school choice context is to seek out a different school, and a nudge from school staff can help move this process along (Welner, 2013).

BACKGROUND BRIEFING

Charter schools sometimes engage in counseling out subgroups of higher need students (Bulkley & Fisler, 2002). Zollers and Ramanathan (1998) uncovered several cases in Massachusetts where students receiving special education services were removed from a charter school when their disabilities were discovered. They concluded that for-profit charter school directors likely engage in counseling out students with "complicated disabilities and expensive needs" as a common practice by suggesting they would be better served elsewhere.

In a 2000 study commissioned by the U.S. Department of Education, researchers found that rather than making accommodations and providing required services, charter schools systematically counseled out students with disabilities (Fiore et al., 2000). Additionally, administrators at a quarter of charter schools in the study reported that they advised parents of students with disabilities that the school was not a good fit for them.

In a 3-year qualitative study of special education in U.S. charter schools, researchers found that the process of advising children with disabilities into or out of charter schools outside the traditional IEP process was a recurring concern among disability advocates (Rhim & McLaughlin, 2001). In more than half of the states in the study disability advocates perceived that some students with disabilities were counseled out of charter schools but that counseling out was not limited to students with disabilities; it also occurred with nondisabled students who were particularly challenging (Rhim & McLaughlin, 2001).

More recently, a study exploring charter operators' knowledge of federal special education legislation found that the most common reasons given by school administrators for counseling out were "a conflict between the child's need and the charter's mission and vision," "unavailability of special education services," the "presence of behavior problems that interfered with other students' learning," and a "lack of qualified staff to address students' needs" (Drame, 2011, p. 60).

In a 2017 study, Kho and Zimmer, using longitudinal student-level Tennessee data, found that students with high numbers of discipline infractions were, relative to better behaved students, about 13–14 percentage points more likely to exit charter schools than traditional public schools. This statistically significant difference suggests that Tennessee charter schools are counseling out students with disciplinary problems. In a 2019 study, Kho and colleagues found that exit rates for lower performing students were disproportionately high, relative to higher performing students, in Tennessee and North Carolina charter schools—and they found this was particularly the case when considering students' behavioral histories. Students with prior suspensions or expulsions were 23% and 15% more likely to exit charter schools in Tennessee and North Carolina, respectively, than were students who had not been previously suspended or expelled in each state. In contrast, Zimmer and Guarino (2013) found no such evidence of counseling out (of lower performing students) in an anonymous major urban school district's charter schools, suggesting that the phenomenon may be minimal or nonexistent in some locales.

FURTHER RESEARCH

We found the process of counseling out usually involves a targeted discussion, nudging certain students and families to consider different school options after they have enrolled in a charter school. Although the counseling out process is sometimes relatively overt, it is usually difficult to document quantitatively for many reasons. For example, even if a charter school publishes high attrition numbers, the numbers do not tell the story of why students and families chose to leave. Yet our interviewees repeatedly told us of counseling out, particularly related to special needs and to discipline.

Students with Special Needs

Dating back to the early days of charter school policies, the failure to adequately serve students with special needs has been an ongoing problem. Counseling a student with special needs to leave a school is a violation of Section 504 and the Americans with Disabilities Act (ADA) requirement that students with disabilities be given access to an educational program that is equivalent to their nondisabled peers. Nevertheless, parents of these children generally acquiesce to the schools' wishes to have them choose a different option. Evaluator and charter school researcher Gary Miron (2014) explained:

> While conducting nine evaluations of charter school reforms for state education agencies between 1997 and 2007, I learned of numerous cases in which families were counseled out and told that it would be some time before the charter school could offer special education supports. Parents can fight—and some do—but these parents are already overextended and tired.

In some instances, however, parents have indeed pushed back or gone public to describe their treatment. As we recently explained (Mommandi & Welner, 2018, p. 61):

> In the fall of 2015, *The New York Times* broke a story about a "Got to Go" list generated by leaders of the Success Academy charter school in Fort Greene, Brooklyn (Taylor, 2015). The article described how the elementary school used a variety of discipline-related approaches to pressure families of the children on this list to withdraw. The targeted children were, it seems, not achieving or behaving as well as the school wished. Several parents interviewed by the *Times* said that school or network staff members explicitly told them the school was not right for their children. Nine of the 16 students on the Fort Greene list eventually withdrew from the school.

Eva Moskowitz, founder and director of the Success Academies, explained that her charter schools are "not the right fit for every student, and that [she believes] in having honest conversations with parents about what is best for their children" (Chadha, 2015).

Similarly, reacting to the got-to-go list, "James D. Merriman, the chief executive officer of the New York City Charter School Center, a group that advocates and supports charter schools, said it was unrealistic to expect any given school to be a good fit for every child" (Taylor, 2015).

In 2016, the parents of 13 Success Academy students with special needs submitted a formal complaint to the U.S. Department of Education alleging that several campuses of the charter network refused to provide students with appropriate services and often retained these students, requiring them to repeat grades. The complaint told the story of one boy with severe learning disabilities who was originally placed in a general education classroom only to be retained. After a new evaluation that recommended small class sizes, the child's parent was told that small classes were not available and that the arrangements were being made for the child to transfer to a public school (Gonzalez, 2016). Earlier, in 2013, the *New York Daily News* reported videotapes of Success Academy staff admitting to the mother of a student that they were not meeting the IEP of that student. After having repeatedly suspended the boy because of behavior in violation of the school's zero-tolerance discipline policy, school staff encouraged his mother to transfer her child back to the public school system. But the staff admitted on the tape that his behavior was related to his speech disability, adding that the network does not offer smaller special education classes in kindergarten (Gonzalez, 2013).

Likewise, a 2019 complaint filed on behalf of a parent of an elementary schooler alleged that the network engaged in a "campaign of harassment" designed to force a student with special needs out of Success Academy Bed-Stuy 1. According to the lawsuit, the school pushed the Brooklyn child out by repeatedly suspending him, calling the child services agency on his mother, and even dropping him off at a police precinct (Zimmerman, 2019).

The 2015 "got to go" list was, therefore, just one instance of an ongoing pattern. Parents of five children with disabilities who were all on that Success Academy charter school list filed a lawsuit in federal court alleging disability-based discrimination under federal law (Advocates for Children New York, 2018). In March of 2021, a federal judge in Brooklyn ordered Success to pay a judgment of over $2.4 million (Klinger & McGrath, 2021).

But these same practices are also found in other charter schools. In 2018, an Arizona mother filed a complaint with the state's charter board against Heritage Academy, days after her son's 1st day of school. Haylee Barthol said the school forced her to withdraw her son on the 2nd day of school because they "didn't have the resources for his issues." Barthol was reportedly told that her son could only continue to attend Heritage if she volunteered at the school every day to supervise him (Harris, 2018).

Roby Chavez, a parent of two children with special education needs enrolled in New Orleans's Bricolage Academy, told board members in March of 2019 he had been told by multiple school staff that the school could no longer provide for them (Jewson, 2019). Chavez also voiced concerns that he and other parents of children with special education needs had with Bricolage's after-school program. Chavez claimed parents were asked to pay extra money for children with disabilities to have extra support. Bricolage's aftercare director allegedly told one parent that maybe the program was not a right fit for their child. Chavez explained this is code for "we don't want your child in our school" (Jewson, 2019). In an interesting twist, Chavez's day job is the communications director for the Louisiana Association of Public Charter Schools.

In a 2018 report examining the challenges and best practices associated with special education and charter schools, the National Council on Disability interviewed a number of stakeholders—parents, children, and state officials—in several states who commented on the practice of counseling out.

> For example, one parent advocate noted that charter admissions personnel might counsel out students by trying to convince parents that the school is not an appropriate fit, making statements such as "We're not sure we can meet your needs. You might want to look for a different school. Have you gotten into other schools off the lottery?" Another advocate commented: "Sometimes it's very blatant and [charter schools] actually use those words, 'this isn't the right school for your kid, you know, maybe you would be happier somewhere else.'" (National Council on Disability, 2018, p. 61)

In the report, an official working at a state department of education explained:

> "[I]n our state . . . we do stress that any new school that is approved must certify that they will accept any, that they will not deny students based on things such as if they have an IEP. . . . We tell [the charter schools] . . . they can't counsel out those students, but unfortunately we know it happens. Even if they don't use the exact words, they make it such that . . . [the school is] not as attractive to all students." (National Council on Disability, 2018, p. 61)

Virtual Charter Schools

Virtual charter schools, many of them for-profit, have been plagued by scandals ranging from management issues to very low achievement results—and problems with access have emerged as well. One recent example was documented by Oklahoma Watch and concerned efforts by Epic Charter Schools to avoid having lower performing students impact accountability ratings. Specifically, former teachers told Oklahoma Watch that "[t]eacher bonuses were dangled like 'a carrot' and used to push for withdrawals of low-performing students" (Palmer, 2019). If withdrawn students reenrolled in the virtual charter school, they were not included in accountability measures (Palmer, 2019).

Disciplinary Counseling Out

Many interviewees shared stories about the ways charter schools are able to counsel out students for behavioral reasons. An attorney explained how it works:

> Virtually always if a school says, "we can expel you or you can withdraw," the student withdraws. I've never had a parent take that risk; they always withdraw. It's sort of unfair because if the charter did go through expelling they would be responsible for educating the kid. But because they can threaten expulsion they won't have to bear the cost of that expulsion financially, because the parents always leave before expulsion.

A law professor who has done similar work confirmed this pattern of practice. She explained that it is not uncommon for expulsion cases to "disappear" after students are told that there will be nothing in their record if they leave. Parents (very sensibly) take the offer, to prevent the child's school record from reflecting the suspension or expulsion. She also contended that disciplinary push-out approaches strategically target lower scoring students as a way to keep their scores from counting against the school: "[K]ids get dumped during test time, I'm convinced it's a problem."

At PPEP TEC High Schools, a network of six charter schools in southern Arizona, all students are enrolled on a 2-week probationary period. During this probationary period, if a school feels an enrolled student failed to follow its discipline matrix, the student may be withdrawn. The student may also be withdrawn after the probationary period if the school decides that it is, for some other reason, not an "appropriate placement" for the student (Zetino, 2017).

In 2005, Houston Independent School District Superintendent Abe Saavedra told state Senator Mario Gallegos that 407 children moved to HISD from charters during the 17 weeks prior to state testing. Gallegos wrote to the state's education commissioner to investigate into alleged student dumping (Gilbert, 2005). Similarly, a researcher who has spent time in New Orleans explained the deep sense of mistrust that emerged over this issue among different school leaders. The principals she met with often accused other schools of kicking students out who would not test well for them:

> I did hear a lot of accusations of other schools . . . [including] one example where a principal [received charter transfer] students midyear, the week before testing. She was concerned about it, the score would count for her, even though there was barely any opportunity to work with the child.

As explained by the leader of an organization in Detroit, "The threat of long-term suspension or expulsion can cause a family to 'voluntarily' leave a school. If long-term suspension or expulsion becomes official, the student cannot get into another school, DPS or charter, without special permission from the School Board. The kid winds up in the alternative system, and most parents would rather leave the school on their own than take that risk" (Institute for Innovation in Public School Choice, 2014).

The worry that voluntary withdrawals may not be very voluntary has prompted some charter sector leaders to look more closely into the issue. A charter board president we spoke with explained his office correlates voluntary withdrawals with the number of times a child has been suspended. As the frequency of suspensions increases, the likelihood of withdrawal correspondingly increases. He could not say whether giving multiple suspensions was an intentional strategy by charter schools to remove particular students, but he confirmed the correlation is there.

A New Orleans–based interviewee told us how she would hear from families of children who received frequent in-school suspensions. These frequent suspensions lead to significant time away from classes and instruction, resulting in ongoing struggles. This cycle combines with counseling to nudge particular students to not reenroll over the summer, pushing them out relatively unnoticed, in the face of scrutiny over high expulsion and out-of-school suspension rates.

Some charter schools may even be counseling out students who are overage and under-credited, because of pressures to meet strict standards. (An interviewee also mentioned age cutoffs, whereby some charters refuse to enroll ninth graders if they are too old.) A *Detroit Metro Times* article describes the situation of teachers at one charter school who were fired after coming to the defense of Etab Ahmed, a 20-year-old immigrant from Yemen who was pushed out of the school after being told to write out a statement in English that she did not understand: "I am Etab Ahmed want to finish the high school through GED. And do not want to continue at Universal Academy—Etab Ahmed 11/10/15" (Gross, 2016).

As a researcher explained to us, "It's not just about suspending; it's about having a climate that is so intolerant of people that they choose to leave." Consider the following additional examples:

- A student was trying to get to school on time in New Orleans and violated school policy by crossing a train track to get to campus. He was given two options, expulsion or voluntary withdrawal—so he withdrew (George-Parkin, 2014).
- "Nineteen of the last 20 children to leave KIPP Academy [in Tennessee] had multiple out-of-school suspensions. Eleven of the 19 are classified as special needs, and all of them took their TCAPs at Metro zoned schools, so their scores won't count against KIPP" (Clawson, 2013).
- "There is no reporting or tracking to monitor potential wrongful expulsion or dismissal of 'less desirable' students by charter schools. The [Alameda County, California] Grand Jury heard testimony that some charter schools may counsel a student to leave that school for a variety of reasons including recurrent misbehavior or lack of achievement. Witnesses testified that this procedure would be unknown were it not for 'whistleblowers'" (Alameda County Grand Jury, 2016, p. 90).

Strict Attendance Policies

The ACLU of Arizona reports that at least 30 charter schools in the state have stricter attendance requirements than is required by law (Zetino, 2017). A typical example is Harvest Preparatory Academy, which has three campuses in the state. As reported by the ACLU, the policy states, "Students are only allowed 5 excused absences throughout the year. Tardies and early departures are included. If a student exceeds the limit, a meeting will be arranged with the parent and school administrator" (Zetino, 2017, p. 24). Other schools have policies stating that absences will result in lowered grades, grade retention, suspension or expulsions, or the student being "dropped" from the school.

In 2017, seven charter schools were cited by the Philadelphia Charter Schools Office for having truancy policies that allow for expulsion and/or suspension for truant behavior. Students truant three times or more at the Boys' Latin of Philadelphia Charter School receive an out-of-school suspension. These policies are in clear violation of Philadelphia truancy law, which states, "Schools shall not expel or impose out-of-school suspension, disciplinary reassignment or transfer for truant behavior" (School District of Philadelphia, 2018).

New Orleans Crocker College Prep has a policy of disenrolling students based on attendance. The 2021 parent handbook outlines this policy, for kindergarten through 8th grade; students may be disenrolled for 15 or more consecutive absences, and pre-kindergarten students "[m]ay be disenrolled if the student fails to attend 74% of school days for two consecutive months" (p. 3).

District Pushout

Interestingly, reporters at ProPublica recently documented the converse phenomenon: "alternative" charter schools serving as a dumping ground for school districts seeking to hide low-performing students from accountability systems (Vogell & Fresques, 2017). They found that traditional high schools in many states are free to use alternative programs like the ones at these charter schools to rid themselves of students whose test scores, truancy, and risk of dropping out threaten the schools' standing. As a result, these alternative schools and programs can become warehouses that poorly serve at-risk students. While alternative schools are not inherently harmful, the ProPublica reporting shows how abuses can arise if policy and financial incentives make it mutually beneficial to charter schools and district schools to enter this sort of devil's bargain.

Students told reporters in San Diego of a similar phenomenon, whereby they "left the district after staff members at their San Diego Unified schools encouraged them to leave because they fell behind in credits or exhibited behavioral problems" (Koran, 2017). A recently retired high school principal acknowledged the counseling out: "All principals have done it. I did it. If students fall behind to the point where no matter what you do they still wouldn't graduate, you have to give them some kind of option." The newspaper documented:

> In the 2015–2016 school year alone, 475 students left the district and transferred to the Charter School of San Diego or one of its two sister schools, Audeo and Laurel Prep Academy. . . . Each school offers independent study programs, which allow students to create schedules tailored to their availability and goals, and online coursework students can complete from home. Students don't have to physically attend school every day. (Koran, 2017)

The 475 students at these three schools were 82% of the 581 total who left district schools for charter schools that year. But as the newspaper also pointed out, these online instructional models are "ridiculously easy to cheat" (Koran, 2017).

CONCLUSION

Issues of special needs and of discipline continue to emerge as flashpoints for denied access, and we certainly see that here. When charter school authorities see students as problematic for these or other reasons (e.g., attendance), they can—and sometimes do—attempt to counsel them out of the school. As with most access-restricting practices, oftentimes the neediest students are those who are left behind.

In the next chapter we turn to two other practices that fall under the broad umbrella of counseling-related practices: mandatory GPA requirements and grade retention policies.

CHAPTER 12

Pass Interference

GPAs and Grade Retention

From BASIS's first year in 1996–1997, students who failed the
comprehensives had to retake them. If they did not pass, they were not
promoted. Most of the parents who were told their children had to repeat
a grade took them out of BASIS instead. (Mathews, 2020)

I always knew that Success Academy left a lot of kids back. I just never
thought that it was, at minimum, one out of six. (Rubenstein, 2018)

As a rule, students do not want to be considerably older than their class-
mates, particularly as they approach adulthood (Baumhardt & Julin, 2018),
nor do they want to be separated from their friends. So grade retention
threats can be powerful at the stage of application and enrollment as well as
any time after the student has been attending the charter school. As Welner
(2013) explained, some charter schools tell unwanted students and their
parents "that if the student remains at the school, she will be retained in
grade. . . . One effect of such policies is to rebuke less successful students
and to suggest that those students may do better elsewhere (and to inform
them that they will have to go elsewhere if they want to graduate on time)."

BACKGROUND BRIEFING

An extensive research base examines the academic and life effects of
grade retention (Griffith et al., 2010; Hong & Yu, 2007; Jimerson, 2001;
Jimerson & Ferguson, 2007; Ou & Reynolds, 2010). In a nutshell, the research finds no sustained academic benefits but finds a clear detriment: an
increased risk of dropping out (Hughes et al., 2017; Jimerson et al., 2002;
Roderick, 1994; Stearns et al., 2007).

A 2010 Mathematica study found a systematic pattern in the rates of
grade repetition at 22 KIPP middle schools. Almost all of the schools in
the study retained students at significantly higher rates than other public
schools in the same districts (Tuttle et al., 2010). Likewise, findings from a

2013 CREDO report analyzing New York City charter schools suggested that the charters were more likely to retain academically low-performing students than were district schools. In Denver, a 2013 study of the widely lauded Denver Schools of Science and Technology (DSST) network of charter schools found that about 10% of students had to repeat an entire year because they were required to pass courses with a C or better (Spillane et al., 2013).

FURTHER RESEARCH

We found that the practices of grade retention, administering placement tests, and having minimum GPA requirements were all ways in which charter schools could push students out of schools and, in some cases, misleadingly inflate test scores.

Grade Retention

As a researcher we interviewed explained, strict grade retention policies could be a mechanism that serves to send selected students back to traditional public schools. The numbers for some well-known charter schools also lend support to our interviewee's claim. In 2004, the founder of the Democracy Prep network told *The American Prospect* that in 2003 more than 20% of the sixth-grade class was held back and that the network lost about half of the eighth graders it planned to retain. At the time, around 15% of the eighth-grade class was held back each year (Garland, 2010).

A 2010 Chalkbeat analysis found that New York City charters Williamsburg Collegiate Charter School, Harlem Village Academy, Leadership Village Academy, and KIPP S.T.A.R. all retained a large number of students in their entering classes each year between 2006 and 2009 (Gittleson, 2010). This suggests that the higher test scores produced at all four schools during that time period might have been the result of students repeating grades and thus retaking tests (Gittleson, 2010).

In a 2018 report on the Denver Schools of Science and Technology (DSST) charter network in Denver, the Century Foundation found that

> [i]n every track, DSST struggles most with the academic performance of students with disabilities. At several schools in the network, the numbers of special needs students are so small that the state does not publish performance data for that subgroup, leading to questions about retention or pushout of this population of learners. Adding to the concern is the comparatively low graduation rate of special needs students at the schools where such data exists. In the class of 2016 at Green Valley Ranch High, during which time the school had a SPED

population of only 3.1 percent (compared to 10.7 percent that year in Denver Public Schools), only 25 percent of students with disabilities graduated within four years. It is worth noting that DSST, compared to most schools, is more likely to hold students back for further academic preparation, and the five- and six-year graduation rate was not available for that subgroup. (Quick, 2018, para. 41, internal citations omitted)

In the 2013 study of DSST cited earlier, the network's CEO explained how DSST: Stapleton "had to keep 25 kids back in ninth grade because they weren't prepared and we weren't going to cheat them out of what they needed" (Spillane et al., 2013, p. 50). Similarly, after Three Oaks Public School Academy in Michigan got a letter from its authorizer, Bay Mills Community College in 2008, informing the school the authorizer intended to revoke the school's charter contract due to low achievement, the K–5 charter school responded by using student retention as one of its turnaround strategies (Moore, 2015).

James Irwin Charter Schools in Colorado Springs describes grade retention as a "gift" (Simpson, 2012). In 2011, 20 of the school's roughly 530 students in grades K–5 were offered the "gift" and three immediately withdrew. In 2009–2010, the last year Texas published grade-level retention data by district type in annual reports, Texas charters had a 10.1% grade retention rate, while all major urban districts had a 4.5% retention rate (Texas Education Agency, n.d.).

Even (noncharter) districts can use retention policies as a way to push out students they do not serve well. In 2011 Harrison School District 2 in Colorado Springs adopted stringent retention policies that resulted in the district holding back about 10% of eighth graders. As a result of this district-wide policy, some students left the district entirely when they learned they could not move on with their peers. The superintendent at the time was quoted in the *Denver Post* as saying, "And we suspect we'll have some others leave once we hold back third-, fifth- and eighth-graders in May. But we have a whole bunch of parents who realize this is the right thing for their child" (Simpson, 2012).

Threatening retention can boost test scores in two ways: It prompts students the school labels as low performing to leave the school, and those who do not leave may generate higher test scores after getting an extra year to prepare for the tests. An analysis of Harlem-based Success Academy's first graduating class found that approximately one out of six students had been held back (Rubenstein, 2018). According to Gary Rubenstein (2018),

One of the ways that Success Academy gets students to leave their school is to tell them that they are going to be left back if they stay at Success Academy. Then the students are given the option of transferring to a different school and not being left back. I've known for a while that this happens since I've heard first hand accounts of this, but I didn't know how common it is.

Placement Tests

One interviewee explained that KIPP charter schools—an acclaimed network of "no-excuses" schools and the nation's largest chain of charter schools—has been known to retain relatively larger numbers of students as part of their "tough love" philosophy. From 2003–2011 KIPP Ujima, a popular charter school in Baltimore, used a diagnostic exam to determine whether new students seeking to enter sixth grade were performing at comparable reading and math levels as the school's fifth-grade classes. If potential sixth graders did not pass the test, they could enroll but would have to repeat fifth grade. The school stopped administering the test in 2011 because of the potential to misinterpret the practice as a way of attracting high-performing students, according to the executive director of KIPP Baltimore at the time (Green, 2011).

Such placement tests are also administered at James Irwin Charter Schools in Colorado Springs, which uses a curriculum based on what they identify as the great ideas and values of Western heritage. Their website explains, "Placement tests are given to students in grades 1–12 to ensure they are placed in the appropriate level to be challenged and successful. . . . If your student's academic ability is different than the grade level expectations for our schools, they would need to be placed on the waitlist for the appropriate grade" (James Irwin Charter Schools, 2015).

Starting in kindergarten, grade promotion at BASIS Charter Schools requires earning a minimum of 60% and passing all course projects during the year. Then, beginning in middle school, students must score a minimum of 60% on all comprehensive exams. For high school, all students are required to pass several AP courses (BASIS Charter Schools, 2015). The grade retention that likely follows from these policies can lead to attrition. For example, during the 2012–2013 school year BASIS Scottsdale enrolled 144 students in the sixth grade but only 32 in the 12th grade (Loew, 2015). Other BASIS schools show a similar pattern. In the nation's capital, BASIS DC enrolled 57 ninth graders in 2016–2017, despite enrolling 95 eighth graders the year before (DC Public Charter School Board, 2016, 2017). In 2013, the DC Public Charter School board rejected a proposal from BASIS to expand in the city, specifically pointing to the concerning number of students who withdrew during the school year. At the time, the head of school was quoted in the *Washington Post* as saying,

> When a BASIS school comes into a new market, there are students who understand and know what the workload is and what it takes to be successful at

BASIS, and there are students who are not prepared to do that kind of work. (Brown, 2013b)

The attrition at BASIS is best understood as intentional—as a feature rather than a bug. Those who enroll without fully understanding its exclusive nature will soon learn and then remove themselves, often under pressure.

Audubon Charter School in New Orleans, referenced earlier, was highlighted by another interviewee for its placement exam that measures adequate proficiency in French for students to enter the first grade. The school's website has a FAQ section that includes the question, "My child does not speak French and did not attend a French Immersion pre-school. Can I still apply for Kindergarten in the French school?" The answer is, "Yes. We do accept Kindergarten students with no prior French experience. Students are required to demonstrate adequate proficiency to enter first grade, therefore your child may be required to have two years of Kindergarten" (Audubon Charter School, n.d.). Audubon also requires that "Applicants who are English Language Learners will be required to take the Internet based Test of English as a Foreign Language (TOFEL)." Students must score 100 or better and parents are responsible for testing costs. Many parents would balk at these requirements.

A California-based interviewee pointed out that even when charters will take all students at all grades, some will have grade-promotion exams. Students must pass the exam in order to move on to the next grade. If they do not pass, they face grade retention, so they often go back to public schools. We also interviewed a portfolio district official who oversees charters and who echoed this concern:

One barrier we've seen, and I think this happens in district [schools] but is more common in our charters, [concerns] students' enrollments in non-entry grades. [This happens when] a student is supposed to go to third grade but the school wants to retain them based on reading level. Our charter schools can have [their] own promotion and retention policies, but [our district] works with them to be sure they are applied equitably.

GPA Requirements

Another way to counsel out students with academic struggles is to have school policies setting firm expectations for minimum GPAs. For example, as the ACLU or Arizona reported in 2017, at Copper Point High School in Tucson, Arizona, students "must receive a 'C' grade or better in a course to receive credit. If students consistently demonstrate poor character or academic progress, a request will be made for a 're-interview' to determine if the school 'continues to be the right fit for them'" (Zetino, 2017, p. 22).

Similarly, at Northpoint Expeditionary Learning Academy (NELA) in Prescott, Arizona,

> the school will request for a "re-interview" of the student if, "the student demonstrates poor academic progress, behavioral concerns or other issues that "indicate the support of the school expectations is waning." According to the school, "This process is designed to help a student determine whether NELA continues to be the right fit for them." In addition, the school states in its handbook that it "does not encourage students with academic or behavior problems to apply." (Zetino, 2017, p. 22)

A 2016 report documented that at Accelerated Achievement Academy in Mendocino County, California, students on academic probation for two consecutive semesters are told they are at a school that does not meet their needs (Leung et al., 2016). An interviewee described a similar policy at Lusher Charter School in New Orleans, where parents and students are asked to sign a contract conditioning continued enrollment at the school upon maintaining an overall core subject GPA of 2.0 (Lusher Charter School, n.d.). If a student's GPA falls below a 2.0, a letter is sent home saying the family must find another school. According to our interviewee, however, parents who were able to push back could sometimes negotiate for their child to stay. As a result, the policy serves to target parents who are scared, or do not have the resources, to challenge it.

Mandatory Summer School

Freire Charter School, one of the oldest charters in Philadelphia, is a college preparatory school with substantial grade-level promotion requirements. According to the 2016–2017 family handbook, at Freire a "passing grade" is 75% or above. If a 5th or 6th grader fails a core class, they can take summer school to be promoted. However, if 5th and 6th graders fail two or more classes, they are simply retained with no summer school option. From 7th grade through high school, students must pass all core and enrichment courses; they must take summer school if they fail in order to be promoted. During their 8th-grade year, all students must complete a portfolio of work, from throughout the year, in order to demonstrate their readiness for high school. They must also present, explain, and reflect on their work to prove that they are high school ready. The portfolio process is also a promotion requirement (Freire Charter School, n.d.).

Although mandatory summer school is a common feature of many school districts to help struggling students move on to the next grade, it usually does not begin until high school. But, as pointed out by a charter leader we spoke with, charter schools are free to have mandatory summer programs at any grade level. And charters can condition grade promotion on successful completion of the summer classes. Students who reject this requirement or are unsuccessful can, however, transfer over to a district public school.

Mandatory College Acceptance

In 2014, Nashville-based LEAD Public Schools proclaimed that every senior in the first five "graduating classes" at LEAD Academy had been accepted into a 4-year college. The network has garnered praise for this improbable feat, especially since the majority of students had come from low-income families (Garrison, 2014). However, the feat was due in part to a provision included in the school's handbook (and even expressly included in LEAD's original, approved charter application): Students were told that they would not graduate—would not receive their high school diploma—unless they had been accepted into a college. Metro school's executive officer of charter schools was quoted by Nashville Public Radio as worrying that this policy might discourage certain students from enrolling at LEAD in the first place (Chatlani, 2018). A provision like this is also a clear message to struggling students to not stay at the charter if you don't see yourself heading toward college acceptance. After questions of legality were raised, the renewal of LEAD's charter took out the offending provision (Chatlani, 2018).

CONCLUSION

Threats concerning grade retention and GPA requirements can quite effectively convince students that they should leave a charter school. When charter schools embrace grade retention practices, despite the large research base on the deleterious effects of the practice, students and their parents can be faced with the choice of either repeating the grade or leaving the school. In some cases, mandatory placement tests serve as a retention mechanism before a student has even set foot in a classroom. Similarly, when charters impose GPA requirements for continued enrollment, struggling students leave and the school benefits from higher average test scores. In addition, the threat of retention and GPA requirements might be enough to make potential families weary of applying or enrolling in the first place if the student has a history of academic difficulties.

One reason a student's grades may suffer is if they are excluded from the classroom via suspensions. In the next chapter we turn to extreme discipline practices that function to restrict access to certain students.

CHAPTER 13

No Excuses

Discipline and Punish

> We expelled 31 students one year, and then the very next year we expelled 30 students. And we kind of hit the reset button on our school. (Casey Mulligan, head of *Mohave Accelerated Schools in* Bullhead City, Arizona, quoted in Flaherty, 2018)

Harsh discipline regimes allow charter schools "to maintain a more controlled school environment through the selective removal of students who these schools deem as more disruptive" (Welner, 2013). These practices have occasionally garnered considerable press coverage. As we noted in Chapter 11, Success Academy's "got-to-go" list made national headlines.

BACKGROUND BRIEFING

Cavalier and frequent use of suspensions is harmful, as it contributes to chronic absenteeism and is correlated with lower achievement; it also predicts an increased risk of grade retention, lower graduation rates, behavior characterized by schools as delinquent, and involvement in the juvenile justice system (Balfanz et al., 2015; Marchbanks et al., 2015; Noltemeyer et al., 2015; Shollenberger, 2015). Yet while there has been a great deal of scholarly attention paid to school discipline practices in their own right, relatively little research has been published that focuses on charter school discipline practices.

In an early study, Horn and Miron (2000) used school-based data from 51 charter schools, representing about half of the Michigan charter schools in operation at the time, to provide evidence that behavior and discipline were among the common reasons students left traditional public school districts for charter schools. That is, families were seeking an environment with fewer behavioral disturbances and more structure. But the researchers found that frequent suspensions in the charter schools "nearly forced" some students to return to the district (p. 22).

We also note two key studies that will be referenced more extensively later on in this chapter:

- A 2016 report by the Civil Rights Project at UCLA that found that Black students are suspended four times the rate of their non-Black and nondisabled peers in charter schools, while students with disabilities are suspended at two to three times the rate of their nondisabled peers in charter schools (Losen et al., 2016).[1]
- A 2016 study of Philadelphia charter schools finding that most of these schools turn too quickly to exclusionary school discipline as a response to student misbehavior (DeJarnatt et al., 2016).

FURTHER RESEARCH

Discipline disparities connected to race and to special needs are pervasive—in traditional public schools and in charter schools. The practices in the two sectors overlap considerably, as undoubtedly do the underlying biases and beliefs. A 2018 report from the University of Pittsburgh's Center on Race and Social Problems showed that in Pennsylvania's Allegheny County Black students are suspended on average seven times more than non-Black students. The disproportionality in discipline is seen across both sectors: charter and district (Huguley et al., 2018). As discussed next, however, the use of exclusionary discipline varies considerably among schools.

When students are repeatedly subjected to exclusionary discipline, they can get caught up in the so-called school-to-prison pipeline—falling further behind in school, becoming more disengaged from school, and becoming more entwined in the criminal justice system (Kim et al., 2010). For students in charter schools, exclusionary discipline also can serve as an impetus to disenroll. Next, we review the discipline disparities found between the sectors and then outline four types of troubling disciplinary practices that research suggests are used by charter schools.

Discipline Disproportionalities

Disciplinary regimes are disproportionately felt by Black students and students with special needs. As noted, these inequities are found in traditional public schools as well as charters, although some evidence suggests that charter schools suspend at higher rates on average, at least when looking at comparable demographics of students. In the 2018 report by the National Council on Disability referenced in Chapter 11, stakeholders—parents, children, and state officials—noted that some charter schools also quietly advise parents that the school is not an appropriate fit for their child because of behavior.

After analyzing discipline data from nearly 5,000 charter schools, gathered by the U.S. Department of Education's Office for Civil Rights, Losen and his colleagues (2016) found that "the charter school suspension rate was 16 percent higher than the non-charter school suspension rate" (p. 2). But it is two other findings that are most relevant to this book: (1) "The 20 highest-suspending charter schools in 2011–12 all suspended more than two-thirds of their student body at least once; all but six of these schools had Black enrollment greater than 50 percent"; and (2) "At 484 charter schools, the suspension rate for students with disabilities was 20 percentage points higher than for those without disabilities" (p. 2). That is, just as we see in noncharters, the extreme use of suspensions is less a sector-wide problem than a severe problem within a subsector of the charter world.

These national trends also show up in local research. Equip for Equality, a nonprofit that advocates for people with disabilities in Illinois, found that in Chicago harsh charter school discipline policies disproportionately affect students with disabilities. While only about 12% of charter school students had an IEP in 2015, 26.2% of students expelled from charter schools had an IEP the previous year (Shapiro & Wysong, 2015). Likewise, a 2016 CityLab geographic analysis of school discipline in Boston, New York, and Washington, DC, showed that in all three cities charter schools out-suspended and out-expelled their district counterparts and that the hyper-disciplinary schools in all three cities were all charter schools located in concentrated majority Black neighborhoods (Joseph, 2016). Similar patterns have been documented at KIPP DC AIM Academy, a middle school in Washington, DC, where students who received special education services were suspended at a rate of 48.2% compared to a 28.2% average for DCPS (Abdul-Alim, 2015), and at Crossroads Charter School, in Charlotte, North Carolina, which suspended nearly three quarters of its Black students in 2011–2012 (Rich, 2016).

Death by Demerits

A way that charter schools use discipline to shape their student population is what one interviewee called "death by demerits," a point-based system in which tallies are kept for each student for behavioral infractions, including very minor infractions. As a result, students continuously, and often rapidly, accumulate demerits that lead to more severe consequences such as in- or out-of-school suspension. In an op-ed she penned in the *Washington Post*, a former charter school English teacher explained, "I once gave out 37 demerits in a 50-minute period. This was the sort of achievement that earned a new teacher praise in faculty-wide emails at Achievement First Amistad High School, in New Haven, Connecticut" (Fisher, 2016).

The cycle of a student accumulating demerits, the parent required to then attend meetings, and the student missing instructional time wears families down and leaves students behind. It also informally pushes them out of these schools.

In fact, when New York City–based Democracy Prep took over the management of a Las Vegas charter school, its new "no-excuses" culture was enough to prompt many parents to pull their children out of the school (Ortiz, 2018).

The broken windows theory—first introduced in 1982 and applied to building maintenance and to policing (Wilson & Kelling, 2015)—is behind these point-based behavior systems, which are commonly found in no-excuses charter school networks. Those buying into this approach to discipline are philosophically committed to "sweating the small stuff." When charter schools sweat the small stuff, they often punish actions that other schools would ignore in order to dissuade worse actions.

For years, the Noble Network of charter schools issued demerits for acts like not sitting up straight or not wearing a school uniform or for "rowdy" or loud behavior and then charged fines to offending students. The superintendent of Noble defended this approach to discipline: "We absolutely live by that. If you allow a lot of windows to be broken, soon that house is going to turn into one where lots of damage is going on" (Ahmad-Ullah, 2014).

Strict discipline codes are especially burdensome for students with certain disabilities. An advocate interviewed by the National Council on Disability (2018) provided the following example:

> If a student . . . has ADHD and the charter school has an existing policy that students who do not do things like track the teacher where they are following along with the teacher and, you know, their eyes are kept on the teacher the whole lesson, if that student has a disability that might prohibit them from being able to effectively be able to track the teacher, they are possibly going to be given demerits, given detentions, maybe even suspended for behavior that really is in many respects a manifestation of their disability. (p. 107)

At New Orleans charter schools run by Collegiate Academies, a civil rights complaint alleged that students were sent home for "discipline infractions such as 'laughing too much . . . hugging a friend and most commonly for being 'disrespectful'" (Dreilinger, 2014). The infraction system described by researchers looking at a Philadelphia charter school was equally troubling:

> Young Scholars-Douglass [charter school] has a code that is both punitive and employs shaming as an enforcement mechanism. Although it opens with "Our goal is to ensure that our school is safe, that learning is occurring 100 percent of the time, and that students are joyful and feel that the adults around them care about them as people," each K-2 student has a "choices meter" which color-codes the student's behavior. The student starts the day on Green but can move up to Blue or Blue Star or down to Yellow, Orange, or worst of all Red. The code specifies that an "elite group" of students will be chosen for special "privileges and opportunities that other students won't experience," including eating in a special location in the lunchroom, getting to be a line leader, and

enjoying dress down Fridays—all of which make the students' status visible to others. (DeJarnatt et al., 2016, p. 45, internal citations omitted)

The family handbook for the recently shuttered Sylvanie Williams College Prep (2018), part of the New Orleans College Prep network, declared, "We have very high expectations for behavior, and we 'sweat the small stuff' to maintain a focused learning environment." Among other things, this means that suspensions are counted against a very strict attendance requirement. The school uses a system of demerits, linked to infractions. "Class 1 Infractions" (a list of 15 bullet points) include things like possession of "chewing gum, toothpicks, rubber bands, toys (of any kind), [and] dolls" (p. 9). Six such infractions garner an in-school suspension. In an interesting turn, the 2020–2021 handbook from another New Orleans College Prep network school, Crocker College Prep (2021), does include the phrase "sweat the small stuff" and outlines a "reward system." However, this reward system operates a lot like a consequence system; that is, students face consequences when they do not reap the rewards. Younger students (pre-kindergarten–4th grade) have the following "rewards":

> Individual students are assigned a color that reflects the choices they have made throughout the school day. A color of blue or green represents a student who has positively contributed to the school environment that day. A color of orange or red indicates that an individual student did not meet expectations that day and may have been assigned one or more consequences as a result of their choices. (p. 10)

For middle school–aged students (5th–8th-graders) the "rewards" take the form of a point system:

> For each class period, a student may earn [or lose, with consequences] up to 5 points for meeting various expectations. Behavior appears twice to reinforce to students that they have the ability to recover from a single mistake or poor choice.
> Transition into class
> Participation/work completion
> Behavior
> Behavior
> Transition out of class. (p. 10)

A lawyer interviewee who has represented many charter school students in the greater Boston area shared how one of her clients was penalized for not complying:

> I had a client, [a] 6-year-old kid the school wanted to sit in scholar-ready position. This kid, he has ADHD, cannot do it. He just can't,

and he is constantly redirected to look at [the] teacher. He has a whole series of diagnoses, and he—there is no way he can constantly stare at the teacher. [The] school wants [his] parent to medicate the kid. The psychiatrist didn't think it was necessary because he was 6, and [the] parent didn't want to medicate him because he was 6. I think you shouldn't have to throw a pharmacological intervention to make a 6-year-old follow a teacher. He was listening. [He] just wouldn't look at [the] teacher ever, and he would get redirected so many times, and then he would be suspended, multiple times in a week, over and over and over.

Another interviewee of ours described an infraction-heavy secondary school she researched that engendered resistance from students—particularly those she saw as most vulnerable:

I would say policies and practices would make it difficult for many traditional students to be successful; disciplinary practices were very, very strict. So I mean looking at the school's disciplinary data, on average students received an infraction once every three days, for very minor infractions. But especially as students get older. Seventh and eighth grade students get older [and] there is more resistance about being treated like an elementary school kid. So I think kids, black males who don't necessarily want to conform, they won't be successful.

A review of New York City charter school discipline policies found that half of the city's charter schools permit suspension or expulsion as a penalty for lateness, absence, or cutting class (Advocates for Children New York, 2015). But some charters have started to reconsider a commitment to no-excuses discipline. The Ascend charter network in New York City, for example, saw suspension rates drop from 9.5 to 4.2% across the network during the 2015–2016 school year (Bellafante, 2017). After reconsidering its commitment to no-excuses discipline, the network began to retrain teachers to focus on social and emotional development in an effort to prevent escalation of conflicts between students, or between teachers and students. Ascend has also moved toward in-school suspensions, all of which may help explain the dramatic drop overall (Bellafante, 2017).

An interviewee pointed to Folk Arts–Cultural Treasures (FACTS, 2016) charter school in Philadelphia, which does a great job implementing restorative justice. She said, "[U]nlike the other codes that occasionally would have rhetoric about restorative justice but would still give you detention for blinking eyes, FACTS actually had a whole section (not in its code but on the web page) with examples of what restorative justice means. It says things like, 'if you fight with someone or you bully someone, what we have [the] perpetrator do is write a paper about all the good things they can say.'"

Zero Tolerance

Interviewees pointed to the persistence of zero-tolerance policies in the charter sector as a mechanism by which charter schools shape their student population. After analyzing every school discipline code provided to the Philadelphia School District by charter schools within Philadelphia during the 2014–2015 school year, researchers found that 74% of charter school discipline codes included categories of offenses that result in some form of automatic suspension or expulsion (DeJarnatt et al., 2016). The researchers called these "de facto zero tolerance policies."

The discipline policies of Philadelphia's Renaissance charter schools (schools that were formerly district-run schools) are expected to align with district policies. For this reason, the discipline policies of General David B. Birney Charter School and Global Leadership Academy Charter School were negatively cited in 2017 by the Philadelphia Charter Schools Office (School District of Philadelphia, 2018). Global Leadership's code of conduct states that "continual disregard of school rules and regulations may lead to dismissal from Global Leadership Academy Charter School" and that students at the school can be suspended for offensive language. District policy clearly states that students cannot be expelled or suspended for these actions (School District of Philadelphia, 2018). To be clear, schools (whether charter or not) can discipline students for such behaviors, but they are prohibited from responding to the behavior by excluding the students from school.

Similar problems arise across the country. In Indianapolis, Tindley Accelerated Schools is a network of five no-excuses charter schools with the motto "College or Die." In a 2014 report regarding school discipline, the Indianapolis chapter of the NAACP highlighted Tindley's policies and practices, which included automatic suspensions for minor infractions, including chewing gum (Elliot, 2016). In the 2016–2017 school year, Tindley Preparatory Academy, a middle school in the network, gave out-of-school suspensions to 82% of its students, according to state data. Another network school, the Charles A. Tindley Accelerated School, suspended two thirds of its students (Hinnefeld, 2018). Starting in the 2018–2019 school year, the Tindley network responded to some of the criticism by moving away from automatic suspensions for minor infractions; it instead adopted a demerit system. Rather than being immediately suspended, students now accumulate points for misbehaving and face suspensions after reaching a certain number of points (Wang, 2018). In short, students can still be suspended for chewing gum.

Similarly, in New York City, Advocates for Children New York (2015) analyzed the policies of 164 charter schools throughout the district. They found that 107 of the schools had discipline policies that permitted suspension or expulsion for any of the infractions listed in the discipline policy, no matter how minor.

Expulsions were also concentrated in charter schools in Washington, DC. In the 2016–2017 school year, 106 expulsions occurred in DC, and 103 of them were in charter schools (Office of the State Superintendent of Education, 2017). In its 2015 annual report, the Washington, DC, Office of Ombudsman for Public Education examined zero-tolerance policies and found some charter schools that required automatic expulsion for certain behaviors, noting, "These policies run counter to national research and federal school discipline guidance discouraging the use of zero-tolerance policies" (p. 20).

The Bay State Banner reporting on Boston schools that overuse suspensions, quoted an attorney who spoke of a fifth grader who said, "[H]e didn't want to go to school anymore because they were just going to send him home" (Pattison-Gordon, 2016). These schools, four out of five of which were charters, were pushing students out of school and thereby burdening both children and parents. Tito Jackson, chair of the Boston city council's Committee on Education explained, "Many of our students come from single parent households, and multiple suspensions can mean a single parent could possibly put their job in jeopardy and oftentimes will move their child from an institution that has these draconian zero-tolerance policies," to the *Banner*.

One way to address problems such as this is to bring charter school disciplinary decisions within the scope of district oversight. In New Orleans, the state-run Recovery School District has taken this step:

> [The RSD] has established a central process to review and approve proposed expulsions for all of the city's public schools using common, agreed-upon standards for expellable offenses. The centralized hearing process has, by all accounts, brought a much more consistent and fair approach to expulsions. Previously, every school defined its own criteria and process for expulsion and expelled students were left to find a new school, without any state or local agency knowledge or involvement. Since the program was put in place, overall expulsion rates appear to have declined and New Orleans now has a reliable count of how many students are being expelled. More importantly, expelled students are closely tracked and supported to ensure that they continue to receive appropriate educational services. (Gross et al., 2016, p. 2)

Of course, suspensions are much more common than expulsions, so expanding this oversight to include suspensions may help to address additional problems detailed.

Another possible improvement is demonstrated by the DC Public Charter School Board, which has taken significant steps toward data transparency. It released several years of charter discipline data, confirming that DC charter schools expelled students at much higher rates than district schools (Brown, 2013a). One year after first publishing those discipline data, the expulsion rate for charter schools dropped to half of what it was in 2011–2012, and the rate of out-of-school suspension dropped by 20% (Chandler, 2014b). Despite the positive steps taken in DC, in 2015 greater than 64% of DC charter school discipline codes included zero-tolerance provisions for acts (including nonviolent acts) that resulted in automatic expulsion; meanwhile, rules for schools operated by the school district disallow zero-tolerance provisions in any circumstance (Council for Court Excellence, 2015). And the 2015 annual report published by the DC Office of the Ombudsman for Education (2015) cautioned that some DC charter schools overused school exclusion through the use of zero-tolerance policies. It concluded that zero-tolerance policies run counter to national research and to federal school discipline guidance. Although the DC charter sector is making strides in reducing the number of suspensions, it is important to keep in mind that when charter schools kick students out, those students are not allowed to return—so they generally transfer to a traditional public school (Davidson, 2017).

Due Process Violations

Another way many charter school discipline policies differ from district schools is in the protection of students' due process rights. A California-based attorney interviewee explained that although many charter schools have official policies that provide a right to a hearing, almost none have a right to appeal. Furthermore, the hearing policies are not necessarily followed. The result, according to the interviewee, is that students are given a perfunctory hearing, expelled, and "dumped back into [the] traditional school system."

Similarly, a 2015 analysis of 164 New York City charter schools' discipline policies revealed that 59 failed to include the right to appeal charter school suspensions or expulsions, 36 failed to include any additional protections before suspending or expelling students with disabilities, and 52 failed to include the right to alternative instruction during the suspension period—all in violation of state law (Advocates for Children New York, 2015). In the same year, a report by the Council for Court Excellence (2015) found that charter school discipline codes in Washington, DC, varied in their adherence to due process procedures; in fact, just 52% of charter school discipline codes allowed for additional due process (e.g., a manifestation determination under IDEA) protections for students with special needs.

In 2018, Advocates for Children New York filed a complaint against several Bronx-based Success Academy charter schools—Success Academy Harlem East, Success Academy Bronx 2, Success Academy Upper West, and Success Academy Fort Greene—to the state department of education. According to the complaint, students with disabilities at these schools managed by Success Academy were not receiving the due process protections that they are entitled to under the IDEA and New York education law (Chapman, 2018). IDEA and New York's education laws guarantee the rights of parents to participate in decisionmaking and to use the administrative due process system to challenge decisions concerning their children's special education needs and rights. Specifically, parents have the right to an IEP meeting as equal participants and decisionmakers prior to any change in placement. They also have the right to "pendency"—to keep their children in the last agreed-on placement while any challenges to the student's proposed placement proceed. The complaint alleged that the four Success Academy schools refused to comply with these IDEA procedures and legal mandates by changing student placements without IEP meetings or written notice and defied pendency orders, resulting in students with disabilities losing months of mandated instruction. The complaint also alleged the schools denied parents their rights to participate in decisionmaking concerning their child's special education placement (Advocates for Children of New York, 2018). In 2019, the findings of a New York State Education Department investigation confirmed the complaints and added that the New York City Department of Education violated several laws in their oversight of Success Academy (Offenhartz, 2019).

Two Philadelphia charters, Khepera Charter School and Laboratory Charter of Communication and Languages, were both cited in 2017 by the city's charter school office because the schools' codes of conduct did not indicate that a formal hearing must take place prior to expulsion, nor did they indicate that an informal hearing must take place prior to a suspension of greater than 3 days. The Philadelphia Charter School Framework states that a school's disciplinary code must identify due process rights related to long-term suspensions and expulsions (School District of Philadelphia, 2018).

In 2016, a judge ordered the North Star Academy Charter School in Newark, part of the Uncommon Schools Network, to return a middle school student to school after a 2-month suspension for a violation of North Star's discipline code. Among other things, the judge found that the continuation of a suspension without notice or hearing was a violation of the child's due process rights (Education Law Center, 2016). Similarly, the Georgia Department of Education placed Savannah Classical Academy (SCA) charter school on probation in 2017 for, among other reasons, not implementing a written due process discipline policy for students (Few, 2017).

Just a year earlier, the U.S. OCR determined, following an investigation of Noah Webster Basic School in Arizona, that the school had failed to implement a student's Section 504 education plan (U.S. Department of Education, OCR, 2015). The 504 plan called for individualized behavior contracts with the student, shortened or simplified assignments, and more time to complete assignments and tests. According to the complaint, the student was subject to punishment for homework incompletion, and he had received 12 "demerit points" related to his inability to complete his homework. The student eventually accumulated more than 30 demerits, triggering a manifestation determination review to determine whether his behavior was a consequence of his disability. School officials concluded that the behavior was not a result of his disability and that the student was eligible for expulsion. After investigating the student's complaint, the OCR found that the school failed to implement the modifications required by the student's Section 504 education plan and that the school's failure to modify "related directly to the bases for the Student's expulsion" (p. 5).

These due process violations by charter schools are another area, however, that has seen some progress in recent years. In California, Assembly Bill (AB) 1360 went into effect in January of 2018 with the support of the California Charter Schools Association. The bill requires, at a minimum, those submitting petitions for charter school authorization to explain "how the charter school will comply with federal and state constitutional procedural and substantive due process requirements." In order to ensure these due process requirements are met, the bill contains specific language that must be contained in the charter petition and specific processes that the charter school must follow when disciplining or removing a student (California Charter Schools Association, 2017).

Manifestation Determination

According to a finding of Philadelphia's Charter Schools Office, Franklin Towne Charter High School "consistently violated" the "manifestation determination" requirement of IDEA (Windle, 2018). This requirement prohibits a school from suspending or expelling a student with an IEP if the wrongful behavior results (manifests) from the disability. That is, the student cannot be excluded from school because of the student's special needs, and the school must provide notice and due process to allow for this to be determined.

Franklin Towne Charter School was not alone. The Philadelphia Charter Schools Office issues notices of deficiency to charter schools for "significant instances of non-compliance or poor performance that may affect student well-being or access" (School District of Philadelphia, 2018). In 2017, four charter schools were cited for manifestation determination violations. The schools (Independence Charter West, Laboratory Charter School of Communication and Languages, West Philadelphia Achievement Charter School, and Wissahickon Charter School) all did not reference manifestation determination in disciplinary hearings for students with special education needs, as required by Pennsylvania Public School Code (School District of Philadelphia, 2018). Wissahickon was also cited for not referencing due process in disciplinary hearings for students with special education needs.

Demanding Conformity

Our study identified several other discipline-related practices that do not fit easily in the aforementioned categories or that are examples of all of them. What they have in common is a demand of conformity by the charter schools—a demand so strong that nonconforming students are denied access or counseled out of schools.

In a 2015 study of "Dream Academy" (pseudonym), a no-excuses charter school serving students from low-income families, sociologist Joanne Golann described the emphasis on control and order. She noted the charter school's belief that a disciplinary emphasis was a prerequisite to raising test scores. But she also pointed out that these compliance-based behaviors stressed as crucial for the low-income students of color enrolled in the school are the same behaviors thought to undermine success for middle-class and wealthy children. According to Golann (2015),

> At school, students develop expectations not only for how they should behave but also for how they should relate to authority. At elite boarding schools, students learn to be at ease with adults, which helps prepare them for leadership positions in which they will need to interact with different types of people (Khan 2011). At Dream Academy, students learn different lessons. Given few opportunities to negotiate or participate in rule-making, students often find themselves at odds—rather than at ease—with their teachers. (p. 10)

Other schools require conformity of speech. In November of 2018 parents and former students of Victory Preparatory Academy in Commerce City Colorado filed a federal lawsuit claiming the charter school violated their First Amendment rights to free speech (Maass, 2018). This lawsuit stemmed from a number of events the previous fall, when all 120 high school students were sent home following a protest. The events stemmed from a series of suspensions of students for Facebook posts and likes, critical of the school's principal. In response, students presented a list of grievances to school administrators and refused to recite the school's pledge during a morning assembly (Maass, 2018). The students were all then sent home for the day. Additionally, according to the attorney representing parents and former students, a number of students were disciplined for participating in interviews with local media, and a student's parents were banned from campus because they published a critical article in their Spanish-language newspaper (Maass, 2018).

In 2018, National Public Radio (NPR) broke a story about the excessive disciplinary practices of Chicago-based Noble charter schools (Rhodes, 2018a). As noted earlier, Noble charters have more than 20 different types of (rather benign) behaviors that lead to demerits. Violating the network's stringent dress code is one way to get a demerit. Students must wear light khakis, plain black leather belts, black leather dress shoes, and tucked-in school-branded polo-style shirts. In addition, students' hair is monitored and can only be a "natural color" without any designs (Rhodes, 2018a). Noble enforces uniformity by employing two full-time auditors who drop in on all of the network's campuses to ensure teachers are upholding school culture. The following excerpt provides further context:

> Teachers told NPR they received professional demerits if an auditor found they weren't issuing demerits for each infraction of Noble's rules. For students, demerits can be costly. Any four demerits (such as failure to wear a black belt) within a two-week period triggers an automatic 2–3 hour detention. Students who rack up 13 or more detentions during a school year have to attend "character development" class at a cost, until this year, of $140. Students who get 26 detentions have to attend two character development classes. Students who receive more than 36 detentions in a year are automatically ineligible for promotion to the next grade. Consequently, a significant percentage of students opt to transfer out of Noble rather than repeat a grade. Data obtained from Noble Network through the Freedom of Information Act shows that, over the past five years, the general arc bends up, toward increasing numbers of demerits. (Rhodes, 2018a)

Noble was quick to dismiss NPR's original coverage, but more egregious disciplinary details then emerged in a follow-up NPR piece (Rhodes, 2018b). Students reported that girls did not have enough time to use the bathroom during their menstrual periods. On some campuses, teachers told NPR that administrators allowed girls to tie a Noble sweater around their waist to hide blood stains. These administrators then sent emails to staff announcing the names of the girls who have permission to wear a sweater tied around the waist so that they do not receive demerits for violating dress code (Rhodes, 2018b).

Vague language found in many school conformity policies serves to allow schools to deny admission (outlined in an earlier chapter, concerning students not being the right "fit") or to push students out who do not conform to aspects of the school's culture or practices. In fact, we found instances of schools using vague language to push students out for the actions of *other people*. For example, at the Wellington School in Palm Beach, Florida, a student was threatened with expulsion after his father posted a negative review of the school on Facebook (Marra, 2017). The PLC Arts Academy at Scottsdale in Arizona asserts the right to disenroll a student "if in the opinion of the Board, the student or student's family members engage in activities which could result in complaints against the school, and endanger the future of the school from any public body, i.e. City of Scottsdale (traffic stipulations and contract), Police Department, State of Arizona" (Zetino, 2017).

Some charter schools also focus on grooming and dress in seemingly extreme ways. In the fall of 2017 at Mystic Valley, a charter school in Malden, Massachusetts, administrators dropped a controversial ban on hair extensions that, in practice, discriminated against Black girls (Wiggs, 2017).

Sisters Mya and Deanna Cook served several suspensions before the story got the attention of civil rights groups. The school claimed the girls' braids violated school dress code policies (Lazar, 2017). There have been multiple instances of schools—district, charter, and private—targeting Black girls in recent years (Lattimore, 2017).

A Newark charter school made headlines in the fall of 2018 for turning dozens of students away from the school on the 1st day of class due to uniform violations. Marion P. Thomas school officials asserted that parents were informed about dress codes prior to the 1st day of school, so when some high school students arrived without their proper uniform they were told to leave. Some headed to a nearby park, where, in one viral video, a student explains that he was asked to leave for having some white on his (otherwise compliant) black shoes (Wall, 2018b).

One researcher interviewee explained that a huge percentage of Philadelphia charter schools have provisions in their disciplinary code that enable them to suspend and even expel kids for things like untucked shirts, not having a belt, folding their arms, rolling their eyes, or sucking their teeth. In fact, at least 28 charter schools in Philadelphia allow a student to be expelled for chronically failing to wear a uniform properly. In addition to directing students how to sit and walk, the discipline code for Young Scholars Douglass Charter School in Philadelphia dictates the proper width of a girl's headband, and it specifies that students' shoes must be entirely black, including "laces, eyelets, buckles, soles, designs and emblems" (DeJarnatt et al., 2016).

Consider also four grooming/dress examples from Colorado. The Classical Academy charter school in conservative Colorado Springs told a student who had attended the school for 12 years not to return unless he cut his shoulder-length hair (Kelley, 2014). Five years later, a Colorado Springs mother sued the nearby (but apparently unrelated) Rocky Mountain Classical Academy after her 5-year-old son was expelled from the school for wearing a stud earring, a violation of the school's dress code policy. The school defended its policy and the child's expulsion because, they claimed, the mother was made aware of the policy when she signed the parent–student handbook (CBS 4 Denver, 2019). At Golden View Classical Academy (again apparently unrelated) in Golden, Colorado, girls must wear skirts on "formal Wednesdays," and the school recommends all girls wear modesty shorts or leggings under any skirts. In addition, "students should present themselves well at school, which means they need to be well-groomed and clean-shaven" (Golden View Classical Academy, 2018). At James Irwin charter schools in Colorado Springs, female students have been on the receiving end of so-called modesty checks: "A lot of girls were upset because they were touching them without permission and then it's also kind of public humiliation in a sense because [it's] in front of all of these girls," [said a 17-year-old female student]. "We're having people pulling at our pants and telling us that it's not ok" (Howland, 2016). Researchers have pointed to the ways such uniform policies can amount to discrimination in all schools, district and charter (Harbach, 2015; Mitchum & Moodie-Mills, 2014).

The National Women's Law Center published a report in 2018 on dress codes in Washington, DC. According to the report, majority-Black high schools had more dress code restrictions than other high schools. Further, charter schools, on average, had more than twice the number of dress code restrictions than traditional public schools. A policy in DC public schools forbids out-of-school suspensions for dress code violations; however, charter schools do not have a similar policy. The report concluded that many punishments for dress code violations exclude students, particularly Black girls, from the classroom in ways that are educationally harmful.

A former teacher at American Preparatory Academy, a network of Utah charter schools, described a set of anti-immigrant policies to the *Salt Lake Tribune* (Wood, 2018). The network's English-only policy meant that APA students who were not native English speakers were prohibited from using their first language on campus. According to the teacher, violations of the policy carried academic consequences, and he had multiple students who were suspended from his class for speaking Spanish. The teacher also explained how anti-immigrant and racist social media posts of the network's top administrator were indicative of long-standing attitudes of the network toward racial and cultural diversity (Wood, 2018).

After 18 months of ethnographic fieldwork, including 92 interviews with administrators, teachers, and students inside a no-excuses charter school, sociologist Joanne Golann concluded,

> [These no-excuses] schools' highly prescriptive disciplinary practices, while arguably contributing to their academic success, have unintended consequences for students. As students learn to monitor themselves, hold back their opinions, and defer to authority, they are not encouraged to develop the proactive skills needed to navigate the more flexible expectations of college and the workplace. (Golann, 2015, p. 115)

Most of these restrictions were likely put in place for reasons of obedience and control, not to shape access. But by demanding conformity in these various ways, schools acting within a choice context do shape who enrolls, who remains, and who declines to enroll in the first place.

CONCLUSION

The overuse of suspensions has long been a problem in district-run public schools, leading to a large body of research about the so-called school-to-prison pipeline. Students miss school, fall behind, and are then even more likely to act out in disapproved ways, leading to a cycle of further suspensions, increased risk of dropping out, and increased likelihood of involvement in the criminal-justice system. When charter schools and other choice schools overuse suspensions, it results in these same harms, but with one additional implication: Students are prompted by the suspensions to transfer out. Moreover, prominent charter networks—most notable Success Academy—have embraced strict discipline as part of their "no-excuses" model. These (overwhelmingly) urban charter networks commit to a rigid and structured type of schooling that embraces a philosophy of "sweating the small stuff." This approach virtually ensures that a cascade of events occur. Students accumulate demerits and suspensions for minor issues, leading to parents being asked to attend required meetings and students missing instructional time. Again, this perpetuates a cycle of falling behind, disengagement, and acting out. Ultimately, many students and their families are worn down. Such disciplinary regimes are justly criticized as demanding conformity. And when students do not conform, they must go.

Recently, a number of high-profile charter networks have begun to publicly back away from previous commitments to no-excuses disciplinary regimes. After a summer of protests following the murder of George Floyd by a Minnesota police officer, KIPP and Uncommon Schools, two pioneers of ultra-strict discipline, both publicly lessened their commitments to no-excuses discipline. Uncommon Schools claimed the network would reduce the use of detentions and end policies such as silent hallways and the use of SLANT (Uncommon Schools, 2020). KIPP (2020) dropped their "Work Hard. Be Nice" motto, acknowledging that the philosophy ignores the effort required to dismantle systemic racism. KIPP's spokeswoman also stated the network's intention to reform its system of rewards and punishments and to start using restorative justice for some student misbehavior (Mathews, 2019).

Similarly, in March of 2021, Chicago's Noble network of charter schools sent a letter to alumni apologizing for their past discipline and promotion policies that they now understood to be racist. The network noted the apology was the beginning of work they planned to do to repair past harms (Karp, 2021).

When students do leave, however—because they are pushed out or for other reasons—what happens to the empty seats left in their charter schools? In the next chapter we consider the often debated issue of backfilling those seats.

Irreplaceable
Backfilling Student Attrition

> You have a space, there are 2,500 kids on a waitlist—why would you not
> fill the space? It never crossed my mind—"Wow, don't backfill because you
> might have to work harder to make that kid a Renaissance kid." My charter
> colleagues should really look closely if their enrollment practices don't look
> equitable. (Stacey Gauthier, Principal at Renaissance Charter School in New
> York City, a school that actively backfills, quoted in Darville, 2014)

To a certain degree, student mobility and attrition are features of all schools.
For example, there are schools in under-resourced communities that serve
vulnerable populations of students who tend to be very mobile because of
housing and employment insecurity. But these issues can play out differently
in charter schools, where officials often limit entry points into their schools
and refuse to backfill seats after other students have left.

Backfill is the practice of keeping available seats full in every grade as
long as demand exceeds supply, and most public schools are required to do
that—or even go beyond that. When charter schools refuse to take in new
students at certain grade levels or refuse to take in transfer students during
the school year, they shift burdens to district schools, and they deny access
to more mobile student populations. The excluded students tend to be
among a community's most vulnerable. As one of our interviewees explained, "[I]t's a big deal for foster and homeless youth." Welner (2013)
summarized the issue as follows:

> Low-income communities across the country tend to have high rates of student
> mobility. Many students exit and enter each year and—most disruptively for
> all—during the school year. Neighborhood public schools generally have no
> power to limit this mobility and must focus instead on minimizing the disrup-
> tion. Charter schools, however, can decide to enroll few or no new students
> during the year or in higher grades. Researchers refer to this addition of new
> students as a choice of whether or not to "backfill" the students [who] charters
> lose through normal attrition or through counseling out.

BACKGROUND BRIEFING

Several studies about the KIPP network of charter schools have examined attrition, retention, and backfill. In a 2011 study, researchers found that KIPP schools have higher levels of attrition than do their local school districts and that African American males in particular were substantially more likely to leave KIPP schools (Miron et al., 2011). These patterns were also probed in a study of 19 KIPP middle schools (Nichols-Barrer et al., 2016). The researchers found no difference, on average, between attrition patterns at KIPP schools and nearby public schools and no difference, on average, in the levels of disadvantage between the students KIPP admits and the students nearby public schools admit. However, researchers did find that KIPP schools tend to replace fewer students overall in the later years of middle school and they found that KIPP tends to replace students who leave with higher achieving students (Nichols-Barrer et al., 2016). This study's findings suggest that enrollment at KIPP is shaped by backfilling policies, not by attrition itself. Similarly, a 2013 study examining attrition in an unnamed large urban district found no evidence to support the claim that charter schools there were selectively pushing out students who were labeled as lower performing (Zimmer & Guarino, 2013).

Additional evidence about the importance of backfilling policies is found in a study of New Orleans charter schools by Jabbar (2016). She noted that several of these schools purposefully over-enrolled students at the start of the school year to prevent backfilling. Because the schools were initially overenrolled, the district could not automatically assign students to their schools midyear when spots opened up.

By not backfilling during the school year, these charter schools reduce the likelihood of enrolling students experiencing a variety of out-of-school disadvantages, including homelessness. A 2018 study found that while Philadelphia's Renaissance charter schools served the same percentage of homeless students as did the city's district schools, the traditional (not Renaissance) charter schools in the city served three times fewer the number of students experiencing homelessness as did the district schools in Philadelphia (Shaw-Amoah & Lapp, 2018). (The vast majority of charters in Philadelphia are traditional, not Renaissance.)

FURTHER RESEARCH

Our research repeatedly pointed to access and equity issues associated with backfill-related policies. In particular, inequitable access for populations that are more mobile appears to arise from the practice of not accepting students midyear. The inequities in access related to backfilling are widespread;

only four states (Connecticut, Georgia, Idaho, and Massachusetts) require that charter schools backfill to varying degrees (Campbell & Quirk, 2019).

No Backfilling

According to a report by Democracy Builders, between 2006 and 2014 charter schools in New York City lost between 6 and 11% of their students each year across all grades (Popadin, 2016). This attrition creates thousands of open seats for new students to fill that many charter schools are nevertheless not filling.

Success Academy—the high-profile and controversial chain of New York City no-excuses charter schools founded by Eva Moskowitz—does not fill any seats in upper grades. According to its website, for example, the network only accepted applications for grades K–5 for the 2017–2018 school year, which means the network made a conscious decision not to backfill after the fourth grade.

During a 2015 radio interview Moskowitz had the following exchange with a reporter:

> *Moskowitz:* We accept through elementary.
> *Lehrer:* And so what happens in the upper grades? You have no entry point into middle or high schools? So all of your students . . . are only those who started in elementary school?
> *Moskowitz:* That's correct. . . . We are comfortable with the notion that we accept through elementary (Lehrer, 2015).

An analysis done by the United Federation of Teachers showed that 178 of the 753 students who started third grade at Success Academy in 2013 were gone by 2016 and that the network did not take steps to backfill those seats (Popadin, 2016; see also Casey, 2016).

In Philadelphia, Freire Charter tests all students in reading and math before they enter, and it does not backfill. Freire's head of school, quoted in *The Notebook*, explained this practice as follows: "If they come in the middle of the year, it's like, how do we make sure that we're addressing their needs, their skill deficits, where the holes and gaps are from the beginning?" (McCorry, 2015). Similarly, Boys Latin, another Philadelphia charter school that does not backfill, has a rigorous admissions process that begins well before the school year (McCorry, 2015). For the charters, these systems help to create an elite, non-disrupted environment; but shaping enrollment in such ways belies the "publicness" that the sector rhetorically embraces.

When charters do not backfill and only accept students at certain grades, communities with recently arrived immigrants or with high mobility are affected the most. In communities with immigrants, for example, newly arrived students are only able to enroll in a charter school if they applied for a seat in the initial grade that was offered (Garcia & Morales, 2016).

Modified Backfill

Other charter schools use a modified no-backfill process. For example, KIPP DC schools backfill when seats are available; however, they only do so at the beginning of the school year, so students needing midyear placement are not accommodated. In fact, that pattern and practice is not unusual in Washington, DC. Charter schools enroll about 44% of all students in the city, and many do take in new students at the beginning of the school year. Yet while charter enrollment tends to increase *between* school years, the pattern is different *during* the school years. During the 2013–2014 school year, for instance, charter schools lost 5% of their students while district school enrollment grew by 2% (Chandler, 2015). Similarly, during the 2015–2016 school year the top five DC high schools with positive net cumulative movement (more students enrolled than left) were all traditional comprehensive high schools, while four out of the five high schools with the most negative net cumulative movement were charter schools (Matos & Brown, 2017).

Part of what is happening in such situations is that some charter schools do not backfill and; they do not enroll students midyear or in the final one or two grades served by the school. For instance, Achievement Prep middle school (serving grades 4 to 8) in Southeast Washington, which has scores that are 40 points higher than nearby schools, does not take applications for seventh or eighth grade. Similarly, the Edgewood campus of DC Prep (also serving grades 4 to 8), which had a 100% math proficiency rate in 2013–2014 for eighth graders, does not take new students in seventh or eighth grade. Flagged by the DC Charter Board as "extremely restrictive," the policy of Latin American Montessori Bilingual is to take no students whatsoever after prekindergarten (Chandler, 2015).

When charter schools are first opened, they often use a related practice called *feeding from below*. For example, if a new charter plans to eventually serve grades K–8, it opens with just grades K–2, and then each year adds a new grade level, to K–3, then K–4, and eventually to K–8. As Welner (2013) notes, "This approach tends to create stability and to screen out more transient students and families."

The failure of many charter schools to accept midyear placements was specifically identified by our interviewees as a big problem. An interviewee with inside knowledge of the DC school system stressed the resulting failure to serve students and the burdens thereby placed on other schools. Others pointed out that the disruption caused by midyear placements can be substantial and is inequitably distributed. When traditional public schools accept these transfers, along with some charter schools, the charters that refuse these students are unfairly shifting that burden. Similarly, an editorial in

Colorado's *Greeley Tribune* (2015) points out that under that state's funding formula, this unidirectional flow of midyear transfers from charters to district schools leaves the latter with educational responsibilities but no funding:

> From early October through the end of the school year, Greeley-Evans School District 6 grew by 766 students last year. But the district got no additional funding for those students, creating a $5.3 million drain on school finances. The district's charter schools, however, lost 220 students during the same time frame, but got to keep the money attached to those students, meaning a revenue boon of $1.5 million.

In *How the Other Half Learns: Equality, Excellence, and the Battle over School Choice,* Robert Pondiscio (2019b) shares insight into Success Academy's backfill policies. When families get off the waitlist for a vacated spot, they are sometimes told their child will have to repeat a grade, so these families are likely to pass on the spot. Using this approach, Success can ensure any backfill students are higher performing.

Oversubscription to Avoid Backfill

An interesting issue can also arise in terms of charter schools wanting to have full enrollment but not wanting the midyear disruptions. This concern is particularly salient in jurisdictions where the school district can assign students midyear to open seats in the charter schools they have authorized. Faced with such prospects, these schools can alter their marketing and recruitment strategies to continue marketing even after their seats are full. For example, Jabbar (2016), referenced earlier, relates the thinking of a New Orleans charter school leader who explained how the school stayed full throughout the year to avoid receiving students in the middle of the year: "There's a community that's always moving. What I've learned, though, is that the more you stay filled, the less that teachers have to handle a revolving door, and if we have a little buffer, or even over-enrolled a couple, then it's not constantly flow in." Similarly, to avoid midyear entrants, another school administrator described to Jabbar how her school overfills by setting higher target enrollments on OneApp. By remaining oversubscribed, the school could lose students midyear without replacing them: "We set our targets for 32 per class. . . . We've only lost less than 10 kids all year. Some of our classes still have 32 in them, which I know our teachers are so excited about [sarcastically]" (p. 16).

Addressing Inequities

This issue of backfilling is, however, on the radar of equity-focused charters that have taken steps to address the accessibility concerns. Charter school networks that backfill as a matter of policy include the Strive Prep network in Denver and the RePublic network in Tennessee and Mississippi (Gorski, 2017; National Alliance for Public Charter Schools [NAPCS], 2016). In DC, the city is attempting to structure a new funding model that will create a financial incentive for charter schools to backfill. The goal of the new model is for all public schools to have multiple membership counts, so schools can be compensated for the students actually enrolled as opposed to those who never showed up or who left midyear (NAPCS, 2016). As another example of such progress, the Indiana Public Charter Board requires that charter contracts include a commitment to using enrollment practices similar to traditional public schools. This is understood as requiring charter schools to fill seats as they become available (NAPCS, 2016).

Although the Strive Prep network in Denver has taken steps on its own to backfill students, charter schools in Denver are not required to enroll students after the start of the school year or to backfill when students leave. Consequently, as is the case in most cities, other schools carry the burden of accommodating transfer and new students midyear—students who have some of the greatest academic needs. In an effort to alleviate this inequity, in 2012 Denver public schools recruited charter schools to participate in "enrollment zones" (Doyle et al., 2017). In Denver, if students live within the boundary of an enrollment zone they can be assigned by the district to any school participating in that enrollment zone, rather than just one neighborhood school—and some charter schools have voluntarily agreed to participate (such participation is mandatory for district-run schools). In addition, all schools participating in enrollment zones must set aside a small number of seats (5% initially) at the start of the year to accommodate students who transfer into the district. Transferring students can then choose from any school with availability in their zone (Doyle et al., 2017). In 2018, DPS moved to reserve a total 2,500 seats across all schools for late-arriving students who want to enroll at a school but who do not live in its boundary (Asmar, 2018). But this appears to be just for students who arrive before school starts in August but after the initial February enrollment period, so it does not address the issue of backfill.

CONCLUSION

Backfilling, including allowing new students to enroll in a school after the school year has begun, is a common practice in traditional school districts. In the charter sector, however, many schools have refused to accept new students midyear even when space opens up to do so. This raises the common access issues discussed throughout this book. But the ramifications of this policy become more pronounced in communities where charters make up a significant portion of a city's schools. Even under the best of circumstances, student mobility is challenging for nearly everyone involved. Accordingly, reforming restrictive backfilling policies addresses an issue of access equity and a way to limit the ability of schools to problematically inflate their test scores.

In the next chapter we review our final category of access-restricting practices in the charter sector: cost-related issues that make charter schools unaffordable for some families.

CHAPTER 15

Show Me the Money
The Price of Attendance

Arizona Revised Statutes Title 15. Education § 15-116(A-B). Public schools; fees; waiver; prohibition

A. A school district governing board or charter school governing body that authorizes the assessment of fees pursuant to this title shall ensure that all fees contain a provision that allows the fees to be waived in the event of economic hardship to the pupil.
B. The nonpayment of fees charged by a public school may not prevent a pupil from enrolling in, applying to or remaining enrolled in a public school.

Assorted monetary charges can discourage many families that can ill afford the added costs. Yet, notwithstanding legal prohibitions like the one set forth above for Arizona schools, charter schools have repeatedly placed such burdens on families. To some extent, the problem we are describing in this chapter is universal—impacting traditional public schools as well as charters. As state funding has tightened, district schools and charter schools alike have had to search for new sources of revenue. Accordingly, some of the fees that charter schools charge are of the same type now charged by many district schools: for lab supplies or band equipment or other extracurriculars. These now typical fees, while problematic, are not what we focus on here. Instead, we focus on charter school charges and expenses that go beyond the ordinary, making the cost of attending a charter school significantly greater.

BACKGROUND BRIEFING

While, as described next, our research turned up numerous examples of charter schools that impose burdensome costs, fines, and fees with predictable access implications, we found very little academic research focused on this issue. The only exception that we uncovered (Weiler & Vogel, 2015) concluded that charter school fees pose a "barrier," with the potential to impede some students from fully participating in charter schools. However, as the researchers noted, charter schools that did have student fees typically kept the number lower than the fees of traditional public schools in Colorado (Weiler & Vogel, 2015). They then point to other fees and costs associated with attending a charter school, such as uniforms, transportation, and suggested donations, that impose other barriers.

FURTHER RESEARCH

Exorbitant or multiple fines and fees, expected donations, and the increasing cost of school-required uniforms are all factors we found that play into the costs of attending some charter schools. In addition, as mentioned in previous chapters, charters sometimes shape access by giving enrollment priority to families that earlier enrolled their children in an associated, private, tuition-charging preschool and by not offering free or reduced-price lunch.

Fines and Fees

Tight school budgets have, for the past several decades, prompted public schools to institute a wide variety of fees (Kiracofe, 2010): athletic fees, lab fees, technology fees, locker fees, workbook fees, band fees, fees for participating in other extracurricular and after-school activities that include supplies or travel, other supply fees, program fees for some elective classes, and fees to pay for gym uniforms. These fees are usually small, and state laws require them to be voluntary or waivable. But schools can poorly communicate those voluntary/waivable messages, and the cumulative costs can amount to more than $200 annually.

It is within this context that we heard complaints about charter school fees that were substantially more burdensome. Two key differences emerged. One is that some charter schools have conditioned the initial or continuing enrollment of a student upon the payment of a fee. The second is simply in degree, with some charter schools charging fees at levels unheard of in district-run public schools.

As a couple of our interviewees explained, fees and charges that are imposed or described during the enrollment process discourage parents who are already jumping through hoops to enroll their children. In this way, the fiscal barrier access issue overlaps considerably with the barrier concerning conditions placed on enrollment. Consider, for example, the Houston Gateway Academy, part of a charter network with schools located in economically disadvantaged communities. The *Houston Chronicle* reported that applicants received a letter setting forth a fee ($100 per child or $200 per family) for parents to pay if they wished to reserve a spot in the school for the following fall—a violation of state law, according to the Texas Education Agency (Mellon, 2013). During the 2015–2016 school year, Houston charter schools collected about $2.3 million in student fees, about $168 per student (Webb, 2017).

Some of these fees were determined by the Texas Education Agency to violate the Texas education code. A fee agreement form used at KIPP Liberation College Prep and KIPP PEACE Elementary, for example, was supposed to be optional but was not presented as such and was tied to student registration. The *Houston Chronicle* spoke to several parents who believed they were duped by the charter network into paying optional fees that seemed required as a condition of registration (Webb, 2017).

Kish Russell, a BASIS San Antonio parent, told the Rivard Report that she knows of families who pulled their children out of BASIS because of fees (McNeel, 2014). Small fees accumulate into substantial sums at BASIS because students must rent lockers, purchase books to annotate, and own communication journals. Although mandatory fees are not allowed, Russell explained that they are indeed often presented to students as such (McNeel, 2014).

Nationwide, the exact scope of these practices is unclear. Parents do not usually publicly object or file complaints. But after the Hillsborough County School District in Florida sent letters to charter school families in 2013 explaining that some fees may be against the law, nine charter schools were flagged by parents (Ackerman, 2016).

As highlighted at the outset of the chapter, Arizona law states the "non-payment of fees charged by a public school may not prevent a pupil from enrolling in, applying to or remaining enrolled in a public school." In Arizona, like in most states, schools may not charge fees that create barriers to enrollment and are required to waive fees if they create economic hardship to students and their families. However, despite this clear prohibition, the ACLU of Arizona found that

> [a]t least 35 charter schools in Arizona charge fees for a range of items, including essential course materials like textbooks, without giving parents a waiver option. Ten charter schools require parents to pay fees tied to enrollment. In addition, at least 41 charter schools charge anywhere from $50 to $1,000 in fees for activities, such as field trips, and supplies. These fees may keep students from low-income families from applying, especially when the school doesn't allow families to waive the fees, and make it so that an education that's supposed to be free is only available to those who can afford it. (Zetino, 2017, p. 18)

A couple of interviewees pointed to the high-profile case of Noble, the Chicago-based charter school network, mentioned in the earlier chapter regarding strict discipline policies. Our interviewees explained how Noble leveled fines for behavior infractions. Starting in 2008, Noble students were charged fines for minor disciplinary infractions such as cell phone use. These fines could accumulate into the thousands of dollars and were especially burdensome for families already living in poverty. Over a 3-year period, the network collected nearly $390,000 from mostly low-income Black and Latinx students and families (Huffington Post, 2013). Here's a concise description from the *Chicago Tribune*:

> At Noble, which runs 14 campuses throughout the city and is often praised by Mayor Rahm Emanuel, students are issued demerits for misdeeds like not sitting up straight or not wearing a full school uniform—minor issues that would be overlooked in district-run schools. They receive demerits for being as little as a minute or less late to school, having a permanent marker in their possession, or "rowdy or loud behavior."
>
> And unlike district schools and most other charters, Noble charges fines for disciplinary infractions. Demerits for minor misbehavior can add up quickly—after four, students get a detention, which comes with a $5 fine.
>
> Noble officials and many parents defend the tough disciplinary code, saying it keeps their schools safe and keeps students focused in the classroom.
>
> "You hear the phrase 'sweat the small stuff' or 'the broken window theory,'" said Noble Superintendent Michael Milkie. "We absolutely live by that. If you allow a lot of windows to be broken, soon that house is going to turn into one where lots of damage is going on." (Ahmad-Ullah, 2014)

Although Noble's leaders claimed that the school had stopped this practice, it appears that the fees continued (Shibata, 2017). In fact, according to a Chicago-based interviewee who we spoke with in 2019, a Noble school was apparently withholding transcripts for students whose families had not paid outstanding fees. These sorts of fines and charges can have the effect of driving away lower income families in particular. Consider the following statement from a Chicago parent:

> We knew nothing about high schools—my kids knew a little and wanted certain schools. We were accepted at our home school and also at a charter school. A teacher told us that the charter was better and so we did that but we had to pay for uniforms, books, and more, and the school fined us money if his shirt was not buttoned properly. We left that and went to our home school. (Institute for Innovation in Public School Choice, 2017, p. 12)

Similarly, a New Orleans parent and community activist described to us her experience at Lusher, the exclusive New Orleans charter school discussed earlier:

> I remember her 9th grade fees were $900, and she was on reduced lunch. I said, "this is not a private school, you get federal funds, she

has an IEP [and] you get her gifted money." The next year it was $1,100 . . . and each year the fees went up. When she didn't pay, they shut her off of EdLine; that's where you get homework and extra credit assignments. If you drop below a C they put you out—well, they say they don't invite you back. But if you're poor and you don't pay fees you get off of EdLine and then your grades drop below a C."

Even more troubling was a practice at Sophie B. Wright Charter School, another charter in New Orleans: Two homeless students were barred from school for 2 months in February of 2017 because they did not have uniforms, which is a clear violation of the federal McKinney-Vento Act (Jewson, 2017). In fact, New Orleans activist and parent advocate Ashana Bigard (2017) shared several examples of students being punished for uniform violations stemming from their families not being able to afford to pay for new clothes and shoes in New Orleans charter schools:

> In a high poverty city with an affordable housing crisis and schools that emphasize strict discipline and compliance, the stories I've shared are the norm. The question is 'why?' If a school's student body is poor enough that 99% of the children receive free or reduced lunch, how is it OK to require parents to buy uniforms they can't afford as a condition of school attendance?

In 2015, the ACLU of Delaware filed a complaint saying charter school policies in that state—such as charging more than $200 in activity fees—were discouraging low-income students from applying and were resegregating public schools (Prothero, 2017). Again, the concern here goes beyond the immediate hardship for these families. These instances illustrate how fees can create a barrier to enrollment. As another example, Twin Peaks Charter Academy (n.d.) in Longmont, Colorado, states on its website,

> We do not charge tuition. Further, we do not charge fees as a condition of a student's enrollment or attendance in any class that is considered part of a public school's educational program. However, we ask families and their students to pay fees to cover the costs associated with consumable course materials, access to Infinite Campus, and benchmark testing. Students who enroll in electives, athletics, or other extracurricular activities will incur additional fees.

These fees to cover costs associated with the range of activities offered by Twin Peaks are steep. For example, a high school family can pay up to $655 a year in athletic and activity fees alone (Twin Peaks Charter Academy, 2020).

Even fee waivers can come at a cost. Tempe Preparatory Academy in Arizona charges various fees, including a $180 book deposit fee and fees to pay at enrollment ranging from $60 to $287 (amounts increasing with higher grade levels). The school offers financial assistance for families where these fees would be a hardship—which sounds sensible, except that "families must pay a fee for the financial aid application, which is used to determine how much financial assistance the school will provide them" (Zetino, 2017).

In 2018, the *Los Angeles Daily News* reported that California state education and labor officials identified the North Valley Military Institute, a public military charter school in Los Angeles that serves a predominantly low-income population, as charging illegal summer school fees. Additionally, state labor officials charged the school with unfairly compensating students who worked at the school as a way to pay for the summer schools fees if they could not otherwise afford them. Students had the option of working at the school for $5 an hour, or their parents could do so for $10 an hour, to offset the cost of summer classes (Gazzar, 2018).

In June of 2018, the Oakland Unified School District ordered the Bay Area Technology School to stop requiring students and their families to purchase uniforms, graduation tickets, and caps and gowns, a practice that had allegedly been going on for years and that had collected thousands of dollars in violation of state education laws (Bondgraham, 2018).

Donations

Requests for parental donations are not unusual in schools today, for many of the same reasons that fees have become common: Schools often face tight budgets. But some charter schools make these donation requests in ways that likely impact access. One extreme example is Cambridge Lakes Charter School in Pingree Grove, Illinois. Reuters reported that this charter school mandated that each student's family invest in the company that built the school (Simon, 2013). California provides three additional examples: (1) Pacific Collegiate School (n.d.) in Santa Cruz, where families contribute 15–20% of the school's budget and the school asks parents to make a donation of $3,500 or more per student each year; (2) The City School (2017) in Los Angeles, which sets the goal of 100% parent participation to raise over $100,000, where the website emphasizes needing everyone's participation to reach the goal; and (3) Bullis charter school in Los Altos, where parents are asked to donate to a foundation set up to help fund the school in an amount of at least $5,000 for each child enrolled (Bullis-Purissima Elementary School Foundation, n.d.). A member of the Santa Clara County Board of Education said she received numerous calls from Bullis parents who felt pressured by aggressive solicitation to make this "donation" (Hechinger, 2011).

Yet another California example surfaced when the Orange County School of the Arts, a popular Southern California charter school, applied to renew its charter with the Santa Ana Unified School District (Javier, 2020). District officials highlighted mandatory meetings where parents were told that they were expected to donate more than $4,000 a year to cover costs related to teaching the arts (Javier, 2020).

Arizona-based BASIS schools engage in this practice as well, using teacher salaries as the enticement. In a 2016 profile in *Forbes* magazine, Mark Reford, the "chief brand officer" for BASIS Educational Ventures, the management company for the charters, lauded teachers as "[t]he most significant variable in the quality of a school" and declared that "teachers are rewarded for excellence and going beyond" (Sullivan, 2016). BASIS teachers' salaries are thousands of dollars less than their traditional public school peers, even though the network gets more per-pupil funding than traditional public schools (Harris, 2018). BASIS then subsidizes these lower teacher salaries by asking parents to make sizable donations. In 2018, the *Arizona Republic* reported that BASIS Scottsdale asked parents for at least $1,500 per child each year and that a donation pledge card noted the money "represents a fraction of the annual cost of a top private school education" (Harris, 2018). Julie Erfle, a former BASIS parent quoted in the article, explained that although the giving was voluntary, BASIS made a big push for parents to donate (Harris, 2018).

In 2018, parent Karina Bland reported in the *Arizona Republic* that she had to attend a mandatory meeting at her son's charter school every year, during which administrators asked parents to donate $1,800 per student to help pay for the school's arts program. Parents could not register their children for the next school year until they filled out a form detailing how they would fulfill the donation request.

Uniforms

In addition, many charter schools require that students wear uniforms, which generally ends up as an added cost for families. This problem is particularly acute if financial assistance is not provided for families struggling economically, as is typically provided in district schools. As one interviewee explained, "[P]arents realize there are uniforms that need to be purchased and aid isn't available—suddenly a barrier is created." She also noted that each child needs more than one uniform, since they cannot wear the same set of clothes every day.

Costs can balloon for families with multiple school-aged children enrolled in these schools. To illustrate, consider the uniform requirements at Washington Latin Public Charter School in Washington, DC. Students are required to purchase daily wear uniforms in addition to uniforms for physical education and for middle school sports (Washington Latin Public Charter School, n.d.). Assuming a family with two enrolled children purchased a few pairs of the cheapest shirts and pants available from the approved vendor, it would cost this family nearly $300 dollars to outfit these children. In schools where uniform infractions are handled as disciplinary violations, it becomes very important for students to be in the correct uniform every day.

Other schools require uniforms that are substantially more costly. At Lake Oconee Academy in Greensboro, Georgia, where 73% of students are White, the school required expensive Land's End uniforms. In 2018, only 12% of students were White in Greene County's other public schools. According to a 2018 Hechinger Report investigation, residents said that policies like the Land's End uniform requirement make it hard for Black families to enroll their kids (Felton, 2018).

Charging Tuition

We came across several charter schools that charge tuition for a private preschool or kindergarten associated with the charter school and then give these paying customers priority for entry into the charter. One example of this is Flagstaff Academy in Longmont, Colorado. Flagstaff offers a fee-based preschool program for ages 3–5 years. Tuition ranges from $3,000 to $6,750, and there is a $100 registration fee. Students who attend preschool have priority entrance into Flagstaff Kindergarten (Flagstaff Academy, n.d.). Another example is found a couple dozen miles to the south, in Denver Language School—a Mandarin and Spanish immersion school—which requires full-day kindergarten for all students, which they claim is necessary for the success of their immersion model. The school website, however, identifies the clear access problem: "[T]he state only covers the cost of half day kindergarten, families are responsible for the additional cost" (Denver Language School, 2016).

One of our interviewees also pointed to the Lycee Francais de la Nouvelle Charter, a French immersion school in New Orleans, as an example of such a school. This is documented in a 2011 report by former Orleans Parish Schools superintendent Barbara Ferguson and education advocate Karran Harper Royal, which described both Lycee Francais de la Nouvelle and Audubon Charter School as having fee-based prekindergarten programs that provide pathways into kindergarten, although school leaders from both schools disputed these claims (Morris, 2011).

In California, Livermore Charter Preparatory Academy—which shares space with an expensive private school enrolling a substantial international student population—has been accused of recruiting students from China and charging them tuition. In August of 2016, the Livermore Unified School District board served a notice of violation against Livermore and its sister school, Livermore Valley Charter School, over the district's concerns, which included claims of illegal tuition charges for those international students (Ruggiero, 2016).

CONCLUSION

Any time families of public school students must pay out of pocket for any school-related activity, there is the potential for some students to be excluded. As price tags go up, this potential likely increases. But something else happens when the fee or other cost is imposed by a charter school: The potential of a student being excluded from an activity also becomes the potential of a student being pushed away from the school itself. As we have seen in this chapter, some charter schools have charged families to "get out of" mandated volunteer hours or to "deal with" disciplinary infractions. Other schools pressured parents to donate money, and some required expensive uniforms. These practices and others that have been documented in previous chapters of this book, in effect, make these charter schools unaffordable to socioeconomically disadvantaged families.

CHAPTER 16

Understanding Access

In the opening chapter of this book we introduced three concepts that help us understand access issues. This framework gives us a useful lens to view the larger context that encases and powerfully influences the charter practices described in the book's main body. The lens highlights how incentives and disincentives surrounding (and incorporated into) choice systems facilitate opportunity hoarding by an area's most efficacious parents, thereby contributing to a system of effectively maintained inequality. Lowering access barriers requires addressing those incentives and placing constraints on the ability of charter schools to game the system.

COMPETITIVE INCENTIVES FOR SCHOOLS TO BE CHOOSERS

In Chapter 6 we described how Oklahoma City's ASTEC charter school required prospective students and parents to fill out a 14-page application with over 80 questions. Like applications for other charter schools described in that chapter, ASTEC's application problematically asks for a student's discipline history and requires parents to state whether the student has ever received special education services (Felder, 2017). In Chapter 5 we shared the example of LISA Academy in Little Rock, which in 2016 sent out recruitment mailers to area neighborhoods except for the three zip codes that encompassed the heavily Black and Latinx parts of town that also had the highest concentrations of subsidized housing (Petrimoulx, 2016). Through the exclusionary mechanisms of targeted marketing and burdensome applications, LISA and ASTEC were actively shaping the pipeline of potential students. The "school choice" that results from these barriers has schools doing much of the choosing.

What might lead charter schools to engage in practices such as these? To make sense of such policies, we turn to the work of Chris Lubienski and his colleagues, who have closely examined the role of incentives in school choice patterns and assumptions (Lubienski, 2003, 2005, 2007; Lubienski & Lee, 2016; Lubienski & Weitzel, 2008; Lubienski et al., 2009). These articles interrogate the market theory basis of competition-based reforms. They explain that charter schools have often responded to competitive incentives in ways that are contrary to the theory's prediction that competition will give schools the necessary nudge to meet the needs of all students. While market incentives are indeed real and potentially powerful, they do not always push in desirable directions.

In a nutshell, the market theory of choice contends that school choice gives families the freedom to choose the schools that are best for their children while simultaneously incentivizing schools to improve as they compete for students. In the competitive drive for improvement, underperforming schools do not survive, high-performing schools proliferate, and more high-quality options are available for all students and families (Chubb & Moe, 1990; Friedman, 1995; Hoxby, 2019). This line of thinking conflates high quality with high standardized test scores.

The market logic also predicts benefits for district-run schools. Because the institution of public schooling has been historically shielded from market competition, this argument goes, it has been resistant to change and has not been incentivized to serve all students. In contrast, once the system is restructured so that schools must compete for students, the district-run schools will be incentivized to change in ways that benefit students and families. As explained by Lubienski et al. (2009), "this incentivist logic presents a compelling critique of 'government-monopoly' school systems and offers an intriguing prescription for competition to force schools to become more effective in meeting the needs of underserved communities" (p. 611).

Yet, as Lubienski and his colleagues conclude, there is a fundamental misunderstanding underlying this belief that market-like competition will incentivize schools to broadly and equitably strive to serve all students—a misunderstanding regarding the nature of competitive incentives for schools. Instead of (or in addition to) encouraging schools to find more effective or equitable practices, competitive incentives can guide schools to adopt strategies that exclude students and that otherwise shape their enrollment. In other words, charter schools are incentivized to selectively compete, and thereby to usurp part of the parental role as the chooser.

A key assumption of market theory, which envisions charter schools as businesses and parents and their children as consumers, is that all potential consumers are treated equally. In reality, however, charter schools perceive students as differently valued consumers because these schools operate within competitive environments that place higher value on specific student characteristics. In order to survive, charter schools must demonstrate academic performance (to stay open and to attract new customers) and hold down costs. Those two pressures work together to incentivize charter schools to pursue the most attractive clients: those students who are high performing and are less costly to educate. These incentives are then exacerbated by policies such as a 2016 law in Arizona that provides schools and teachers with a financial bonus for each student who passes an AP

(Advanced Placement) or IB (International Baccalaureate) exam for college credit in mathematics, English language arts, or science (Altavena, 2018).

Because of such pressures, competitive incentives guide schools to adopt organizational strategies around student enrollment—which is directly relevant to the question of equitable access. As Lubienski explains, the incentive to shape enrollment hijacks incentives to improve in ways that broadly serve all students. Even when charter schools are legally prohibited from nonrandom selection of students, the competitive incentives to admit "better" students are strong enough that charter schools take steps to shape the pool of applicants from which they must randomly select a student body (Lubienski, 2003, 2005; Lubienski et al., 2009).

Further, Lubienski (2007) describes two ways that charter schools in competitive climates position themselves to admit these more desirable students. The first focus is on how the schools figuratively position themselves through image management and marketing to enhance their relative status in market hierarchies. Drawing on institutional perspectives, he argues that organizations (charter schools) often react to competitive pressures by adopting behaviors such as marketing and other promotional activities. Charters' marketing focus often has more to do with symbolic management of a school's image than, for example, its educational practices. Lubienski's analysis of school marketing in competitive, racialized education contexts explains how this marketing targets particular audiences instead of offering information broadly about school effectiveness, thus suggesting a degree of selectiveness on the part of schools in competitive environments.

Lubienski's second focus highlights the ways that charter schools position themselves to be more accessible and desirable to certain populations of consumers. For example, Lubienski et al. (2009) documented how groups of schools in DC, Detroit, and New Orleans used locational decisions to assert competitive advantages by avoiding certain types of students. They concluded that instead of opening options for all students, competitive incentives may cause schools to arrange themselves in ways that limit access for the most disadvantaged.

Through decisions about areas such as location and marketing, charter schools can impose disparate costs (e.g., for transportation) on different families and thus shape their pool of applicants. As discussed throughout this book, such costs are also imposed through charter schools' decisions about the nature and availability of services for students perceived as disciplinary problems, students whose first language is other than English, and students with special needs. For example, in Chapter 10 we cited a 2017 ACLU report that found multiple and repeated violations of special education laws by charters in Arizona. One finding was that close to half of the state's charter schools analyzed in the report asked during the enrollment process if students had a disability and needed special education services (Zetino, 2017). Other examples included a charter that put any student with an IEP on a waiting list because its special education department was full, plus a charter organization where special education placements were limited by a cap of 10 students for each school site (Zetino, 2017).

In short, the surest path to success for charter schools is to seize the niche of serving "lower cost" students with higher test scores and stronger out-of-school opportunities and privileges. An added perk of this strategy is a group of parents with greater capacity to privately fundraise. This dynamic plays out across the socioeconomic continuum, with enrollment of the more advantaged students and families within any given community providing the school a relative advantage. Markets are rarely perfectly open systems, where competitors see all customers as equally worth reaching. When chef Wolfgang Puck opened his Spago restaurant on the Sunset Strip near Los Angeles, he benefited from developing an exclusive and wealthy clientele. This is a common business model, whether concerning aspirational goods such as Rolex watches or merely exclusive goods such as elite colleges. While market incentives will also serve the proletariat through low-end restaurants, Target watches, and shady for-profit colleges, this sort of market stratification cannot serve the egalitarian purposes of public education.

At their best, charter schools are open-access institutions that necessarily provide equitable opportunities for application, admission, and retention to all potential applicants. But as long as charters also face pressures to produce higher test scores, keep costs down, and minimize peer disruptions, the incentives will push them to admit "better" students by, for example, shaping the pool of applicants from which they select students and then shaping the pool of students they retain (Lubienski et al., 2009). This is a key part of the story told in this book.

OPPORTUNITY HOARDING: PARENTS AS CHOOSERS

When schools respond to these incentives to restrict or shape access, they generally do so by actively allocating opportunity based on parental efficacy. In 1998, sociologist Charles Tilly introduced the concept of opportunity hoarding, which he describes as a mechanism through which groups use bounded networks to monopolize access to valuable resources. Central to the concept is the control of rationed resources by certain groups, excluding other groups from access to those resources and, thus, to the benefits of resource accrual. Applied to education, we can conceptualize any given school as an institution with a limited capacity for enrollment. If those enrollment opportunities are perceived as differentially valuable, a stratified marketplace for enrollment (a valuable resource) will likely arise.

Long-standing racist and exclusionary mechanisms, such as residential sorting and associated school assignment policies into catchment areas, have facilitated the hoarding of schooling opportunities for some at the expense of others. Although school choice systems had been envisioned by Coons and Sugarman (1978) and others as having the potential to de-link schooling opportunities from residence, in practice the two mechanisms are additive (Bifulco & Ladd, 2006; Kotok et al., 2015; Siegel-Hawley & Frankenberg, 2015). In particular, charter schools can, as we have seen, add another mechanism for opportunity hoarding. When school choice systems result in differential access, they contribute to a system where efficacious parents—parents with more money, time, and privilege—are already able to sequester superior educational experiences for their children.

Parents with the capacity to do so will often try to hoard those lim-ited opportunities by erecting boundaries around access. An obvious ex-ample in the charter context concerns enrollment preferences for insiders, such as a school's employees and founders. But because charter schools themselves are incentivized to place their thumbs on the choice scales so as to enroll students from more advantaged families, we have seen the emergence of the larger array of exclusionary and stratifying practices dis-cussed throughout this book. In this way, parental opportunity hoarding interacts with those incentives for charter schools to take exclusionary steps, thus generating greater social inequality (Anderson, 2010; Lewis & Diamond, 2015).

Demand-side arguments for school choice rely heavily on the view that parents are uniquely familiar with their children's needs and uniquely con-cerned about their children's well-being. If given a choice, therefore, parents will seek out the highest quality options for their children. These choices then drive school improvement, according to the market argument, because when per-pupil funding follows children into the schools that they attend, schools that are in high demand will thrive while schools that experience low levels of demand will face closure unless they improve and thereby in-crease their appeal to families.

Elements of this market theory are consistent with our daily experiences. We can generally expect parents to seek benefits for their children, for ex-ample. As noted, however, children will lose in the competition for resources when their parents are not able to actively seek or are relatively ineffective at competing for those resources. In addition, this argument is complicated by research documenting how the choices of individual parents are often driven by factors that have very little to do with school quality. When this happens, those parents' choices may not be driving school improvements and may even be working against equity-oriented policy goals. These studies tell us, for example, that White parents in particular tend to self-select into schools with White students and that more affluent parents tend to be able to cast a wider net when considering choice options, in part due to having greater access to transportation and more social capital (i.e., access to social net-works and other sources of useful information) (Bell, 2009; Holme, 2002; Schneider et al., 1997). The policies and practices of the schools themselves, as discussed throughout this book, must be understood within this context. Any given hurdle will be differentially approached by parents, with some demographic groups being predictably more likely to clear that hurdle and others more likely to shy away from it or trip over it.

The process of sorting students through choice policies then results in self-fulfilling prophecies of "good" and "bad" schools, where the good schools are those that enroll the most students from more advantaged (Whiter and wealthier) families (Bifulco et al., 2009; Holme, 2002; Wells et al., 2009). Once school reputations are established, upper–middle class and affluent White parents have greater access to the most exclusive schools (Holme, 2002; Johnson & Shapiro, 2003). Similarly, among choice schools located in under resourced communities and communities of color, creaming involves avoiding children and families that are most disadvantaged (Lacireno-Paquet et al., 2002). In these ways, contemporary school choice policies and processes often exacerbate stratification and segregation (Roda & Wells, 2012).

Tilly's (1998) concept of opportunity hoarding helps us understand this empirical research as part of a larger system that reproduces inequalities. Parents can be expected to seek advantages for their children, and our analyses of these parents do not contend that policymakers should discourage (or encourage) such advantage-seeking. It is merely an acknowledgement that, on average, this has been and will continue to be how parents act. The issue, then, is not parents' behavior; it is whether policies should make children's access to educational opportunities dependent on how effectively privileged, or relatively more privileged, parents are able to take advantage of, or manipulate, the system. Imagine the clear absurdity of allocating slots to the best schools by placing admissions tickets on a high shelf that the tallest parents could reach much easier than others. The absurdity of a choice system that allocates opportunities to children based on parental efficacy in working within that system should be no less obvious.

Our conclusion is that policies should not facilitate such opportunity hoarding. Yet many of the choice systems we examined do just that, providing restricted pathways that help parents with relative advantages pass those advantages along to their children. In the most egregious cases, the pathways were actively blocked to families seen as less desirable.

To see the interplay of efficacious parents and charter school access restrictions, recall the example of Colorado's Stargate charter school, which we discussed in Chapter 6. At Stargate, students are only admitted if they pass an IQ test. The resulting student body demographics were far out of line with the surrounding school district. Or consider the example of the BASIS network of elite college preparatory schools primarily located in Arizona, which we discussed in Chapter 3. In 2018, the top five high schools in America according to U.S. News and World Report were all BASIS schools, and the BASIS website proudly proclaims itself "America's Best

Charter Schools." To what can we attribute BASIS's success? In addition
to not providing transportation, BASIS schools decline to participate in the
federal subsidized school lunch program—in a state where more than half
the students were eligible for free or reduced-priced lunch in 2018–2019
(Arizona Department of Education, 2019). In the 2018–2019 school year,
BASIS enrolled 15,630 students in 22 schools. Less than 1% of students
were EBs, and only 2.7% of students had disabilities (Arizona Department
of Education, 2019).

Despite these demographics, BASIS has benefited from Title IV grant
money from the U.S. Department of Education; these grant funds are intended to go to charter leaders interested in opening schools that serve
disadvantaged students. Disadvantaged-serving schools, as defined by the
grant, serve at least 40% racially and ethnically diverse, economically disadvantaged, special education, or EB students. How did BASIS qualify for
these funds? Technically the network has a population that is more than
40% racially and ethnically diverse, in most part due to a 39% Asian enrollment notwithstanding the relative affluence of the enrolled students
(Arizona Department of Education, 2019).

As mentioned previously, market theorists contend that choice gives
families the freedom to choose what's best for their children and incentivizes
schools to improve in order to compete for students. Another key assumption is that the universe of potential customers is populated by parents who
have equal and accurate information and have an equal chance to "buy" (or
access) the product. BASIS and Stargate are among the starkest examples
of flaws in this assumption. BASIS shapes access by designing its schools
for, appealing to, and being most accessible to privileged and efficacious
parents. Stargate straightforwardly excludes all children who do not soar
on their IQ test. As a result, parents are able to hoard opportunities for
children who are already relatively advantaged, which, in turn, contributes
to a stratified system.

EFFECTIVELY MAINTAINED INEQUALITY

When schools and parents enact these scenarios, they are playing out
power relations and pursuing goals that are contextually and structurally defined. Both the process and the outcome are predictable, in part
because many parents can be expected to use their relative advantages to
seek levers that maintain those advantages and pass them along to their
children.

Sociologist Samuel Lucas (1999) identifies and explains these processes
and outcomes with a concept he calls *effectively maintained inequality*
(EMI). According to the EMI hypothesis, outcomes such as educational at-
tainment have two dimensions: a quantitative dimension (e.g., the number

of years of education obtained) and a qualitative dimension (e.g., the quality of education pursued). Lucas (2001) explains,

> Effectively maintained inequality posits that socioeconomically advantaged actors secure for themselves and their children some degree of advantage wherever advantages are commonly possible. If quantitative differences are common the socioeconomically advantaged will obtain quantitative advantage. If qualitative differences are common the socioeconomically advantaged will obtain qualitative advantage. (p. 1652)

As applied to education, EMI contends that socioeconomically well-off children are most likely to receive a qualitative educational advantage (Lucas, 2001). The types of education obtained effectively reproduce patterns of advantage and disadvantage, even though quantitative outcomes are largely equalized as a result of free and compulsory schooling laws (Lucas, 2001). Moreover, the EMI lens helps us see patterns in how parents in our system are—when one avenue of opportunity hoarding is closed off through a policy change—able to seek out new quantitative or qualitative ways to pass their advantages along to their children (see also the approaches for passing along advantages described in Cheadle, 2008; Lareau, 2003, 2011; Parcel & Dufur, 2001; and Potter & Roksa, 2013).

The EMI literature has mostly focused on ability grouping (or tracking), a practice that cogently illustrates the qualitative educational difference. Tracking, however, is not the only form of qualitative differentiation. As the examples throughout this book highlight, stratification within a choice system can lead to differentiation that closely resembles tracking (see Burris, 2014).

Additional qualitative educational differentiation can arise from distinctions and choices among school sectors—district and charter. In a study of patterns of selection into Boston charter schools, Walters (2018) found that students who score lower on tests, come from low-income households, and are racially minoritized are less likely to apply to charter schools. He concluded that parenting and household "advantages" may contribute to higher achieving students disproportionately choosing charter schools instead of district schools. As discussed in Chapter 2, these sector differences that emerge at the application stage are also important because they call into serious question the generalizability of lottery-based studies. Boston, in fact, is the location of many of the lottery-based studies that show test score benefits of charter schools; but what policy meaning do we attach to that when we cannot generalize to the broader population of Boston families?

In Colorado's Greeley 6 school district, charter schools enroll about 24% of all students, but those charters enroll 40% of the district's White students (Colorado Department of Education, 2018). In fact, the stratification looks much worse once one drills down to the enrollment in the district's five charter schools. One school is 96% Latinx (see Table 16.1). Three

Table 16.1. 2018–2019 Charter Schools Student Membership, Greeley, CO

School	% Latinx	% White	% FRPL*
Frontier Academy (K–5 & 6–12)	21	74	17
Salida del Sol Charter	96	3	83
Union Colony (Elem & Prep)	53	36	59
University Charter	35	61	30
West Ridge Academy	32	61	33
District 6 (excluding charters)	67	25	70

* "Free or reduced price lunch," a commonly used proxy for poverty.

of the remaining four charters enroll White students (and non-poor students) at a level that is highly disproportionate to the district. The race and wealth stratification between district schools and nearby charters is so great that it was noted in a segment on Comedy Central's *Daily Show* (Amira & Pennolino, 2019).

The application for admission for University Charter offers some clues as to why the charter school has a Whiter and wealthier student body compared to its neighboring district schools. Parents are asked if their child has ever been suspended or expelled from another school (if yes, an explanation is required). The application also includes a general information section that informs parents of various testing and records requirements, including a birth certificate (University Schools, n.d.):

- Students are selected by a lottery draw when an opening occurs. When your child's name is drawn, you will be notified and requested to submit a permanent school record and transcript from any previously attended schools, health records, and any other pertinent information that may be of help in determining admission.
- *High School Parents:* Upon admittance to our high school program, your child will take placement tests in reading, writing and mathematics to assist in developing an appropriate class schedule.
- *All Parents:* Upon admittance to University Schools, a registration packet must be completed. A birth certificate, current physical and immunization record must accompany the registration packet. . . . Parents are responsible for transportation.

In fact, charter schools in Greeley have come up in a few of this book's chapters. In Chapter 6, we shared the example of West Ridge Academy, which requires placement tests for students in grades 3–8. The school also printed materials only in English, notwithstanding the district's very large

Spanish-speaking population. In Chapter 14, we discussed how a unidirectional flow of midyear transfers from Greeley's charters to district schools leaves the latter with educational responsibilities but no funding. Greeley serves as a microcosm that illustrates the problematic results of an unequal society where more advantaged parents use their relative advantages within a charter school milieu to seek levers that maintain those advantages and pass them along to their children.

Examining the much larger system of New York City, Sattin-Bajaj and Roda (2018) analyzed the specific policy provisions built into choice plans that prompt middle-class parents to act in ways that secure advantages for their children. They point to the imbalanced racial/ethnic and class composition of many gifted and talented programs and high-performing high schools as evidence of the harmful collective effects of policies that reward opportunity hoarding.

As noted, school choice can also interact with and amplify residence-based opportunity hoarding. In Chapter 4, we shared the example of Anderson Creek Charter School, which was strategically located right outside of Anderson Creek Club, a luxury gated golf community near Fayetteville, North Carolina, that offers "resort-like amenities." A team of researchers examined the evolution of the charter school sector as a whole in North Carolina between 1999 and 2012 and found that this extreme example is emblematic of a larger practice: Charters are increasingly serving the interests of relatively successful White students in racially imbalanced schools (Ladd et al., 2015).

CHAPTER 17

Pursuing Equity Against the Tide

ATTEMPTS TO ADDRESS ACCESS HURDLES

Throughout this book we described examples of individual charter schools, authorizers, districts, cities, and states taking steps to expand charter school access. We did this for several reasons. It is important to recognize the range of policy and practice within the charter sector. It is also important to show that despite the competitive incentives to reduce access, some educators and policymakers are taking steps to increase access. Most importantly, these positive steps illustrate ways that a larger percentage of charters can increase equity. Here we revisit some of those examples while emphasizing that the work of good actors pushing back within an unfair system is no substitute for addressing the larger systemic issues of inequity that afflict choice policies. Detrimental policy disadvantages children as well as those charter schools (and authorizers) that attempt to swim against the tide. Sustainably good public policy does not incentivize bad behavior and then disingenuously hold up the praiseworthy exceptions as exemplars. Exceptions are, almost by definition, limited in scale. The rules and incentives themselves need to change.

Mystery Shopper Programs

The DC charter board has taken the unique step of instituting a "mystery shopper" program in an effort to make sure city charters are not dissuading students with special needs from applying to charter schools. Launched in 2012 by the DC Public Charter School Board (PCSB), the mystery shopper program has staff posed as parents call schools and ask several questions about enrollment, including specific questions about enrolling students with disabilities. Staff are trained to know appropriate "special education language" and create scenarios before making calls, which may be in English, Spanish, or another language. If a school answers questions inappropriately on two occasions during an enrollment season, it is contacted by PCSB staff, who offer to retrain charter staff in open enrollment rules and procedures. Schools may also be issued a notice of concern, which is taken into account when schools are up for renewal (DC PCSB, n.d.).

Massachusetts also implemented a mystery shopper program in 2013, where staff from the Department of Elementary and Secondary Education call charter schools anonymously to inquire about their special education services to determine if charter schools are discouraging parents from enrolling their child (Prothero, 2014).

In their Equity-Focused Charter School Authorizing Toolkit, Philadelphia nonprofit Research for Action includes an equitable enrollment phone call script based on the Washington, DC, program. The sample language is intended for authorizers to use when validating or checking up on charter school enrollment practices (see Tool 14 in Research for Action, 2019).

Intentional Diversity

Racial and socioeconomic segregation is unacceptably high in district schools, and it is even higher in charter schools (National Center for Education Statistics [NCES], 2019). Charter school growth appears to drive segregation by socioeconomic status (proxied by free lunch eligibility), and such segregation grew faster in the charter sector than in traditional public schools in the largest school districts in the country (Marcotte & Dalane, 2019).

In response to these and other concerns, a subgroup of charter schools is attempting to create "diverse-by-design" learning environments (also known as intentionally diverse charter schools), led by the Diverse Charter School Coalition (diversecharters.org). In Chapter 8, we discussed the ways enrollment preferences are used by some charters to limit access, but this tool can also be used for equitable aims. For example, High Tech High (n.d.), a San Diego–based network that serves students from kindergarten through 12th grade, uses a zip code–based weighted lottery that helps achieve its goal of diversity. In Brooklyn, the standalone Community Roots charter school reserves 40% of seats for students who live in public housing (Prothero, 2016). Similar schools and approaches are scattered throughout the United States.

The 2015 reauthorization of the Elementary and Second Education Act (ESEA), known as the Every Student Succeeds Act (ESSA), removed old federal barriers to weighted lotteries like those used in High Tech High schools (Prothero, 2016). But change on the ground has come slowly. In 2018, only 125 diverse-by-design or intentionally diverse charter schools were identified across the country (Potter & Quick, 2018). The small number of intentionally diverse schools might be due to varying state policies; schools are less likely to use weighted lotteries when state charter laws are unclear about whether those policies are allowed. Intermediary organizations in the charter sector, as well as influential funders like the Gates and Walton foundations, can help build the political will to make state contexts more encouraging of diverse charters. They can also directly pressure charter schools to prioritize diversity.

This pressure is crucial because, as Jabbar and Wilson (2018) found, maintaining a diverse student body requires constant effort from charter schools in the absence of incentives to do so. They conclude that absent incentives, the efforts of intentionally diverse charter schools are easily threatened by "leadership turnover, internal tensions in school communities, and plain old inertia" (p. 20).

Intentional diversity can and should also focus on students with special needs. A small effort in this direction was launched in 2020 by the Bill and Melinda Gates Foundation. The Charter Students with Disabilities Pilot Community, a $10 million pilot initiative aimed at improving charter school programs for middle and high school students with mild and moderate disabilities, consists of 10 CMOs that collaborate to improve systems, learning experiences, and outcomes for students with disabilities. One of the awardees is Denver-based STRIVE Preparatory Schools, which has had "center-based" special education programs for years. (In Denver, some charter schools are expected to offer special education center-based programs in exchange for access to district properties.) STRIVE's commitment to enrolling students with special education needs is reflected in its enrollment: About 15% of STRIVE students have disabilities, which is higher than the district average (Asmar, 2020).

Unified Enrollment Systems and Common Applications

As we discussed in Chapter 6, navigating the array of charter school options and their associated applications, timelines, and other hurdles can easily become an overwhelming task for families. At least six cities (Camden, Denver, Indianapolis, Newark, New Orleans, and the District of Columbia) have taken steps to address these access issues by adopting unified enrollment systems (Hesla, 2018). Although the specifics of each system vary from city to city, unified enrollment systems have the potential to support more equitable access to charter schools by allowing families to fill out one application and adhere to a single deadline for all charter and district schools to which they wish to apply (Hesla, 2018).

We acknowledge here that unified enrollment systems raise concerns among those who object to treating charter schools in ways that equate them to district-run or neighborhood schools. That is, a system that presents parents with a menu of charter and noncharter schools—usually as part of a portfolio reform—serves to promote enrollment in charter schools and to further a system reliant on school closure and churn. In pointing to unified enrollment systems as a positive step for access, we are not weighing in on these other concerns. But, as we note later, a common application system can be created for only charter schools, with district-run schools treated separately.

New Orleans provides perhaps the best example of how this change can be helpful in addressing access. For years, students and families in New Orleans had to navigate a bewildering set of charter school applications. In response, the Orleans Parish School Board in 2011 launched OneApp, a unified application and enrollment system administered by EnrollNOLA, which allows families to apply to all participating schools with a single application. It "manages admissions, readmissions, and transfers for 92% of New Orleans public schools and 84% of its students" (NOLA Public Schools, 2020.

One catch here is that, until recently, New Orleans's most sought after charter schools opted not to participate in the common application process (Clark, 2018). Further, in the 2018 application cycle, nearly a third of New Orleans students were not admitted to any of their top three choice schools (Williams, 2018). In 2021, the city's three most sought after charter schools, Benjamin Franklin, Lake Forest, and Lusher, still did not participate in the OneApp process. Several other in-demand charter schools, those with language immersion and Montessori programs, did participate in the OneApp process but had an earlier deadline than the majority of schools (Hasselle, 2021).

Another approach used by several cities is called the common application system, which is similar to a unified enrollment system. The key difference is that the common application systems for charter schools do not include traditional district schools. In common application systems, all or many charter schools in a city agree to have a common application with common deadlines (Hesla, 2018). Several cities have launched such common applications for their charter schools, including New York, Philadelphia, St. Louis, Kansas City, Oakland, and Houston (Hesla, 2018). The new Houston common application system, for example, allows parents to apply to more than 50 charter schools in five charter networks by submitting a single online application. But, again, not all Houston charter schools participate in "ApplyHouston," which is Texas's first common charter school application system (Dempsey, 2018).

District and Charter School Collaborations

Denver has garnered national praise for collaboration between district leadership and charter schools (Whitmire, 2014). Leaders in these two sectors signed the District-Charter Collaborative Compact in 2010, in which the district pledged more funding for charters and greater access to district property and school buildings, while charter schools committed to improving student access and equity (Center for Reinventing Public Education [CRPE], 2010). While some Denver charter schools have not embraced these changes, recall that the STRIVE network welcomed both elements—taking advantage of access to school buildings and increasing special education enrollment by beginning to house special education centers in several STRIVE schools. In 2012, Denver was awarded $4 million by the Bill & Melinda Gates Foundation to continue building on the collaborative work. Since then, Denver district and charter schools have implemented a common enrollment system, a unified accountability system, and cross-sector professional development specifically targeted to better serve students with special needs and emergent bilinguals (EBs) (CRPE, 2016).

But a similar effort at district charter collaboration seems to have met with less success. In 2012 the Urban Hope Act was signed into law in New Jersey, allowing new types of charters known as "renaissance schools" (similar to the Philadelphia charters using the same term) to open in three cities: Camden, Trenton, and Newark. In exchange for adhering to district enrollment patterns by drawing on neighborhood catchment areas, renaissance charter schools are funded at higher rates and given incentives to build facilities (Mooney, 2014). Additionally, unlike other charter schools, renaissance schools must be approved by local school boards (Mooney, 2014). The Urban Hope Act also stipulates that if a renaissance school operates on land owned by the state's Schools Development Authority, it must serve as a default school for all children in the attendance zone unless a child has enrolled elsewhere.

By requiring that renaissance schools provide access to all children within their attendance areas and by designing a system that required the charters to operate more like traditional neighborhood schools, the Urban Hope Act aimed to address accusations of charter school cream skimming. However, a 2018 report by the New Jersey Auditor explains, with a focus on Camden, how the stated enrollment aims of renaissance schools have fallen short:

> All buildings utilized by the renaissance schools during the 2016–17 school year and seven of ten utilized by the renaissance schools during the 2017–18 school year were on land owned by either the district or SDA; however, we found neighborhood students were not automatically enrolled in their neighborhood renaissance school, where applicable, in accordance with the Act. Instead, the enrollment process for all renaissance schools was implemented by the district as a choice program, requiring parents and guardians to opt in if they prefer their child attend a renaissance school. Renaissance school neighborhoods overlap with those of traditional district schools, creating ambiguity as to which neighborhood school a student is entitled to attend.
>
> Under the current process, students are guaranteed a seat in their neighborhood district school but only receive preference at their neighborhood renaissance school. Although students are required to submit an application through Camden Enrollment to be eligible to attend a renaissance school, no application

is necessary to attend the neighborhood district school. Without a requirement that all district students apply through Camden Enrollment, the district cannot prove that all parents and guardians were adequately informed of their child's eligibility to attend or if they opted not to accept enrollment in their neighborhood renaissance school.

The current policy could result in a higher concentration of students with actively involved parents or guardians being enrolled in renaissance schools. Their involvement is generally regarded as a key indicator of a student's academic success, therefore differences in academic outcomes between district and renaissance students may not be a fair comparison. (p. 4)

These implementation struggles in New Jersey nicely illustrate the access struggles presented throughout this book. Without deliberate and diligent care, a school-choice system existing within a stratified society will itself become stratified.

Additionally, the New Jersey Auditor report found that between 2015 and 2018, the opt-in enrollment system severely limited the participation of neighborhood students in Renaissance schools; fewer than half of these neighborhood students were enrolled in their neighborhood Renaissance school (New Jersey State Auditor, 2018).

Beyond such implementation shortfalls, we should note here that charter school critics have similar concerns about these collaborations as those that we noted with regard to the unified enrollment systems. They point out that district charter collaborations have the effect of endorsing and institutionalizing the growth of charter schools, usually as part of a portfolio district approach that equates charter schools and district-run schools (Burris & Ravitch, 2018). Setting aside the merits of that critique, we are comfortable praising the access-focused elements of these reforms. Those elements, however, will provide no advantages if the policies are not enforceable and, in fact, enforced—as demonstrated by the New Jersey example.

Accommodation of Status Concerns

In DC the charter school board has taken steps to make it easier to enroll in the city's charter schools for students whose family members may have a hard time proving residency status or may be wary of attempting to prove that status. In an effort to ease residency verification, the Office of the State Superintendent of Education—which oversees both DC public schools and DC public charter schools—requires all schools to allow a home visit as a way to verify residency in cases where families cannot provide any of the traditional pieces of documentation needed (My School DC, n.d.).

Transportation

One of the clearest access barriers to charter schools and all other schools of choice is transportation. A charter is not accessible to a child who cannot physically get to that school. Consider the situation in Detroit, which does not provide any transportation for charter school students even though a large share of Detroit students, around 46% in 2017–2018, attend charters (NAPCS, 2019). Although Detroit has public bus networks in the city center, the city generally has a very limited public transportation infrastructure to support its residents. In addition to transportation issues, the city has low rates of car ownership among low-income families. In a 2018 report drawing on interview data collected from district administrators, charter school leaders, charter authorizers, and stakeholders, Professor Carolyn Sattin-Bajaj (2018) concluded that, "[t]aken together, limited access to cars coupled with poor public transportation and restrictive school transportation policies complicate the full exercise of choice in Detroit."

The charter school laws in 15 states address this concern by specifying who must provide transportation to charter school students (Connecticut, Delaware, Florida, Idaho, Iowa, Kansas, Massachusetts, Minnesota, New Hampshire, New Jersey, Ohio, Oklahoma, Oregon, Pennsylvania, and Texas) (Education Commission of the States, 2018). In addition, a 16th state (Louisiana) requires that all local education agencies provide transportation for students living farther than 1 mile away from a school. Because charter schools operate as individual local education agencies, this law mandates that they provide transportation for their own students who live more than a mile away (Sattin-Bajaj, 2018). These state-level transportation requirements are especially important in New Orleans, where almost all of the district's students attend charter schools (Babineau et al., 2018).

However, despite the state law mandating charter schools provide transportation, challenges persist in New Orleans. To the extent that a charter school's transportation hurdles are significantly greater than those of other schools, transportation remains an access barrier likely to shape enrollment. A recent example concerns Einstein Charter Schools, a network of charters that, until recently, did not provide so-called yellow bus transportation to students. Instead, the network gave students bus tokens that could be used to ride buses operated by the New Orleans Regional Transit Authority. The network argued that by providing free bus tokens they were complying with the law. However, after a 2017 complaint by an Einstein parent, the Orleans Parish School Board ordered the school to provide yellow bus transportation to students, and the network complied near the end of the 2017–2018 school year (Nobles, 2018a). The new system continues to be difficult for some parents, who must accompany children to the school's designated bus stops that are sometimes almost a mile from their homes (Nobles, 2018b).

The charter school law in Colorado is one that does not specify who must provide transportation for charter school students. However, the school district in Denver has taken some steps to address transportation barriers facing those students. The district launched the Success Express busing program in 2011, a flexible public busing option that serves students in district and charter schools in the northeast and far northeast parts of the city. A report from the University of Colorado Denver emphasized the importance of such transportation programs that work in parallel with unified enrollment systems (Ely & Teske, 2014). The authors found evidence that Denver's Success Express busing system reduced absences and truancy while providing increased school options for students and families.

Denver's school district has since expanded the program, but the routes still serve only a portion of the city. Professor Ely, one of the 2014 report's authors, later stated that, while the system certainly has its shortcomings, the number of practical policy options is very limited and "as far as better systems, [he doesn't] think there is one. The more you have kids coming from the same neighborhood, going to different schools, the more expensive and complicated the transportation service needs to be. [He doesn't think they] really have an answer aside from these piecemeal or ad-hoc solutions" (Robles, 2017). Given the geographic size of the district and the sprawling nature of its semi-urban and suburban areas, as well as the limited geographic scope of Success Express, parents in Denver still face transportation-related obstacles to using the unified enrollment system to its full extent. But as Ely suggests, these obstacles are simply an artifact of the widely dispersed attendance resulting from choice portfolio approaches.

THE RULES AND INCENTIVES MUST CHANGE

Let's return again to the example of BASIS, a network of elite college preparatory schools that we discussed in the context of opportunity hoarding and in Chapters 3, 12, and 15. A quick recap: For-profit BASIS Schools is a management organization based in Scottsdale, Arizona. The first BASIS school opened in 1998. There are currently 28 BASIS schools, 21 of which are located in Arizona (BASIS.ed, 2019). BASIS students are more likely to be White, less likely to qualify for free or reduced-price lunch, less likely to have special education needs, and less likely to be ELLs (Arizona Department of Education, 2019). The network does not provide transportation and declines to participate in the federal subsidized school lunch program. Academically speaking, BASIS emphasizes a rigorous curriculum and uses testing in promotion and retention decisions at all levels. For example, in middle school, students must pass end-of-year comprehensive exams in each subject to be promoted to the next grade. BASIS schools dominate the outcomes-based U.S. News and World Report rankings.

What rules and incentives have fostered BASIS's proliferation? One key element is that the network has benefited tremendously from features of Arizona's charter law. Arizona has no cap on charter schools, allows multiple authorizers, and for-profit entities are not excluded from applying to open a charter (Arizona State Board for Charter Schools, 2019).

In 2016 Governor Doug Ducey unveiled three noteworthy proposals—all adopted into law—that implicitly endorsed some of BASIS's more exclusionary practices and that aided in the network's expansion: (1) an incentive program tied to college-credit exams, (2) a results-based funding program tied to state exam scores, and (3) a construction loan program tied to the state's school ratings system.

The first of Ducey's proposals resulted in the "college credit by examination incentive program," which gives bonuses to schools based on the number of students who pass an AP or IB exam for college credit. When funds were distributed for the first time in the fall of 2018, BASIS received the most money of any network or district, which is unsurprising given the BASIS requirement that students pass AP exams for promotion.

The official purpose of the results-based funding program, which also came out of Ducey's 2016 slate of proposals, is to financially reward and replicate successful schools (Rau, 2017). Money is awarded based on student performance on AzMERIT tests; this is a shift from most state and federal school funding formulas that provide funding primarily based on enrollment. The program initially set aside $39 million annually for schools with higher test scores, and in 2020 that funding was increased to $69 million (Arizona State Legislature, 2020). In 2017, BASIS schools were awarded $2.6 million, and in 2018 an additional $2.95 million. Again, BASIS schools received the most funding in the state.

According to a 2018 *Arizona Republic* analysis (Harris et al., 2018), a disproportionate amount of this performance funding benefited White students. While White students account for 38% of overall public school enrollment and Latinx students account for 45% of that enrollment, 53% of students at charters that received performance funding were White, while only 25% were Latinx.

In 2014, then candidate Ducey made a campaign pledge to "fully fund the wait lists" at Arizona's top charter schools, including BASIS. In 2017, the Arizona Public School Credit Enhancement Program began. In short, this program allows public schools who meet certain criteria to take out loans backed by the state, thus advantaged by the state's credit rating. The loans fund infrastructure projects, often in the form of expansions and new schools. To get access to state-backed funding, a school must have a waiting list and be rated "A" under the Arizona's letter grade system. The program is open to all public schools, but it was likely intended for (and has only been used by) charter schools. In 2017, BASIS issued $31 million in bonds through this program (Duda, 2019). In fact, although BASIS and the Great Hearts charter network together educate around 3% of Arizona students, they tapped into two thirds of the construction loans given out to the state's charter schools (Harris et al., 2018).

With some hindsight and perspective, it would have been surprising if a charter network like BASIS hadn't emerged from the policy environment created in Arizona. Governor Ducey and the policymakers before him created a petri dish with all the necessary nutrients. Imagine two potential charter operators surveying the scene, one of whom is considering a BASIS-like model that will forcefully shape enrollment toward very high achievers. The other potential operator might be considering, for example, an arts-themed school that would enrich the lives of students with few resources to engage in such creative activities in their communities. Both schools may open, but only the first is zeroed in on the state's incentives, which will help it thrive.

More generally, the laws and the formal and informal rules for charter schools and for schooling in general reward the enrollment of students who have rich opportunities to learn outside of school. This shows up in everything from GreatSchools.org (Hasan & Kumar, 2019) to states' A–F rating systems (Howe & Murray, 2015), to peer effects (Caldas & Bankston, 1997), to disruptions and instructional time (Rogers et al., 2014). It is then compounded by school finance systems that systematically fail to provide the additional funding needed to support the education of students who have greater needs and fewer resources and opportunities to learn outside of school (Baker et al., 2018). Changing access-related practices in charter schools (and in other schools operating within choice systems) will require changing these incentives.

CHAPTER 18

Looking Ahead

Designing a Healthier System

Charter schools straddle borders. They are sometimes nonprofit, sometimes for-profit, and sometimes a mix of both. They are sometimes open and available but sometimes elitist and inaccessible. Many resemble public institutions, while many others are best described as private corporations. If we view the charter sector as a monolith, we miss all these things. We also miss the possibilities for thoughtful reforms that can increase access and publicness.

As the nation crafts a future where schooling for many children will likely continue to take place in charters, we need to understand nuances as well as broad trends. That understanding will allow us to step back and consider what that future should look like. What sort of incentives and disincentives do we want in place? What sort of rules, regulations, and constraints might we consider that will allow for creativity but clamp down on abuses?

In their role as public institutions, charter schools must be broadly accessible (as must district schools). Yet the examples in this book illustrate that charters can and do limit access and shape enrollment in multiple ways. These practices are often cumulative for any given school, effectively placing some schools off limits for subgroups—often poorly served and vulnerable subgroups—of the nation's children.

Yet charter schools, and the access issues we focus on in this book, are best understood as part of a larger, inequitable system. Leaders of charter schools interact with policies at multiple levels of governance and time that reward their schools for exclusionary practices. If policymakers hope to improve access to educational opportunities, in charter schools and elsewhere in the system, they will have to deliberately create mechanisms encouraging practices that challenge existing inequalities. Equity in access to charter schools requires policymakers' explicit attention at multiple levels.

This is a policy choice. If the system continues to incentivize charter schools to act inequitably, the nation will continue to see only sporadic attempts at equitable behaviors by individual actors. We applaud the efforts of some charter school leaders who have begun to address access barriers. They illustrate how the sector as a whole can strive toward equity. But a great deal more progress is needed. That progress hinges on mustering the political will to break the bipartisan bulwark that has thus far prevented regulation that could reign in the sorts of charter school abuses discussed in this book.

We have started to see that political will, notably in California (Cano, 2019)—home to the nation's largest number of charters—but also evident in the positions taken by the 2020 field of Democratic presidential candidates. In fact, the "unity task force" recommendations that Joe Biden agreed to include this item, which is very similar to an item in the Democratic Party Platform: "Require charter schools, charter school authorizers and charter school management companies to abide by the laws and regulations applicable to traditional public schools including transparency on civil rights protections, admissions, discipline procedures and finances" (Biden-Sanders Unity Task Force, 2020). If this political trend toward addressing legitimate concerns about the charter sector continues, the reform recommendations we set forth in this chapter will become plausible, because political compromise from charter supporters may be necessary. Intermediary organizations such as the philanthropies that support charter schools can also step up to build the needed political will for change.

At the end of the day, if the nation wants to move beyond merely depending on individuals to act in equitable ways notwithstanding pressures to do otherwise, the incentives for charter schools must change (Tanimura, 2012). In part, this means changing funding incentives and test-based accountability incentives. It also means that multiple levels of governance should adopt and enforce rules that hold charter schools accountable for equitable access.

CHANGING INCENTIVES

According to a December 2019 report from the Education Trust, an equitable system of school finance would provide two to 2.5 times as much funding for schools enrolling EBs (emergent bilinguals) in order to meet their unique needs. Similarly, a school would receive two to three times more when enrolling a student from a low-income family than the school would receive when enrolling a student from a higher income family. Students with disabilities vary greatly in terms of the additional resources they need in order to support their education, and funding should match a student's unique needs.

While these figures provided by the Education Trust should not be treated as definitive, they are a good starting point for discussion. If, for example, the needs of a student living in poverty are two to three times more than a student growing up in a wealthier environment, then consider the enrollment incentives when the state school finance formula provides only 20% or 30% more funding for such children. Each time a charter school (or any school) enrolls a student whose needs for educational resources exceed the school's capacity, the school faces an awful choice: Either under-resource that child or move resources away from other children. This same dilemma arises with other needs—most notably students with IEPs and emergent bilinguals. By fully funding students' educational needs, policymakers would remove these perverse enrollment incentives.

Test-based accountability policies also create strong incentives. Charter schools can, under extreme circumstances, be closed or nonrenewed if their test scores are too low. More importantly, test score pressures create incentives to attract and enroll some students while discouraging others. Pursuant to that nation's ubiquitous accountability policies, the rewards and penalties attached to state assessments are designed to be powerful and to shape schools' policies and practices. Ideally, the schools respond by increasing learning by adopting evidence-based approaches; but the surest way for a school to have high-scoring students is to enroll high-scoring students. The incentives to do so are not particularly subtle, and merely admonishing schools to be nobler will be insufficient.

Those incentives, however, do not stand alone. Ending test-based accountability policies will not end opportunity hoarding. Advantaged students and their families will still seek advantages within the stratified educational system. Accordingly, the task facing policymakers is two-fold: Reduce stratification of quality and opportunities (so that the differences in educational quality between winners and losers is minimized) and limit the ease with which more efficacious parents can seize exceptional advantages. We can shift away from the current system and provide a strong reward for moving toward a system where the advantage seeking is more difficult and the relative payoff is minimal.

CHANGING RULES

The task of changing the rules, particularly to interrupt the current approaches that some charter schools use to facilitate opportunity hoarding, falls primarily on state lawmakers and charter school authorizers, although the federal government can also step up. In a 2019 report for the Century Foundation, professors Julie Mead and Preston Green (2019) addressed the ways charter school policy might intentionally focus on equity:

> Structuring intentional equity needs parallel commitments from federal officials, state officials, and charter school authorizers. If all policy is a codification of values, then the value of equal educational opportunity should be apparent in charter school policy at all three levels. Congress and the U.S. Department of Education have roles to define federal policy, clarify that charter schools are no less accountable for equitable access, and provide oversight to states to ensure that both planning and oversight include measures specific to charter school

operation. State legislatures play a primary role by ensuring that the statutes that enable charter schools explicitly address equity throughout. Finally, authorizers must be on the forefront to guarantee that charter schools respect "[t]he rights of all students to enjoy equitable access to the schools of their choice, to receive appropriate services, and to be treated fairly" while also protecting "[t]he public interest in ensuring that publicly funded programs are accountable, transparent, well governed, efficient, and effectively administered." (p. 9)

The Federal Role

Codifying equitable access as a central value in our school choice system can shift our current incentive structures. At the federal level, laws and regulations attached to ESSA and IDEA funding should pressure states to include requirements for fair and open access in their own laws and regulations. Similarly, new charter schools and expanding charter networks often obtain startup federal funding through the Charter Schools Program (CSP) administered by the U.S. Department of Education (DoE). The CSP grant awards are supposed to fund the creation and expansion of new "high-quality" charter schools, and the DoE offers nonregulatory guidance that touches on many issues related to equitable and open access. For instance, the guidance discusses the voluntary use of race to achieve diversity; lottery, recruitment and admissions policies; and the involvement of religious organizations with charter schools. But, while some states, including California, have taken the position that a charter school wishing to accept CSP funds should follow the terms of the nonregulatory guidance, it has no legally binding authority. Through regulatory rule making, the Biden administration can change that and include additional guidance to make access a guiding principle in CSP grant applications and implementation.[1]

The Roles of States and Charter School Authorizers

While federal officials can exert indispensable pressure, the real onus for changing charter sector rules falls on states and on the authorizers of charter schools. Working together, states and authorizers can prevent and address access-related inequities during each of the three distinct phases of the charter school enrollment cycle: before, during, and after enrollment. Next, we set forth specific recommendations, many of which are drawn from reports published by equity-focused organizations over the past several years (Dingerson, 2014; Education Law Center, 2019; Leung et al., 2016; Mead & Green, 2012, 2019; NAACP, 2017; Potter & Nunberg, 2019; Research for Action, 2019; Zetino, 2017).

Pre-Enrollment. The pre-enrollment phase of the charter school enrollment cycle includes all the decisions made about a charter school that can shape access before a family decides to apply. We grouped access-related concerns that arise before enrollment into Chapter 3, "Description and Design: Which Niche?," Chapter 4, "Location, Location, Location: Decisions About Site and Transportation," and Chapter 5, "Narrow-Casting: The Power of Marketing and Advertising."

In Chapter 3, we argued that in many cases when charter schools attempt to distinguish themselves through their description and design they also shape their pool of future students, sometimes in inequitable ways. Take, for example, a charter school designed to cater to gifted students that ends up enrolling a more affluent and Whiter student body that reflects these students' richer opportunities to learn and thrive within a racist society.

Such practices related to description and design that shape access can be most effectively addressed at the authorizer level. Authorizers should require that charter school applicants explicitly detail how design (e.g., curricular and pedagogical approaches) will not infringe on equitable access. They should require clear plans from applicants, pressing charter schools with niche designs to take steps at the outset to ensure that the description and design of the school does not have the effect of shaping enrollment in ways that undermine public policy. This aligns with the suggestion from Potter and Nunberg (2019) that states adopt charter proposal standards requiring founders to plan explicitly for special student populations, including children with disabilities and children whose first language is not English. (The suggestion also addresses concerns raised in Chapter 10, which we discuss later.)

Research for Action suggests authorizers include questions and prompts related to equity in new charter school applications. The organization also provides model language that can be used in applications related to supporting all students, student recruitment, enrollment, retention, and discipline. For example, and specifically related to school description and design, RFA suggests charter school applications include the following prompt: "Explain why the proposed curriculum is likely to successfully differentiate education for students with disabilities. Cite research or evidence that supports the appropriateness of the school's approach to serving students with disabilities" (Research for Action, 2019, p. 23).

In Chapter 4, we showed how charter school location also shapes access. Unlike district schools, most charter schools do not provide transportation, so a charter school located in a city without a robust public transportation system is likely inaccessible to many families who live across town. State-level laws and regulations are best positioned to require that charter schools meet the same standards as district schools for the provision of transportation—and to ensure that funding is fairly provided to meet this need. As of 2018, only 16 states specify who must provide transportation to charter school students (Education Commission of the States, 2018). The complication here is that charter school growth, and the growth of school choice in general, heightens the need for transportation. But placing the transportation burden on families can powerfully influence charter school accessibility.

In Chapter 5, we explained how marketing and advertising practices are used by some charter schools to narrow-cast to preferred students and families. A charter school in a city with a large immigrant population can choose, for instance, to advertise only in English. Or the nature of the messaging can clearly communicate which students will "fit" and which will not. As of 2019, only 15 states require charter school authorizers to even ask applicants for their marketing and advertising plans (Potter & Nunberg, 2019). Other states should add this requirement, and authorizers should mandate that these plans commit the schools to equitably market to prospective students from diverse backgrounds and circumstances.

During Enrollment. The during enrollment phase includes the time after parents or guardians decide they are interested in applying to a school up until their child is enrolled in that school. We grouped the access-related concerns that arise during enrollment into five chapters: Chapter 6, "Hoop Schemes: Conditions Placed on Applications"; Chapter 7, "The Steering Wheel: The Art of Dissuading Applications"; Chapter 8, "Send Us Your Best: Conditions Placed on Enrollment"; Chapter 9, "Putting in the Hours: Requiring Parents to Volunteer"; and 10, "Not in Service: English Learners, Special Education, and Free and Reduced Price Lunch."

In Chapter 6, we considered application-related obstacles that discourage and sometimes turn away families that lack the time and resources needed to overcome them. These obstacles include long and burdensome applications with inconvenient deadlines, obligatory in-person visits, and entrance assessments. Then, in Chapter 7, we considered the access implications of steering. This can arise, for example, when a charter school requires or encourages parents to visit with school officials to discuss fit prior to enrollment or as a condition of enrollment.

Imagine a charter school that has an application that is several pages long (and that must be picked up in person). Once the application is filled out, parents must attend an in-person meeting with school leadership to learn more about the school and discuss it as an option for their child. In response to a question from the school interviewer, or through the normal course of the conversation, parents may mention that their children have special needs and IEPs. The interviewer responds that the school may not be a good fit, but the district school down the road would be perfect. At this point, prospective students must sit for a math exam to determine their grade level placement. In this scenario, all these hoops are faced by parents who are merely attempting to submit an application for entry into charter schools.

But policymakers can provide some relief. A combination of state-level guidance and authorizer oversight can address many types of these initial enrollment phase concerns. States should forbid unreasonably burdensome applications and incentivize common applications for charter schools. If the authorizers are school districts, they can insist that their charters participate in common applications providing one-stop shopping for all charter schools. Authorizers should provide model student application and enrollment forms that emphasize equitable access for charter schools under their oversight (Research for Action, 2019). Authorizers should also review charter school applications during the initial approval process and continue oversight during charter renewal, again prohibiting unreasonably burden-some applications. States and authorizers should, for instance, forbid essays and complicated enrollment forms (NAACP, 2017). Similarly, states should ban the use of admissions criteria—in charters as well as noncharters—such as entrance assessments that serve to limit access to marginalized groups. Authorizers should implement such bans through monitoring and oversight. Currently, 13 states allow charter schools to use selective admissions crite-ria, such as academic records or test scores, interviews, performances, or "interest" screens (Potter & Nunberg, 2019). Similar prohibitions against steering should be adopted (or strengthened) and enforced.

After completing the initial application process, families must continue to navigate complicated processes and policies. In Chapter 8, we described how some charter schools screen students who might present disciplinary burdens. They do this, for example, by requesting prior discipline-related records, and they sometimes limit access through the use of enrollment preferences. State laws vary in this regard as well. Some states, like Texas, allow a charter school to deny admission to children with juvenile court adjudications, prior criminal offenses, or prior disciplinary records.[2] As recommended by the NAACP (2017), however, charters "should not be allowed to select and reject students based on their educational or behav-ioral histories or needs" (p. 28). States should hold charter schools to the same standards as district schools, which are generally not able to screen or deny admission to students with prior disciplinary or criminal records.

Chapter 8 also discusses other types of enrollment preferences, some of which seem to make a great deal of sense. For example, there is an obvi-ous logic to admitting siblings of already enrolled students and children of faculty and staff. However, these preferences can cumulatively make the school relatively inaccessible to families and children who are not in the right social network. Other preferences have an even more predictable dis-criminatory impact. Some charters favor children who earlier attended the school-run private preschool; others prefer students with a demonstrated academic interest in the school's focus or require that students enter with a given achievement level, such as a GPA of B or higher.

Authorizers should step in when enrollment preferences are making charter schools inaccessible to marginalized groups of students. Enrollment preferences can be used to diversify a school's enrollment, or they could be disallowed; but they should never limit access to such marginalized students. States should prohibit preferences based on demonstrated academic interest or performance. States should also incentivize enrollment preferences that serve to increase access for high-need students and families. For example, states should encourage (or, at the very least, not prohibit) charter schools that equitably use diversity-related factors such as socioeconomic status in their lottery processes.

The focus of Chapter 9 was the use of sweat-equity contracts, or mandatory volunteering policies that expressly or implicitly require parents to commit a certain number of hours of work as a condition of their children's enrollment. Recall the 2014 report by Public Advocates (Hammel, 2014) that revealed the pervasive nature of requirements for volunteer hours in California charter schools. Requirements for volunteer hours were most prevalent in Los Angeles County, where California's charter schools are concentrated and where many families live in poverty. These schools that subtly or not so subtly tell parents they are expected to volunteer are effectively removing a large subset of potential students. States should explicitly prohibit charter schools from requiring mandatory parent volunteer hours; only five states did so as of 2019 (Potter & Nunberg, 2019). As part of their oversight responsibilities, charter authorizers should make sure charter schools are sending parents a message that they must volunteer.

In Chapter 10, we discussed how lacking essential services such as language support, special education support, and free and reduced-price lunch allows a charter school to shape its student population in powerful ways. Federal law demands that all public schools appropriately accommodate students with disabilities and that they respond to the needs of ELLs, but these laws are insufficient in themselves. Access issues related to provided services undoubtedly contribute to the pervading trends of underrepresentation of these groups in charters (see Adamson & Galloway, 2019; Adamson et al., 2015).

State education agencies should track the enrollment trends of EBs, also known as English learners, in order to understand whether EBs are accessing their communities' charter sector in rough proportion to local population. States can also allow or even encourage charter schools to opt into providing EB students with weighted preference in their enrollment lotteries. Additionally, states should follow Massachusetts and Connecticut in requiring charters seeking authorization or renewal to develop EB recruitment and retention plans and set appropriate enrollment goals for EBs.[3] Similarly, authorizers should require charter schools to articulate in detail how the learning needs of EBs and children with disabilities will be met. Charters should detail plans for program development and evaluation as well as plans for securing appropriate staff and for the provision of staff development. Authorizers should also run secret shopper programs, similar to the one implemented in Washington, DC, mentioned in Chapter 17. In these programs, individuals contact charter schools under the authorizer's purview and pose as interested parents of children with disabilities to document whether those charter schools are steering students away. These secret shopper programs should also include "parents" of children whose first language is not English and of children with disciplinary histories.

A related approach worth paying attention to in the future comes from Colorado's state-level authorizer, the Charter School Institute (CSI), which set up a "student services screener" tool in 2017 that CSI claims has had promising early outcomes, showing "service to students who qualify for special education and those who qualify for 504 plans [trending] upward" (CSI, n.d.). Using the tool, CSI staff work with charter schools to consider those schools' performance across six indicators, including discipline and enrollment. They pay particular attention to "students with disabilities, students with 504 plans, English Language Learners, and Gifted and Talented students."

Beyond this, states and authorizers should ensure that charter schools within their purview are complying with federal laws concerning responsiveness to the needs of these special populations. They both have a role in monitoring whether charter schools are serving a fair share of students with all types of disabilities, including costlier students with low incidence disabilities—and stepping in when they fail to do so. States' school funding formulas should be rewritten to address perverse incentives. For example, in Pennsylvania, where students are classified into three tiers based on disability severity, the state funding formula requires districts to pay charters only one rate for special education students, arbitrarily based on what the district spends on its own special education students. The predictable and harmful result is what we see in the Philadelphia school district, which has a higher concentration of needier students. The district must then send Philadelphia's charter schools more money for special education students, even though their special education students are lower needs, and therefore less costly to educate (Hanna & Graham, 2020).

As one much-needed affirmative step, authorizers should require that charter schools specify plans for providing services for students with disabilities, including with respect to enrollment, provision of special education services, and evidence of a sufficient budget. Authorizers should also be proactive in ongoing monitoring of schools concerning the education of students with disabilities, and they should be prepared to hold schools accountable for persistent violations by revoking, nonrenewing, and closing the schools, as necessary, to address significant failures in the area of special education.

Finally, Chapter 10 addresses similar issues regarding a key service generally provided to lower income families: the provision of free or reduced-price meals. Federal law allows charter schools to participate in this program, but it does not require it. In fact, as of 2019, only seven states specifically require that their charter schools provide free and reduced-price meals (Potter & Nunberg, 2019). States and authorizers across the United States should expand such requirements, refusing to allow charter schools to operate unless they provide daily meals to eligible students.[4]

After Enrollment. The access-related issues that arise after the school year begins are detailed in Chapters 12 through 16. Accessibility during this post-enrollment period raises two key issues. First, are some students who begin the year at a particular charter school discouraged from remaining at school? Second, when seats open up at a charter school during the year, are students who are not currently enrolled able to access the school if they wish to do so?

Chapter 11 examines the practice of charter schools encouraging particular students to leave. For instance, students who are counseled out of charter schools may have special education needs or discipline concerns. Students may be told there is a conflict between their needs and the school's mission or that there is an unavailability of staff or resources to address their needs, or perhaps that behavior problems interfere with learning. When this happens to students with disabilities, the schools are likely violating federal law, which forbids schools from denying needed services to special education students. But parents vary greatly in having the efficacy and resources to know their rights and advocate for them, which is an IDEA enforcement challenge seen in district-run public schools as well.

Problems of denied services are heightened in the school choice context because of the potential for counseling out. As described in Chapter 11, some charters see students with special needs as customers who should simply shop elsewhere. At a minimum, therefore, authorizers should proactively work to ensure compliance with special education laws. But they should also step in to ensure that charters are not turning away students perceived as having behavioral or disciplinary challenges. Again, charter schools hold themselves out as public, which entails serving the full community. State laws should also require charters or authorizers to collect and report data on student exits, which will help illuminate which schools lose students midyear for reasons other than what might be normally expected (e.g., because they move residences).

Related practices, concerning required-minimum GPAs and mandatory grade retention, are discussed in Chapter 12. Generally speaking, district schools cannot precondition enrollment on minimum GPA requirements, since the vast majority of public schools are required to serve all students, including those who are academically struggling. (To be clear, the access-focused critiques and recommendations we set forth here should apply to all schools holding themselves as public, including so-called exam schools such as Boston Latin and Bronx Science.) District-run public schools can retain students in grade, but this is rarely done as a way to pressure the student to transfer schools. But these practices, when used in charter schools, do shape enrollment decisions.

Charter schools that require students to maintain certain GPA requirements give no choice to the families of students who struggle to meet them; they must leave. As set forth in Chapter 12, other charter schools use the threat of grade retention to accomplish this same purpose. In light of the large body of research linking grade retention to subsequent increases in dropping out of high school (see Hughes et al., 2017; Jimerson et al., 2002; Roderick, 1994; Stearns et al., 2007), states and authorizers should both be keeping a close eye on those practices. We are not suggesting that grade retention be prohibited, but the practice can be abused in ways that discriminatorily shape access. Meanwhile, states should prohibit all schools, including charter schools, from requiring minimum GPAs.

In Chapter 13, "No Excuses: Discipline and Punish," we discuss the consequences of the harsh disciplinary regimes embraced by many charter schools, particularly the subset of charter schools embracing the "no excuses" approach. In response to the practices described in that chapter, we offer two sets of recommendations, one focused on removing perverse incentives, and one focused on adding positive practices. Many authorizers currently reward schools that abuse push-out discipline. They replicate high-quality charters (aided by access to federal funds through the Charter Schools Program), defined as those with high test score growth—without considering whether those scores are aided by the use of suspension and expulsion to push out less desirable students. These authorizers should change such practices and place a higher value on charter schools' willingness to work with all students.

Making that change will, however, require implementing a second recommendation. In order to diagnose disproportionate and inappropriate discipline, authorizers and others need accurate and complete data. Yet as of 2019, only 18 states required charter schools to report data on student discipline and make these data available to the public (Potter & Nunberg, 2019). States should require the reporting of discipline data, and they should require charter schools to follow the same state-level regulations regarding discipline as do district-run public schools. States should also create and manage transparent data reporting systems to make discipline and mobility rates in district and charter schools meaningfully available to the public. (One example of such a system is in Washington, DC.) In turn, authorizers should require that proposals include a clear and detailed articulation of fair discipline standards, plus clear data-sharing procedures regarding in- and out-of-school suspension, expulsion, and student attrition.

In Chapter 14, "Irreplaceable: Backfilling Student Attrition," we discussed the exclusive-to-charter-schools practice of either not backfilling or partially backfilling open seats. Only four states in 2019 required charter schools to open seats to students on waitlists as they become available midyear (Potter & Nunberg, 2019). States should require, and authorizers should ensure, that schools backfill to enroll new students when others leave. Apart from backfill, many charters only enroll students at the beginning of school years and sometimes only at the start of select grades (usually middle or high school thresholds, such as only ninth grade for high schools). A charter school that only accepts students at the start of the year and at certain grades will be entirely inaccessible to, for example, a family with children who moved to town midyear. Charters, like neighborhood public schools, should be required to replace students who leave with new, interested students (including students just entering the neighborhood or district).

The final access-restricting practice in the book, concerning burdensome costs, is covered in Chapter 15, "Show Me the Money: The Price of Attendance." Half of all states with charter school laws allow the schools to charge fines and fees that are different from those typically charged by other public schools (Potter & Nunberg, 2019). States and authorizers should each require that all school fees are reasonable and comply with the same standards as district-run public schools. Fines should be completely prohibited, except perhaps in cases of damage to school property.

THE IMPORTANCE OF COLLECTING AND REPORTING DATA

One theme of these recommendations is the importance of data collection and transparency. The level of detail is crucial. Authorizers should, for example, require schools to report annually on all student withdrawals and disciplinary actions, including the reason for the departures and disciplinary action as well as documentation that students' due process rights were addressed (see "Tool 11 Equity Data Form" in Research for Action, 2019, p. 41). Importantly, these data must be disaggregated or be able to be disaggregated by factors including race/ethnicity, gender, age, grade level, free/reduced meal status, disability status, and English proficiency status. To the extent possible without identification of individuals (because of low counts for a given "cell" or category), these reports should be available to the public.[5]

When authorizers, policymakers, and the public lack data, they cannot identify and address access-related equity concerns. At the federal level, the U.S. DoE should compel states to provide disaggregated charter school attrition data in addition to enrollment data.

At the state level, data collection and data reporting infrastructures should be created to help the public to easily compare charters to district schools (as has been done in Washington, DC) on access-related measures. Among other benefits, this encourages nondiscriminatory charter sector operations. Since 2012, the Washington, DC Office of the State Superintendent of Education (OSSE) has published annual reports on all district and charter schools. These reports provide comparable information across schools. Access-related measures that are reported include enrollment data by subgroup, including race/ethnicity, FRPL status, ELL status, disability status, foster care status, and the percentage of homeless and migrant students. The reports also include student reenrollment data, month-by-month mobility data, and discipline data (OSSE, 2020).

Authorizers should set clear, uniform, and consistent data-sharing requirements as part of their charter school contracts to illuminate access-related issues such as staff expertise in special education and language acquisition, school-level backfill, discipline, and enrollment.

Relatedly, charter school authorizers should provide a standard and easy-to-use outlet for families to submit complaints against charter schools related to student rights, charter agreements, and state or federal law (see "Tool 5 Model Complaint Form" in Research for Action, 2019, p. 17).

Massachusetts, one of 11 single-authorizer states, has the nation's most robust system of collecting and reporting quantitative and qualitative data related to charter schools (Ladd & Fiske, 2021). The Massachusetts charter school framework evaluates schools on specific equity-oriented performance criteria, through an elaborate system of periodic site visits by inspectors to charter schools (Rausch et al., 2018). In addition to periodic visits aimed at addressing specific issues, charter schools have two site visits in the 1st year and a site visit every 5 years in preparation for renewal. Fifth-year visits lead to a summary report that serves as the basis for the decision on whether the charter should be renewed or placed on probation. The site visit process is designed to ensure that charter school officials understand the ways in which they are falling short on the state performance criteria, and thereby to strengthen any internal pressures on the schools to make changes. Additionally, ongoing inspection reports provide useful information to state policymakers—information based on qualitative data that is far more detailed than would be available without this type of accountability system. The site visit reports remain part of each school's permanent record (Ladd & Fiske, 2021).

HOLDING AUTHORIZERS ACCOUNTABLE

The National Association of Charter School Authorizers (NACSA, 2018) calls for authorizers to safeguard "[t]he rights of all students to enjoy equitable access to the schools of their choice, to receive appropriate services, and to be treated fairly" (p. 6). Because authorizers hold such a critical role in the process, this safeguarding is crucial—but it is not taking place at anywhere near the level needed. Authorizer quality varies widely from state to state, and even within states. In some states, various nonprofits and other noneducational entities can serve as authorizers. Other states allow charter schools to shop around until they find a friendly authorizer. Still other states allow authorizers to charge fees that are meant to cover the cost of monitoring charter schools. Such fees incentivize authorizers to allow low-quality charter schools to open, particularly when the states do not specify how authorizers must use the money; some authorizers use the money for noncharter-monitoring purposes (Phillips, 2019a; 2019b). Similar problematic incentives are created in states that allow authorizers of virtual charters to retain a percentage of per-pupil funding. One result in states like Colorado is that small districts take in surprising amounts of state money by authorizing poorly performing cyber charters that enroll students in far-away communities (Herold, 2016).

In California, home to the highest number of charter school authorizers, a 2019 *Los Angeles Times* series on charter oversight explained how a combination of poor incentives, poor authorizing standards, and decentralization allow low-quality authorizers to flourish in the state. California has a fractured and decentralized authorizer system that allows authorizers to avoid consequences for poor practices. A lack of oversight of authorizers is combined with loose regulation of virtual charter schools, limited regulation of authorizer fees, and a policy permitting a charter school located in one jurisdiction to be sponsored by a neighboring district (a type of authorizer shopping). This creates an amalgamation of counterproductive incentives, pushing the approval of schools of varying quality because authorizers generate revenue through the authorizing fee (Phillips, 2019a, 2019b).

Research for Action's Equity-Focused Charter School Authorizing Toolkit (2019), cited throughout this chapter, includes a total of 15 tools with accompanying examples of best practices from around the country related to how school district authorizers can work together with charter schools to promote equitable access.

Since authorizer accountability is a state issue, states should legislate high-quality authorizer standards. The practices recommended by NACSA and the tools provided by RFA are a good starting point, but they should be strengthened and given the force of law.

CONCLUSION

After the publication of "The Dirty Dozen" (Welner, 2013), the antecedent of this book, the Schott Foundation (n.d.) used it to create an infographic called "CharterLand." Based on the children's game Candy Land, the infographic invites people to work their way through the dirty-dozen obstacles. Along the way, they must navigate "Marketing Meadows," "Hoop 'n Hurdle Hills," and "Push-out Path." It's clever. But it is also unacceptable that something as serious as our children's access to schools can be turned into an obstacle game.

The National Alliance for Public Charter Schools (NAPCS) (2014a), the sector's primary advocacy organization, contends that charters are beneficial because, among other things, they are "open to ALL students" and "do not have special entrance requirements" (emphasis in original). Charter schools, the NAPCS tells us, are helping all children "have the opportunity to achieve at a high level," as demonstrated by the fact that "charter schools are some of the top-performing schools in the country," "charter schools are closing the achievement gap," and "a higher percentage of charter students are accepted into a college or university" (NAPCS, 2014b).

But claims like these are undermined—sometimes directly and sometimes indirectly—when charter schools use access-shaping approaches such as those presented in this book. The truth is that some charters do have special entrance requirements and are not open to all children. Also, because charter schools often shape their enrollment, outcomes such as college matriculation and test scores are not comparable. That is, when enrollment patterns are biased by the approaches set forth in this chapter, researchers are only able to partially control for differences among the students.

NAPCS also repeatedly and vehemently insists that charter schools be referred to as, and understood to be, public schools. But publicness includes at least two elements: legal status as public and behavior as public, in service of public goals. Publicness depends on access. Public schools should, as fundamental institutions within our democracy, minimize barriers to access.

As we emphasized in Chapter 2, these access issues are central to nearly every core issue about charter schools (see Figure 2.1). Consider, for instance, debates over funding and finance, which often center on cost effectiveness. Proponents of charter schools claim that their school produce higher test scores for less money (see Flanders, 2017). But the nonrandom charter school enrollment that is biased due to access barriers can impact all parts of the equation: test score differences, cost to educate, and even the adequacy of funding (Vasquez Heilig, 2018). Regarding the latter, state funding formulas for special education are particularly important. In Pennsylvania, charters tend to have significantly lower percentages of students with high-cost special education needs, yet we have seen that Pennsylvania state policy dictates that districts pay charters a flat fee for all students with special education needs, regardless of their level of need. This creates incentives for charters to overenroll students who need low-cost services and drive the harder-to-serve students back into district-run schools (Education Voters of Pennsylvania, 2020; Hangley, 2020). Meanwhile, researchers and advocates will continue to argue over charter school effectiveness, confounded by the elevated ability of (and incentives for) charters to shape their enrollment.

The future role of charter schools, within our democracy and our educational system, will depend on levels of actual access. This access will, in turn, depend on the rules and incentives within which charters and their leaders make their decisions. In this book we could not quantify the different access-shaping practices of charter schools. But the evidence is indisputable that the practices, the rules, and the incentives exist and are denying opportunities to children throughout the nation. This must change if charter schools are ever going to truly be public schools.

Notes

Chapter 1

1. The research reported here was supported by a grant from the Atlantic Philanthropies. We wish to acknowledge that the phrasing (school's choice) used on our book title was earlier used, in a slightly different form (schools' choice), by Princeton sociology professor Jennifer Jennings in a 2010 article.

Chapter 2

1. In this book, we use *emergent bilingual* to describe students who are not yet proficient in English. Emergent bilingual was proposed by García (2009) as a preferable term to LEP (limited English proficiency) and ELL (English language learner) because it does not focus on a deficit.

2. In addition to the regression- and lottery-based approaches discussed here, a relatively small number of charter-outcome studies have used fixed-effects and instrumental variable approaches, which have their own sets of strengths and weaknesses (see discussion in Zimmer et al., 2019).

Chapter 6

1. As of the summer of 2018, the Education Law Center of Philadelphia was representing the grandmother and seeking redress from the school. The school's initial response was that its letter saying that it was "unable to accept" the student was mistakenly sent and that the grandmother should have understood the school to be saying instead that the student's IEP would be reevaluated (Graham, 2018).

Chapter 8

1. An Act To Make Various Changes to the Laws Affecting Charter Schools, H.B. 800, S.L. 017-173.

Chapter 13

1. This report from the Civil Rights Project prompted a strong rebuttal from Nate Malkus (2016) of the American Enterprise Institute. Malkus reanalyzed the same data set, using different assumptions and approaches, and he concluded that charters on average have lower discipline rates. The UCLA researchers then responded to Malkus (Losen et al., 2016), pointing out (among other things) the following: (a) He acknowledged that the data show charter schools enrolling many fewer students with disabilities; and (b) "students with disabilities tend to be suspended at two times or greater the rate experienced by those without disabilities,

therefore enrolling fewer such students seems likely to drive suspension rates down" (p. 9). The UCLA response then notes that "the AEI report excludes a comparison of rates for Black students and excludes a comparison of rates for students with disabilities—the two areas our report highlights as being higher for secondary-level charter schools" (p. 9). That is, the two different analyses arguably tell a similar story: for comparable subgroups of students, charters suspend on average at higher rates, but because charter schools enroll fewer students with disabilities, their overall suspension rates appear to be lower. But for our purposes, this dispute need not be resolved. Within each sector, some schools suspend at extraordinarily high rates. But high suspension rates in charter schools carry the additional feature of pushing students to disenroll—the access issue that we are focused on here.

Chapter 18

1. The CSP was the subject of a great deal of scrutiny during the 2019–2020 election cycle, with prominent Democratic candidates for president calling for its elimination. The Network of Public Education prompted much of this scrutiny with its analysis showing over $1 billion spent on charter schools that either never opened or that opened and have since been shut down between 2006 and 2014 (Burris, 2019; Burris & Bryant, 2019; U.S. Department of Education, Office of Inspector General, 2018). The suggestions here assume that the program will continue in some form, but they could also be carried over to any other grant program or funding for charter schools.

2. A charter school may exclude from admission a student who has a documented history of a criminal offense, a juvenile court adjudication, or discipline problems (Texas Education Code § 12.111(a)(6)(A)).

3. See Mass. Gen. Laws Ch. 71, §89(e)(xiv) and Conn. Gen. Stat. § 10-66bb(d) (15).

4. See, for example, California's statue at *Cal. Educ. Code § 47613.5*.

5. Mead and Green (2019) suggest that the U.S. Department of Education should clarify that "cell size" (the number of students in a group) cannot be used to avoid collecting or reporting data to the state, or from the state to the federal government, and that states must regularly consider how they will ensure that schools that serve small populations of student subgroups are appropriately serving those populations.

References

Abdul-Alim, J. (2015, December 2). *KIPP D.C.'s high suspension rates raise alarms.* Afro. http://afro.com/kipp-d-c-s-high-suspension-rates-raise-alarms/

Academy for Advanced and Creative Learning. (2018). *Enrollment checklist.* http://academyacl.org/enrollment/

Ackerman, S. (2016, July 16). *Questions about charter school fees.* RedefinEd. https://www.redefinedonline.org/2013/07/charter-school-fees-under-scrutiny-in-florida-district/

ACLU Southern California. (2017, April 24). *Illegal admissions policies persist at some California charter schools following review* [Press release]. https://www.aclusocal.org/en/press-releases/illegal-admissions-policies-persist-some-california-charter-schools-following-review

Adamson, F., Cook-Harvey, C., & Darling-Hammond, L. (2015). *Whose choice? The processes and effects of charter school selection in New Orleans.* Stanford Center for Opportunity Policy in Education. https://edpolicy.stanford.edu/sites/default/files/publications/scope-report-student-experiences-new-orleans.pdf

Adamson, F., & Galloway, M. (2019). Education privatization in the United States: Increasing saturation and segregation. *Education Policy Analysis Archives,* 27(129). https://doi.org/10.14507/epaa.27.4857

Advocates for Children of New York. (2015). *Civil rights suspended: An analysis of New York City charter school discipline policies.* http://www.advocatesforchildren.org/sites/default/files/library/civil_rights_suspended.pdf

Advocates for Children of New York. (2018, November 29). *Complaint filed against Success Academy Charter Schools and NYC DOE for failure to uphold rights of students with disabilities.* https://www.advocatesforchildren.org/node/1312

Ahmad-Ullah, N. (2014, April 7). Chicago's Noble charter school network has tough discipline policy. *Chicago Tribune.* http://articles.chicagotribune.com/2014-04-07/news/ct-charter-noble-discipline-met-20140407_1_noble-students-charter-chicago-public-schools

Alameda County Grand Jury. (2016, June 1). *2015–2016 Alameda county grand jury final report.* https://www.acgov.org/grandjury/final2015-2016.pdf

Alonzo, M. (2014). Arizona charter schools often ignore Latino students and English-Language learners. *Phoenix New Times.* http://www.phoenixnewtimes.com/news/arizona-charter-schools-often-ignore-latino-students-and-english-language-learners-6462476

Altavena, L. (2018, Oct. 31). Did your kids pass an AP exam? Their got a bonus. *Arizona Republic.* https://www.azcentral.com/story/news/politics/arizona

-education/2018/10/31/ap-exam-bonuses-arizona-teachers-achievement
-gap-performance-doug-ducey-education/1753872002/

Altenhofen, S., Berends, M., & White, T. G. (2016). School choice decision making among suburban, high-income parents. *AERA Open, 2*(1), 1.

Altheide, D. L., & Schneider, C. J. (2012). *Qualitative media analysis* (Vol. 38). SAGE.

Amira, D. (Writer), & Pennolino, P. (Director). (2019, January 29). Sallie Krawcheck (Season 24, Episode 52) [TV series episode]. In T. Noah (Executive Producer), *The Daily Show with Trevor Noah*. Comedy Central.

Anderson, E. (2010). *The imperative of integration*. Princeton University Press.

Andre-Bechely, L. (2007). Finding space and managing distance: Public school choice in an urban California district. *Urban Studies, 44*(7), 1355–1376.

Angrist, J. D., Pathak, P. A., & Walters, C. R. (2013). Explaining charter school effectiveness. *American Economic Journal: Applied Economics, 5*(4), 1–27.

Arias, B., & Morillo-Campbell, M. (2008). *Promoting ELL parental involvement: Challenges in contested times*. National Education Policy Center. https://nepc .colorado.edu/publication/promoting-ell-parental

Arizona Department of Education. (2018). *Free/reduce-price percentage*. http:// www.azed.gov/hns/frp/

Arizona Department of Education. (2019). *Enrollment data*. https://www.azed.gov /accountability-research/data/

Arizona Department of Education. (2021). *Accountability and research data*. https:// www.azed.gov/accountability-research/data

Arizona State Board for Charter Schools. (2019). *Charter school law*. https://asbcs .az.gov/board-staff-information/statutes-rules-policies

Arizona State Legislature. (2020). *Highlights of the FY 2020 budget*. https://www .azleg.gov/jlbc/20AR/bh2.pdf

Arsen, D., Plank, D., & Sykes G. (1999). School choice policies in Michigan: The rules matter. *School Choice and Educational Change*. https://education.msu.edu/epc /forms/Arsen-et-al-1999-School-Choice-Policies-in-Michigan-Rules-Matter.pdf

Asmar, M. (2018, June 29). *Denver's new plan gives its neediest students a shot at coveted schools, but waitlists could grow*. Chalkbeat. https://www.chalkbeat .org/posts/co/2018/06/29/denvers-new-plan-gives-its-neediest-students-a-shot -at-coveted-schools-but-waitlists-could-grow/

Asmar, M. (2020, March 9). *Denver charter network STRIVE Prep wins 1.4 million grant focusing on students with disabilities*. Chalkbeat. https://co.chalkbeat .org/2020/3/9/21178701/denver-charter-network-strive-prep-wins-1-4-million -grant-focused-on-students-with-disabilities

Audubon Charter School. (n.d.) *Admissions FAQs*. http://www.auduboncharter .com/AdmissionsFAQs.aspx

Babineau, K., Hand, D., & Rossmeier, V. (2018). *The state of public education in New Orleans, 2018*. Cowen Institute. https://www.researchgate.net/profile /Kate-Babineau/publication/328492385_State_of_Public_Education_in_New _Orleans_2018/links/5bd0d8ce92851cabf265b5fe/State-of-Public-Education -in-New-Orleans-2018.pdf

Bailey, M. J. H., & Cooper, B. S. (2009). The introduction of religious charter schools: A cultural movement in the private school sector. *Journal of Research on Christian Education, 18*(3), 272–289.

Baker, B. (2012a, May 3). *Charter schools are . . . public? Private? Neither? Both?* National Education Policy Center. http://nepc.colorado.edu/blog/charter-schools-are%E2%80%A6-public-private-neither-both

Baker, B. (2012b, June 5). *The commonwealth triple-screw: Special education funding and charter school payments in Pennsylvania.* https://schoolfinance101.wordpress.com/2012/06/05/the-commonwealth-triple-screw-special-education-funding-charter-school-payments-in-pennsylvania/

Baker, B., & Weber, M. (2017). *Newark's schools: The facts.* New Jersey Education Policy Forum. https://schoolfinance101.files.wordpress.com/2017/12/baker-weber-newark-12-13-17.pdf

Baker, B. D., Weber, M., Srikanth, A., Kim, R., & Atzbi, M. (2018). *The real shame of the nation: The causes and consequences of interstate inequity in public school investments.* Education Law Center. https://drive.google.com/file/d/1cm6Jkm6ktUT3SQplzDFjJIy3G3iLWOtJ/view

Balfanz, R., Byrnes, V., & Fox, J. H. (2015). Sent home and put off track. In D. Losen (Ed.), *Closing the school discipline gap: Equitable remedies for excessive exclusion* (pp. 17–30). Teacher's College Press.

Ballou, B. (2018, March 2). For 10 years, parents paid to opt out of volunteering. The problem: It's illegal. *Sun Sentinel.* http://www.sun-sentinel.com/local/broward/pembroke-pines/fl-reg-pines-volunteer-hours-20180227-story.html

Basco, J. (2016, September). Will Austin ISD trustees renew district's marketing plan? *Community Impact Newspaper.* https://communityimpact.com/austin/education/2016/09/21/will-austin-isd-trustees-renew-districts-marketing-plan/

BASIS.ed. (2019). *Find a school.* https://www.basised.com/find-a-school/

BASIS Charter Schools. (2015). *Parent student handbook 2014–2015.* http://basisschools.org/pdf/BASIS%20Charter%20Handbook%20FINAL.pdf

Baum, L. (2015). *State laws on weighted lotteries and enrollment practices.* National Alliance for Public Charter Schools. http://www.publiccharters.org/sites/default/files/migrated/wp-content/uploads/2015/06/NPC035_Weighted Lotteries_Digital.pdf

Baumhardt, A., & Julin, C. (2018, June 15). *Louisiana ends policy that held thousands of students back a grade or more.* Northern Public Radio. http://www.northernpublicradio.org/post/louisiana-ends-policy-held-thousands-students-back-grade-or-more

Becker, H. J., Nakagawa, K., & Corwin, R. G. (1997). Parent involvement contracts in California's charter schools: Strategy for educational improvement or method of exclusion? *Teachers College Record, 98,* 511–536.

Bell, C. A. (2007). Space and place: Urban parents' geographical preferences for schools. *The Urban Review, 39*(4), 375–404.

Bellafante, G. (2017, March 9). A Brooklyn charter school looks past no excuses. *The New York Times.* https://www.nytimes.com/2017/03/09/nyregion/brooklyn-charter-school-discipline.html

Belsha, K. (2017, June 28). English learners often go without required help in Chicago schools. *Chicago Reporter.* http://chicagoreporter.com/english-learners-often-go-without-required-help-at-chicago-schools/

Benjamin Franklin Charter School. (2016). *Parent handbook.* http://media.wix.com/ugd/2ff70a_f772d682bc824ac0bce4c1e7ca9f261b.pdf

Bennett, D. (2016, October 21). *Why we chose a charter school—then chose to leave it.* WBUR. http://www.wbur.org/edify/2016/10/21/commentary-choosing -charter-or-not

Bergman, P., & McFarlin, I. (2018). *Education for all? A nationwide audit study of schools of choice* (no. w25396). National Bureau of Economic Research.

Berliner, D. (2009, March 9). *Poverty and school potential: Out-of-school factors and school success.* National Education Policy Center. https://nepc.colorado .edu/publication/poverty-and-potential

Betts, J., & Tang, E. (2014, August). *A meta-analysis of the literature on the effect of charter schools on student achievement.* Center on Reinventing Public Education, University of Washington. http://www.crpe.org/publications /meta-analysis-literature-effect-charter-schools-student-achievement

Biden-Sanders Unity Task Force. (2020, August). *Combating the climate crisis and pursuing environmental justice* [Press release]. https://joebiden.com/wp -content/uploads/2020/08/UNITY-TASK-FORCE-RECOMMENDATIONS.pdf

Biegel, S., Kim, R. J., & Welner, K. G. (2019). *Education and the law.* West Academic Publishing.

Bifulco, R., & Buerger, C. (2015). The influence of finance and accountability policies on location of New York state charter schools. *Journal of Education Finance, 40*(3), 193–221.

Bifulco, R., & Ladd, H. F. (2006). School choice, racial segregation, and test-score gaps: Evidence from North Carolina's charter school program. *Journal of Policy Analysis & Management, 26*(1), 31–56.

Bifulco, R., Ladd, H. F., & Ross, S. L. (2009). Public school choice and integration evidence from Durham, North Carolina. *Social Science Research, 38*(1), 71–85.

Bifulco, R., & Reback, R. (2014). Fiscal impacts of charter schools: Lessons from New York. *Education Finance and Policy, 9*(1), 86–107.

Bigard, A. (2017, July 18). New Orleans charter schools are punishing students for being poor. *AlterNet.* https://www.alternet.org/2017/07/new-orleans-charters -punish-students/

Black, D. W. (2021). *NEPC review: "Religious charter schools: Legally permissible? Constitutionally required?"* National Education Policy Center. http://nepc .colorado.edu/thinktank/religious-charters

Bland, K. (2018, July 16). I feel good about choosing a charter school. Except for one thing. *Arizona Republic.* https://www.azcentral.com/story/news/local /karinabland/2018/07/16/arizona-school-choice-charter-schools-tax-dollars -open-enrollment/784068002/

Blume, H. (2015, December 2). PAC shielded $2.3 million in donations by L.A. charter school backers. *Los Angeles Times.* http://www.latimes.com/local /education/la-me-charter-donations-20151202-story.html

Bondgraham, D. (2018, August 10). Oakland's Baytech charter school violated multiple state laws. *East Bay Express.* https://eastbayexpress.com /oaklands-baytech-charter-school-violated-multiple-state-laws-2-1/

Booker, K., Zimmer, R., & Buddin, R. (2005). *The effects of charter schools on school peer composition.* Rand Corporation. http://www.rand.org/pubs /working_papers/WR306/

Borg, L. (2017, November 6). Woonsocket Beacon charter school broke admission-lottery rule. *Providence Journal.* http://www.providencejournal.com

/news/20171106/woonsocket-beacon-charter-school-broke-admission-lottery
-rule

Brewer, T. J., & Lubienski, C. (2017, April 13). *Review of "Differences by design? Student composition in charter schools with different academic models."* National Education Policy Center. http://nepc.colorado.edu/thinktank/review-charters

Brinson, D. (2011). *Turning loss into renewal: Catholic schools, charter schools, and the Miami experience.* Public Impact. http://publicimpact.com/publications/Seton_Miami_Case_Study.pdf

Brown, A. (2012, September 30). *Counseled out: How some Twin Cities charter schools push kids with disabilities towards district schools.* TC Daily Planet. http://www.tcdailyplanet.net/should-special-education-students-be-counseled-out-charter-schools/

Brown, E. (2013a, January 5). D.C. charter schools expel students at far higher rates than traditional public schools. *Washington Post.* https://www.washingtonpost.com/local/education/dc-charter-schools-expel-students-at-far-higher-rates-than-traditional-public-schools/2013/01/05/e155e4bc-44a9-11e2-8061-253bccfc7532_story.html

Brown, E. (2013b, April 16). D.C. charter school board rejects request from BASIS to expand. *Washington Post.* https://www.washingtonpost.com/local/education/dc-charter-board-rejects-request-from-basis-to-expand/2013/04/16/32a735ee-a69a-11e2-8302-3c7e0ea97057_story.html

Brown, E., & Makris, M. V. (2018). A different type of charter school: In prestige charters, a rise in cachet equals a decline in access. *Journal of Education Policy, 33*(1), 85–117.

Buchanan, N. K., & Fox, R. A. (2003). To learn and to belong: Case studies of emerging ethnocentric charter schools in Hawai'i. *Education Policy Analysis Archives, 11*(8), 1–23.

Bulkley, J., & Sattin-Bajaj, C. (2011). Are ELL students underrepresented in charter schools? Demographic trends in New York City, 2006–2008. *Journal of School Choice, 5*(1), 40–65.

Bulkley, K., & Fisler, J. (2002). *A review of the research on charter schools.* Center for Reinventing Public Education. http://www.cpre.org/review-research-charter-schools

Bullis-Purissima Elementary School Foundation. (n.d.) *2016–2017 annual campaign.* http://www.bcsfoundation.com/annual-campaign

Bulman, R. C. &. Kirp, D. L. (2000). The shifting politics of school choice. In S. Sugarman & F. Kemerer (Eds.), *School choice and social controversy: Politics, policy, and law* (pp. 36–67). Brookings.

Burris, C. C. (2014). *On the same track: How schools can join the twenty-first-century struggle against resegregation.* Beacon.

Burris, C. C. (2018, January 28). How Mike Pence expanded Indiana's controversial voucher program when he was governor. *Washington Post.* https://www.washingtonpost.com/news/answer-sheet/wp/2018/01/28/how-mike-pence-expanded-indianas-controversial-voucher-program-when-he-was-governor/

Burris, C. C. (2019). *Still asleep at the wheel.* Network for Public Education. https://networkforpubliceducation.org/wp-content/uploads/2020/02/Still-Asleep-at-the-Wheel.pdf

Burris, C. C., & Bryant, J. (2019). *Asleep at the wheel*. Network for Public Education. https://npe.wpengine.com/wp-content/uploads/2019/12/Asleep-at-the-Wheel-ONLINE-VERSION.pdf

Burris, C. C., & Ravitch, D. (2018, November 4). Perspective: Why it matters who governs America's public schools. *Washington Post*. https://www.washingtonpost.com/education/2018/11/04/why-it-matters-who-governs-americas-public-schools

Caldas, S. J., & Bankston, C. (1997). Effect of school population socioeconomic status on individual academic achievement. *The Journal of Educational Research*, 90(5), 269–277.

California Charter Schools Association. (2015, January 29). *Department of Education and charter schools association agree with civil rights group: Public schools can't force parents to volunteer* [Press release]. https://www.publicadvocates.org/resources/news/department-education-charter-schools-association-agree-civil-rights-group-public-schools-cant-force-parents-volunteer/

California Department of Education. (2021). *Free or reduced-price meal (student poverty) data*. https://www.cde.ca.gov/ds/ad/filessp.asp

California State Auditor. (2010). *California's charter schools*. http://www.bsa.ca.gov/pdfs/reports/2010-104.pdf

California Teachers Association. (2019). *State of denial: California charter schools and special education students*. https://aarjb2jw4n53e35fhbquj418-wpengine.netdna-ssl.com/wp-content/uploads/2020/03/State-of-Denial-Report.pdf

Campbell, N., & Quirk, A. (2019, August 6). *Student mobility, backfill, and charter schools*. Center for American Progress. https://www.americanprogress.org/issues/education-k-12/reports/2019/08/06/472090/student-mobility-backfill-charter-schools/

Cano, R. (2019, August 28). *Charter schools, unions call a truce in an epic battle as Newsom brokers a deal*. Cal Matters. https://calmatters.org/education/k-12-education/2019/08/charter-school-deal-california-newsom-teachers-unions/

Carpenter, D. (2006). Modeling the charter school landscape. *Journal of School Choice, 1*(2), 47–82.

Carter, P. L., & Welner, K. G. (Eds.). (2013). *Closing the opportunity gap: What America must do to give every child an even chance*. Oxford University Press.

Casanova, C. (2008). Charter schools: A step in the right direction or a fourth left turn for public education. *Whittier Journal of Child and Family Advocacy, 1*(1), 231–252.

Casey, L. (2016, February 18). *Student attrition and 'backfilling' at Success Academy charter schools: What student enrollment patterns tell us*. Albert Shanker Institute. http://www.shankerinstitute.org/blog/student-attrition-and-backfilling-success-academy-charter-schools-what-student-enrollment

CBS 4 Denver. (2019, December 19). *Lawsuit filed against school that expelled 5-year-old boy for wearing earring*. https://denver.cbslocal.com/2019/12/19/rocky-mountain-classical-academy-expelled-earring-boy-colorado-springs/

Center for Reinventing Public Education. (2010). *District-charter collaboration compact*. https://www.crpe.org/sites/default/files/Denver_Compact_Dec10_0.pdf

Center for Reinventing Public Education. (2016). *Denver district-charter collaboration compact*. https://www.crpe.org/sites/default/files/city_summary_denver_1.2016.pdf

Center for Research on Education Outcomes. (2009). *Multiple choice: Charter school performance in 16 states.* http://credo.stanford.edu/reports/MULTIPLE_CHOICE_CREDO.pdf

Center for Research on Education Outcomes. (2013). *National charter school study.* Stanford University. https://credo.stanford.edu/publications/national-charter-school-study

Center for Research on Education Outcomes. (2019a). *Charter school performance in South Carolina.* https://credo.stanford.edu/sites/g/files/sbiybj6481/f/sc_report_final_08292019.pdf

Center for Research on Education Outcomes. (2019b). *Charter school performance in Pennsylvania.* https://credo.stanford.edu/publications/charter-school-performance-pennsylvania

Center for Research on Education Outcomes. (2019c). *Charter school performance in Ohio.* https://credo.stanford.edu/publications/charter-school-performance-ohio

Center for Research on Education Outcomes. (2019d). *Charter school performance in New Mexico.* https://credo.stanford.edu/publications/charter-school-performance-new-mexico-0

Center for Research on Education Outcomes. (2019e). *Charter school performance in Washington.* https://credo.stanford.edu/publications/charter-school-performance-state-washington

Center for Research on Education Outcomes. (2019f). *Charter school performance in Idaho.* https://credo.stanford.edu/sites/g/files/sbiybj6481/f/idaho_report_final.pdf

Center for Research on Education Outcomes. (2019g). *Charter school performance in Maryland.* https://credo.stanford.edu/publications/charter-school-performance-maryland

Chadha, J. (2015, October 30). *Success Academy founder responds to criticisms it weeds out students.* WNYC News. http://www.wnyc.org/story/success-academy-founder-and-principals-respond-criticisms/

Chandler, M. A. (2014a, October 8). D.C. Charter board reviewing admissions preference for children of employees. *Washington Post.* https://www.washingtonpost.com/local/education/dc-charter-board-reviewing-admissions-preference-for-children-of-employees/2014/10/08/dcfc57b4-4efe-11e4-8c24-487e92bc997b_story.html

Chandler, M. A. (2014b, September 4). Suspensions and expulsions down in D.C. charter schools. *Washington Post.* https://www.washingtonpost.com/local/education/suspensions-and-expulsions-down-in-dc-charter-schools/2014/09/04/0d47e472-346c-11e4-9e92-0899b306bbea_story.html?utm_term=.61f80e9a6880

Chandler, M. A. (2015a, March 17). D.C. auditor finds improvements in financial oversight of charter schools. *Washington Post.* https://www.washingtonpost.com/local/education/dc-auditor-finds-improvements-in-financial-oversight-of-charter-schools/2015/03/17/dd83d2ca-cc0d-11e4-8a46-b1dc9be5a8ff_story.html

Chandler, M. A. (2015b, October 31). Charters grapple with admissions policies, question how public they should be. *Washington Post.* https://www.washingtonpost.com/local/education/public-charter-schools-grapple-with-admissions-policies/2015/10/31/c40a4390-7128-11e5-8d93-0af317ed58c9_story.html

Chapman, B. (2018, December 12). NYC kids with disabilities shortchanged by Success Academy charters. *NY Daily News.* https://www.nydailynews.com/new-york/education/ny-metro-success-academy-kids-with-disabilities-20181129-story.html

Charles, C. Z. (2003). The dynamics of racial residential segregation. *Annual Review of Sociology, 29,* 167–207.

Chatlani, S. (2018, December 27). *Nashville charter school chided over college acceptance requirement.* WPLN News. https://wpln.org/post/nashville-charter-school-chided-over-college-acceptance-requirement/

Chattanooga Charter School of Excellence. (2021). *Parents.* http://www.chattanoogacharter.com/parents

Cheadle, J. E. (2008). Educational investment, family context, and children's math and reading growth from kindergarten through the third grade. *Sociology of Education, 81,* 1–31.

Chetty, R., Hendren, N., Kline, P., & Saez, E. (2014). Where is the land of opportunity? The geography of intergenerational mobility in the United States. *The Quarterly Journal of Economics, 129*(4), 1553–1623.

Chi, W. C., & Welner, K. G. (2008). Charter ranking roulette: An analysis of reports that grade states' charter school laws. *American Journal of Education, 114*(2), 273–298.

Chubb, J. E., & Moe, T. M. (1990). *Politics, markets, and America's schools.* Brookings Institution Press.

Clark, J. (2017, September 21). *Einstein charter schools deemed non compliant for providing inadequate transportation.* WWNO. http://wwno.org/post/einstein-charter-schools-deemed-noncompliant-providing-inadequate-transportation

Clark, J. (2018, November 20). *The do's and dont's of OneApp.* WWNO. https://www.wwno.org/post/dos-and-donts-one-app

Clark, M. A., Gleason, P. M., Tuttle, C. C., & Silverberg, M. K. (2015). Do charter schools improve student achievement? *Educational Evaluation and Policy Analysis, 37*(4), 419–436.

Clawson, L. (2013, May 21). *Nashville charter schools "lose" problem students to public schools-just in time for testing.* Daily Kos. https://www.dailykos.com/stories/2013/5/21/1210512/-Nashville-charter-schools-lose-problem-students-to-public-schools-just-in-time-for-testing

Cobb, C. D., & Glass, G. V. (1999). Ethnic segregation in Arizona charter schools. *Education Policy Analysis Archives, 7*(1), 1–36.

Cohen, R. (2018, May 18). Cash incentives for charter school recruitment: Unethical bribe or shrewd marketing technique. *The Intercept.* https://theintercept.com/2018/05/18/charter-school-recruitment-financial-incentives/

Colombo, H. (2016, February 6). Charter school approval fuels new questions. *Indianapolis Business Journal.* http://www.ibj.com/articles/57079-charter-school-approval-fuels-new-questions

Colorado Charter School Institute. (n.d.). *Serving all students.* http://resources.csi.state.co.us/wp-content/uploads/2018/08/Serving-All-Students_FINAL.pdf

Colorado Department of Education. (2018). *2017–2018 pupil membership.* https://www.cde.state.co.us/2017-18pupilmembership

Colorado Department of Education. (2020). *2019-2020 pupil membership.* https://www.cde.state.co.us/cdereval/2019-2020pupilmembership

Colorado Department of Education. (2021). *2020-2021 pupil membership*. https://www.cde.state.co.us/cdereval/pupilcurrent

Colton, H. (2017, March 22). *New Mexico charter school system plagued by governance issues*. KUNM. http://kunm.org/post/new-mexico-charter-school-system-plagued-governance-issues

Community Unit District 300. (2016). *May 19 special meeting presentation*. https://www.youtube.com/watch?v=edSc6EYVrV8&ab_channel=CUSD300

Conti, D. (2014, February 18). *Environmental charter school admissions lottery raises, dashes hope*. TribLive. http://triblive.com/news/education/5613263-74/charter-lottery-schools

Coons, J. E., & Sugarman, S. D. (1978). *Education by choice: The case for family control*. University of California Press.

Council for Court Excellence. (2015). *Equity in school discipline*. http://www.courtexcellence.org/uploads/publications/Equity_in_School_Discipline_Report___FINAL_31115.pdf

Crocker College Prep. (2021). *Family handbook*. https://www.crockercollegeprep.org/apps/pages/index.jsp?uREC_ID=1449164&type=d&pREC_ID=1609956

Cucchiara, M. (2016). Thinking locally: Attending to social context in studies of marketing and public education. *Peabody Journal of Education, 91*(1), 121–130.

Daley, A. (2018, February 7). *School switches from private Christian to public charter*. WCNC. http://www.wcnc.com/article/news/school-switches-from-private-christian-to-public-charter/275-515769682

Darling-Hammond, L. (2013). Inequality and school resources. In P. Carter & K. Welner (Eds.), *Closing the opportunity gap: What America must do to give every child an even chance*, (pp. 77–94). Oxford University Press.

Darling-Hammond, L. (2015). *The flat world and education: How America's commitment to equity will determine our future*. Teachers College Press.

Darville, S. (2014, March 11). *The quieter charter school divide: What you need to know about "backfill."* Chalkbeat. https://www.chalkbeat.org/posts/ny/2014/03/11/the-quieter-charter-school-divide-what-you-need-to-know-about-backfill/

Davidson Institute. (n.d.). *The Charter School of Wilmington*. https://www.davidsongifted.org/Search-Database/entry/R13136

Davidson, J. (2017, February 14). Feds cite D.C. charters for high suspension rates, particularly for Black students. *Washington Post*. https://www.washingtonpost.com/news/powerpost/wp/2017/02/14/feds-cite-d-c-charters-for-high-suspension-rates-particularly-for-black-students

DC Office of the Ombudsman for Public Education. (2015). *2015 annual report*. http://sboe.dc.gov/sites/default/files/dc/sites/sboe/publication/attachments/DCO_2015%20Annual%20Report_final_large5.pdf

DC Public Charter School Board. (n.d.) *Review of the Washington DC Mystery Shopper Program*. https://dcpcsb.org/review-washington-dc-mystery-shopper-program

DC Public Charter School Board. (2015). *Sibling founder and staff preference*. https://dcpcsb.org/admission-preference-policy

DC Public Charter School Board. (2016). *BASIS DC PCS equity report*. https://osse.dc.gov/page/2016-17-school-year-equity-reports

DC Public Charter School Board. (2017). *Washington Yu Ying PCS school performance*. https://osse.dc.gov/sites/default/files/dc/sites/osse/publication/attachments

/2017_Equity_Report_Public%20Charter%20School_Washington%
20Yu%20Ying%20PCS.pdf

DC Public Charter School Board. (2018, May 14). *Basis DC PCS student location map*. http://www.dcpcsb.org/basis-dc-pcs-student-location-map

DeAngelis. C., Wolf, P. J., Maloney, L., & May, J. F. (2018). *Bigger bang, fewer bucks? The productivity of public charter schools in eight U.S. cities*. Department of Education Reform, University of Arkansas. http://www.uaedreform
.org/bigger-bang-fewer-bucks-the-productivity-of-public-charter-schools-in
-eight-u-s-cities/2

Decker, J., Eckes, S., & Plucker, J. (2010). Charter schools designed for gifted and talented students: Legal and policy issues and considerations. *Education Law Reporter, 259*(1), 1–18.

Decker, J. R., & Carr, K. A. (2015). Church-state entanglement at religiously affiliated charter schools. *Brigham Young University Education and Law Journal, 2015*(1), 77–105.

DeJarnatt, S. L., Wolf, K., & Kalinich, M. K. (2016). Charting school discipline. *The Urban Lawyer, 48*(1), 1–46.

Dempsey, R. (2018, January 10). Houston parents have many school choices. That can be tricky. *Houston Chronicle*. https://www.houstonchronicle
.com/local/gray-matters/article/Houston-parents-have-many-school-choices
-That-12485244.php

Denver Language School. (2016). *Home page*. http://www.denverlanguageschool.org/

Denver Public Schools. (2021). *Enrollment guides*. https://schoolchoice.dpsk12.org
/enrollment/guide/

Desimone, L. (1999). Linking parent involvement with student achievement: Do race and income matter? *Journal of Educational Research, 93*(1), 11–30.

Di Carlo, M. (2014, January 22). Extended school time proposals and charter schools. *Albert Shanker Institute*. http://www.shankerinstitute.org/blog
/extended-school-time-proposals-and-charter-schools

DiMartino, C., & Jessen, S. B. (2016). School brand management: The policies, practices, and perceptions of branding and marketing in New York City's public high schools. *Urban Education, 51*(5), 447–475.

DiMartino, C., & Jessen, S. B. (2018). *Selling school: The marketing of public education*. Teachers College Press.

Dingerson, L. (2014). *Public accountability for charter schools: Standards and policy recommendations for effective oversight*. Annenberg Institute for School Reform at Brown University. https://files.eric.ed.gov/fulltext/ED558016.pdf

Doyle, D., Kim. J., & Rausch, L. (2017). *Beyond the fringe: Charter authorizing as enrollment grows*. National Association of Charter Schools. http://www.qualitycharters
.org/wp-content/uploads/2017/11/Beyond-the-Fringe_HMS-Report.pdf

Drame, E. R. (2011). An analysis of the capacity of charter schools to address the needs of students with disabilities in Wisconsin. *Remedial and Special Education, 32*(1), 55–63.

Drame, E. R., & Frattura, E. (2011). A charter school's journey toward serving all learners: A case study. *Urban Education, 46*(1), 55–75.

Dreilinger, D. (2013, August 2). New Orleans public schools inadequate for non-English speakers, critics say. *Times-Picayune*. http://www.nola.com/education
/index.ssf/2013/08/groups_to_file_complaint_alleg.html

Dreilinger, D. (2014, November 20). Civil rights complaint targets New Orleans charter group Collegiate Academies. *Times-Picayune.* https://empathyeducates.org/civil-rights-complaint-targets-new-orleans-charter-group-collegiate-academies/

Dreilinger, D. (2015a, May 26). Recent history of special education in New Orleans. *Times-Picayune.* www.nola.com/education/index.ssf/2015/05/new_orleans_special_education_3.html

Dreilinger, D. (2015b, March 3). Flagrant special ed violations, cover-up alleged at New Orleans Charter Lagniappe. *Times-Picayune.* http://www.nola.com/education/index.ssf/2015/03/new_orleans_charter_school_vio.html

Duda, J. (2019, November 25). Arizona charter school gets $213M in 'achievement district' financing. *AZ Mirror.* https://www.azmirror.com/2019/11/25/arizona-charter-schools-get-213m-in-achievement-district-financing/

Dynarski, S. (2017). *Online schooling: Who is harmed and who is helped.* Brookings. https://www.brookings.edu/research/who-should-take-online-courses/

Dynarski, S., Hubbard, D., Jacob, B., & Robles, S. (2018). *Estimating the effects of a large for-profit charter school operator.* National Bureau of Economic Research. http://www.nber.org/papers/w24428

Eakins, P. (2006, June 11). Intolerance, or a strict education?—Students, parents concerned about prayer at Escondido Charter High. *San Diego Union Tribune.* http://www.sandiegouniontribune.com/sdut-intolerance-or-a-strict-education-students-2006jun11-story.html

Eastman, N. J., Anderson, M., & Boyles, D. (2016). Choices or rights? Charter schools and the politics of choice-based education policy reform. *Studies in Philosophy and Education, 36*(1), 61–81.

Eckes, S. (2015). Haven charter schools: Separate by design and legally questionable. *Equity & Excellence in Education, 48*(1), 49–70.

Eckes, S., & Carr, K. (2014). Niche charter schools: Legal and policy considerations. In N. Fox & P. Buchanan (Eds.), *Proud to be different.* (pp. 167–185). Rowman & Littlefield.

Edwards, D. S. (2021). Just out of reach? Unrestrained supply, constrained demand, and access to effective schools in and around Detroit. *Educational Evaluation and Policy Analysis.* https://doi.org/10.3102/0162373721996738

Ed-Data. (2018). *Oakland Unified.* http://www.ed-data.org/district/Alameda/Oakland-Unified

Education Commission of the States. (2018). *Charter schools: Does the state specify the students who may be given enrollment preference?* http://ecs.force.com/mbdata/mbquestNB2C?rep=CS1706#:~:text=New%20Jersey-,Yes.,a%20siblings%20of%20enrolled%20students.

Education Commission of the States. (2018). *Charter schools: Does the state specify who must provide transportation to charter school students?* http://ecs.force.com/mbdata/mbquestNB2C?rep=CS1707

Education Law Center. (2016, May 19). *Lawsuit enforces due process rights of students in NJ charter schools* [Press release]. http://www.edlawcenter.org/news/archives/nj-charter-schools/lawsuit-enforces-due-process-rights-of-students-in-nj-charter-schools.html

Education Law Center. (2019, February). *Safeguarding educational equity: Protecting Philadelphia students civil rights through charter oversight.* https://www.elc-pa.org/wp-content/uploads/2019/02/ELC_report-Safeguarding-Civil-Rights.pdf

Education Trust. (2019). *5 things to advance equity in state funding systems*. https://
edtrust.org/resource/5-things-to-advance-equity-in-state-funding-systems/

Education Voters of Pennsylvania. (2020). *Fixing the flaws in Pennsylvania's special
education funding system for charter schools: How an outdated law wastes
public money, encourages gaming of the system, and limits school choice*. http://
educationvoterspa.org/wp-content/uploads/2020/06/Complete-and-Final-Ed
-Voters-charter-special-ed-report.pdf

Einhorn, E. (2016, November 30). *Detroit just created its first intentionally diverse
charter school. Here's why it might not stay that way*. Chalkbeat. http://www
.chalkbeat.org/posts/detroit/2016/11/30/detroit-just-created-its-first-intentionally
-diverse-charter-school-heres-why-it-might-not-stay-that-way/

Elliot, S. (2016, March 8). *Viral video of a teacher tearing a student's paper sparks
renewed school discipline debate*. Chalkbeat. http://www.chalkbeat.com
/posts/in/2016/03/08/viral-video-of-a-teacher-tearing-a-students-paper-sparks
-renewed-school-discipline-debate/

Ely, T., & Teske, P. (2014 February). *Success express: Transportation innovation in
Denver public schools*. Center for Education Policy Analysis School of Public
Affairs, University of Colorado Denver. https://www.crpe.org/sites/default/files
/MHC_Success_Express_2014.pdf

Enrollment Preferences Task Force. (2015, December). *Final report*. http://udspace
.udel.edu/handle/19716/17397

Epstein, K. (2016, January 15). *Charter school teachers fired: Two teachers fired for blowing whistle on lack of special education, English language
learner instruction*. Post News Group. https://www.postnewsgroup.com
/charter-school-teachers-fired/

Ertas, N., & Roch, C. H. (2014). Charter schools, equity, and student enrollments:
The role of for-profit educational management organizations. *Education and
Urban Society, 46*(5), 548–579.

Espinoza v. Montana Department of Revenue, 591 U.S. ___. 2020. https://www
.supremecourt.gov/opinions/19pdf/18 -1195_g314.pdf

Estes, M. B. (2004). Choice for all? Charter schools and students with special needs.
Journal of Special Education, 37(4), 257–267.

Fan, X., & Chen, M. (2001). Parental involvement and students' academic achievement: A meta-analysis. *Educational Psychology Review, 13*(1), 1–22.

Felder, B. (2017, July 23). *Oklahoma charter school applications could be barrier to
enrollment*. The Oklahoman. https://tulsaworld.com/news/state-and-regional
/charter-school-applications-could-be-barrier-to-enrollment/article_704c0807
-ce1b-59cf-9f3a-0d9c31fb6e8c.html

Felton, E. (2018, June 17). *"It's like a Black and White thing": How some elite charter schools exclude minorities*. NBC News. https://www.nbcnews.com/news
/education/it-s-black-white-thing-how-some-elite-charter-schools-n878656

Ferrer, E., Shaywitz, B. A., Holahan, J. M., Marchione, K. E., Michaels, R., & Shaywitz, S. E. (2015). Achievement gap in reading is present as early as first grade
and persists through adolescence. *The Journal of Pediatrics, 167*(5), 1121–1125.

Few, J. (2017, July 31). State places Savannah Classical Academy on probation.
Savannah Now. http://www.savannahnow.com/news/2017-07-30/state-places
-savannah-classical-academy-probation

Fiore, T., Harwell, L., Blackorby, J., & Finnigan, K. (2000). *Charter schools and students with disabilities: A national study. Final report.* Office of Education Research and Improvement. https://eric.ed.gov/?id=ED452657

Fisher, H. (2016, September 16). Mesa charter school sued, accused of teaching religious doctrine. *East Valley Tribune.* https://www.eastvalleytribune.com /arizona/mesa-charter-school-sued-accused-of-teaching-religious-doctrine /article_7824de10-7936-11e6-824c-ff2e8d570ede.html

Fisher, J. (2016, August 11). Schools that accept "no excuses" from students are not helping them. *Washington Post.* https://www.washingtonpost.com /posteverything/wp/2016/08/11/schools-that-accept-no-excuses-from-students -are-not-helping-them/

Flagstaff Academy. (n.d.). *About Flagstaff Academy preschool.* https://www .flagstaffacademy.org/apps/pages/preschool-welcome

Flaherty, J. (2018, August 16). Charter school official's boast of mass expulsions causes anger, investigation. *Phoenix New Times.* https://www.phoenixnewtimes. com/news/arizona-investigated-charter-school-after-official-boasting-of-mass -expulsions-10717025

Flanders, W. (2017). Bang for the buck: Autonomy and charter school efficiency in Milwaukee. *Journal of School Choice, 11*(2), 282–297.

Folk Arts Cultural Treasures Charter School. (2016). *Code of conduct.* https://www .factschool.org/wp-content/uploads/2016/12/Code-of-Conduct-2017-2018 _English.pdf

Fong, K., & Faude, S. (2018, June 21). Timing is everything: Late registration and stratified access to school choice. *Sociology of Education, 91*(3), 242–262.

Food Research and Action Center. (2017). *School meals legislation and funding by state.* http://frac.org/wp-content/uploads/state_leg_table_scorecard.pdf

Fox, R. A., Buchanan, N. K., Eckes, S. E., & Basford, L. E. (2012). The line be-tween cultural education and religious education: Do ethnocentric niche charter schools have a prayer? *Review of Research in Education, 36*(1), 282–305.

Frankenberg, E., Siegel-Hawley, G., & Wang, J. (2011). Choice without equity: Charter school segregation. *Education Policy Analysis Archives, 19*(1), 1–96.

Freire Charter School. (n.d.). *Student and family handbook 2016–2017.* http:// freirecharterschool.org/wp-content/uploads/2015/03/FCMS-Student-Family -Handbook-2016-17.pdf

Friedman, M. (1955). The role of government in education. In R. A. Solo (Ed.), *Economics and the public interest* (pp. 123–144). Rutgers University Press.

Gallagher, N. (2015, December 31). Special education students drawn to Maine char-ter schools. *Portland Press Herald.* http://www.pressherald.com/2015/12/13 /special-education-students-drawn-to-maine-charter-schools/

Garcia, D. (2008). Academic and racial segregation in charter schools: Do parents sort students into specialized charter schools? *Education and Urban Society, 40*(5), 590–561.

García, O. (2009). Emergent bilinguals and TESOL: What's in a name? *TESOL Quarterly, 43*(2), 322–26.

Garcia, P. K., & Morales, P. Z. (2016). Scaling up success for English language learn-ers in charter schools: Exploring the role of charter school authorizers. *Journal of School Choice, 10*(4), 495–515.

Garcy, A. M. (2011). High expense: Disability severity and charter school attendance in Arizona. *Education Policy Analysis Archives, 19*(6), 1–30.

Garda, R. A., Jr. (2011). Culture clash: Special education in charter schools. *North Carolina Law Review, 90,* 655.

Garland, S. (2010, October 10). Repeat performance. *The American Prospect.* http://prospect.org/article/repeat-performance-0

Garrison, J. (2014, March 4). Nashville charter school LEAD Academy boasts 100 percent college acceptance. *Tennessean.* https://www.tennessean.com/story /news/education/2014/03/04/nashville-charter-school-lead-academy-boasts -100-percent-college-acceptance/6025067/

Gazzar, B. (2018, June 26). LA charter school's summer program fees are illegal, state says. *Los Angeles Daily News.* https://www.dailynews.com/2018/06/26 /la-charter-schools-summer-program-fees-are-illegal-state-says/

George-Parkin, H. (2016, February 24). Life after getting expelled: What really happens when students are kicked out of school. *Teen Vogue.* https://www .teenvogue.com/story/high-school-expulsion

Gilbert, J. (2005, March 25). Senator questions heavy charter school transfers. *Houston Chronicle.* http://www.chron.com/news/article/Senator-questions -heavy-charter-school-transfers-1660153.php

Gittleson, K. (2010, June 9). *Augmenting the UFT's "Vanishing Students" report.* Chalkbeat. https://ny.chalkbeat.org/posts/ny/2010/06/09/left-behind-but-not -gone-forever-augmenting-the-ufts-vanishing-students-report/

Glatter, R., Woods, P., & Bagley, C. (1997). *Choice and diversity in schooling: Perspectives and prospects.* Routledge.

Godsey, M. (2015, November 12). Is there a right kind of school discipline? *The Atlantic.* https://www.theatlantic.com/education/archive/2015/11/the-right-kind-of -school-discipline/415506/

Golann, J. W. (2015). The paradox of success at a no-excuses school. *Sociology of Education, 88*(2), 103–119.

Golden View Classical Academy. (2018). *Dress code and uniform policy.* https:// static1.squarespace.com/static/5b44d65275f9ee1074333b71/t/5ca3ab6771c10 bd5769c268b/1554230120815/2018-2019+Family+Handbook.pdf

Goldring, E. B., & Phillips, K. (2008). Parent preferences and parent choices: The public-private decision about school choice. *Journal of Education Policy, 23*(3), 209–230.

Gonzalez, J. (2013, August 30). Success Academy parent's secret tapes reveal attempt to push out special needs student. *New York Post.* http://www .nydailynews.com/new-york/education/success-academy-tapes-reveal -attempt-transfer-student-article-1.1441098

Gonzalez, J. (2016, January 20). Success Charter Network schools formally accused of violating rights of disabled students. *New York Post.* http://www .nydailynews.com/new-york/education/success-charter-network-accused -disability-violations-article-1.2503503

Goodnough, A. (2007, August 24). Hebrew charter school spurs dispute in Florida. *The New York Times.* https://www.nytimes.com/2007/08/24/education /24charter.html

Gorski, E. (2017, May 30). *Inside one Denver charter school operator's push to serve all students.* Chalkbeat. https://www.chalkbeat.org/posts/co/2017/05/30 /inside-one-denver-charter-school-operators-push-to-serve-all-students/

Graham, K. (2018, July 26). She says her granddaughter's acceptance to Philly charter was rescinded because of her special-education status. *The Inquirer.* http://www .philly.com/philly/education/she-says-her-granddaughters-acceptance-to-philly -charter-was-rescinded-because-of-her-special-education-status-20180726.html

Great Philly Schools. (n.d.). *Apply Philly charter.* https://greatphillyschools.org /articles/2018-2019-standard-application

Great Philly Schools. (2016a). *2017–18 charter school common application.* https://web.archive.org/web/20170228154330/http://greatphillyschools.org /articles/2017-2018-common-application

Great Philly Schools. (2016b). *MaST community charter school.* https:// greatphillyschools.org/schools/mast-community-charter-school

Great Schools. (2018). *Academy for Advanced and Creative Learning.* https://www .greatschools.org/colorado/colorado-springs/4182-Academy-For-Advanced -And-Creative-Learning/

Greeley Tribune. (2015, June 20). *When money doesn't follow students, the numbers don't add up in Greeley, Evans schools.* http://www.greeleytribune .com/news/opinion/tribune-opinion-when-money-doesnt-follow-students-the -numbers-dont-add-up-in-greeley-evans-schools/

Green, E. (2011, April 5). KIPP Ujima to discontinue placement tests. *Baltimore Sun.* http://articles.baltimoresun.com/2011-04-05/news/bs-md-ci-kipp-entrance -exam-20110401_1_jason-botel-kipp-ujima-kipp-baltimore

Green, E. L., & Shapiro, E. (2019, November 26). Minority voters chafe as democratic candidates abandon charter schools. *The New York Times.* https:// www.nytimes.com/2019/11/26/nyregion/charter-schools-democrats.html

Green, P. C., Baker, B. D., Oluwole, J. O., & Mead, J. F. (2015). Are we heading toward a charter school bubble: Lessons from the subprime mortgage crisis. *University of Richmond Law Review, 50,* 783.

Griffith, C. A., Lloyd, J. W., Lane, K. L., & Tankersley, M. (2010). Grade retention of students during grades K–8 predicts reading achievement and progress during secondary schooling. *Reading & Writing Quarterly, 26,* 51–66.

Gross, A. (2016, April 20). Begging for answers: Eight teachers were just fired from a Detroit charter school without cause or notice. *Detroit Metro Times.* http:// www.metrotimes.com/detroit/begging-for-answers-why-were-eight-teachers-at -a-detroit-charter-school-fired/Content?oid= 2438569#

Gross, B., DeArmond, M., & Denice, P. (2015). *Common enrollment, parents, and school choice: Early evidence from Denver and New Orleans.* Center for Reinventing Public Education. https://www.crpe.org/sites/default/files/cpe-report -common-enrollment-denver-nola.pdf

Gross, B., Tuchman, S., & Yatsko, S. (2016). *Grappling with discipline in autonomous school: New approaches from D.C. and New Orleans.* Center for Reinventing Public Education. https://www.crpe.org/sites/default/files/crpe -grappling-with-discipline-6.2016-final.pdf

Gulosino, C. A., & Lubienski, C. (2011). Schools' strategic responses to competition in segregated urban areas: Patterns in school locations in metropolitan Detroit. *Education Policy Analysis Archives, 19*(13), 1–30.

Haimson, L. (2012, March 22). "At KIPP, I would wake up sick, every single day." *New York Public School Parents.* https://nycpublicschoolparents.blogspot .com/2012/03/at-kipp-i-would-wake-up-sick-every.html

Hamilton, L. S., & Guinn, K. (2005). Understanding how families choose schools. In J. Betts & T. Loveless (Eds.), *Getting choice right: Ensuring equity and efficiency in education policy* (pp. 40–60). Brookings.

Hammel, H. (2014). *Charging for access: How California charter schools exclude vulnerable students by imposing illegal family work quotas.* Public Advocates. http://www.publicadvocates.org/wp-content/uploads/charging_for_access _how_california_charter_schools_exclude_vulnerable_students_by_imposing _illegal_family_work_quotas.pdf

Hangley, B., Jr. (2020, June 30). Charters deny 'cherry picking' students, but data show special ed disparities. *The Notebook.* https://thenotebook.org/articles/2020/06 /30/charters-deny-cherry-picking-students-but-data-show-special-ed-disparities/

Hanna, M. (2019, June 4). Pa. charter-school students lag in math, with cyber results "overwhelmingly negative," study says. *Philadelphia Inquirer.* https:// www.inquirer.com/news/pennsylvania-charter-school-performance-cyber-credo -stanford-20190604.html

Hanna, M., & Graham, K. (2020, February 20). Philly schools overpaying charters millions of dollars for special-education students, district says. *Philadelphia Inquirer.* https://www.inquirer.com/education/charter-schools-philadelphia-special -education-costs-20200221.html

Hannah-Jones, N. (2016, June 9). Choosing a school for my daughter in a segregated city. *The New York Times Magazine.* https://www.nytimes.com/2016/06/12 /magazine/choosing-a-school-for-my-daughter-in-a-segregated-city.html

Harbach, M. J. (2015). Sexualization, sex discrimination, and public school dress codes. *University of Richmond Law Review, 50,* 1039.

Hardy, K. (2011, September 28). Chattanooga charter schools grow. *Chattanooga Times Free Press.* http://www.timesfreepress.com/news/news/story/2011/sep/28 /charter-schools-grow/60123/

Harnett Dispatch. (2014, January 21). *Questions raised about Anderson Creek charter school, taxpayers paying 1.2 million.* http://harnettnews.org/?p=1660

Harris, C. (2018, August 16). Glendale charter school drops student because of his disability, mom alleges. *Arizona Republic.* https://www.azcentral.com/story /news/local/glendale-education/2018/08/16/glendale-charter-school-heritage -elementary-accused-kicking-out-special-needs-child/991341002/

Harris, D., Valant, J., & Gross, B. (2015). *The New Orleans OneApp.* Education Next. http://educationnext.org/new-orleans-oneapp/

Harris, E. (2015, November 2). Lawsuit accuses Brooklyn charter school of failing to provide special education services. *The New York Times.* http://www .nytimes.com/2015/11/06/nyregion/lawsuit-accuses-brooklyn-charter-school -of-failing-to-provide-special-education-services.html

Harris, S. (2018, May 07). At BASIS charter schools, another way to boost teacher pay: Parent donations. *Arizona Republic.* https://www.azcentral.com/story /news/local/arizona-education/2018/05/07/basis-charter-schools-seek-big -donations-parents-subsidize-low-teacher-pay/473963002/

Hasan, S., & Kumar, A. (2019). *Digitization and divergence: Online school ratings and segregation in America.* Social Science Research Network.

Hasselle, D. (2021, January 10). With One App deadline looming, see which public schools close their rounds first. *Times-Picayune.* https://www.nola.com/news /education/article_76ce5d50-5381-11eb-992a-43c4c64e9bbf.html

Hastings, J. S., Kane, T. J., & Staiger, D. O. (2005). *Parental preferences and school competition: Evidence from a public school choice program* (no. w11805). National Bureau of Economic Research. https://www.nber.org/papers/w11805

Hatfield, J., & Malkus, N. (2017). *Differences by design? Student composition in charter schools with different academic models.* American Enterprise Institute. https://www.aei.org/wp-content/uploads/2017/02/Differences-by-Design.pdf

Hechinger, J. (2011, November 14). Taxpayers get billed for kids of millionaires at charter school. *Bloomberg.* http://www.bloomberg.com/news/2011-11-15/taxpayers-billed-for-millionaires-kids-at-charter-school.html

Henig, J. R., & MacDonald, J. A. (2002). Locational decisions of charter schools: Probing the market metaphor. *Social Science Quarterly, 83*(4), 962–980.

Herold, B. (2012, September 14). *Questionable application processes at Green Woods, other charter schools.* Chalkbeat. http://thenotebook.org/articles/2012/09/14/questionable-application-processes-at-green-woods-other-charter-schools

Herold, B. (2016, November 3). A virtual mess: Inside Colorado's largest online charter school. *Education Week.* https://www.edweek.org/ew/articles/2016/11/03/a-virtual-mess-colorados-largest-cyber-charter.html

Hesla, K. (2018). *Unified enrollment: Lessons learned from across the country.* National Alliance for Public Charter Schools. https://www.publiccharters.org/sites/default/files/documents/2018-09/rd3_unified_enrollment_web.pdf

Hess, F. (2018, December 14). *Straight up conversation: Seton education partners Stephanie Saroki de Garcia.* Education Next. https://www.educationnext.org/straight-conversation-seton-education-partners-stephanie-saroki-de-garcia/

Hiatt, F. (2017, January 1). The right kind of school choice for Trump to promote. *Washington Post.* https://www.washingtonpost.com/opinions/school-choice-for-children-who-have-none/2017/01/01/60479c34-cead-11e6-b8a2-8c2a61b0436f_story.html?noredirect=on&utm_term=.21014d1ca0d3

High Tech High. (n.d.) *About High Tech High.* hightechhigh.org/about-us/

Hillsdale College. (2016). *The Barney charter school initiative.* https://www.hillsdale.edu/educational-outreach/barney-charter-school-initiative/

Hinchcliffe, K. (2017, April 24). *House committee approves charter school growth, enrollment "perks" for charter partners.* WRAL. http://www.wral.com/house-committee-approves-charter-school-growth-enrollment-perks-for-charter-partners/16662477/

Hinnefeld, S. (2018, May 3). *Suspension rates extremely high at some schools.* https://inschoolmatters.wordpress.com/2018/05/03/suspension-rates-extremely-high-at-some-schools/

Hirsch, E. D., Jr. (1995). *Core Knowledge sequence.* Core Knowledge Foundation.

Holme, J. J. (2002). Buying homes, buying schools: School choice and the social construction of school quality. *Harvard Educational Review, 72*(2), 177–206.

Hong, G., & Yu, B. (2007). Early grade retention and children's reading and math learning in elementary school. *Educational Evaluation and Policy Analysis, 29*(4), 239–261.

Horizon Science Academy. (2021). *Admission procedures.* http://www.horizondenison.org/admission-procedures/

Horn, J., & Miron, G. (2000). *An evaluation of the Michigan charter school initiative: Performance, accountability, and impact.* Evaluation Center, Western Michigan University.

Horning, C. N. (2013). The intersection of religious charter schools and urban Catholic education: A literature review. *Journal of Catholic Education, 16*(2), 364–387.

Horvat, E. M., Weininger, E. B., & Lareau, A. (2003). From social ties to social capital: Class differences in the relations between schools and parent networks. *American Educational Research Journal, 40*(2), 319–351.

Howe, K. R., & Murray, K. (2015). *Why school report cards merit a failing grade.* National Education Policy Center. https://nepc.colorado.edu/publication /why-school-report-cards-fail

Howe, K. R., & Welner, K. G. (2002). School choice and the pressure to perform: Déjà vu for children with disabilities? *Remedial and Special Education (RASE), 23*(4), 212–221.

Howell, C. (2018, August 17). 3 more state charter schools denied. *Northwest Arkansas Democrat Gazette.* http://www.nwaonline.com/news/2018 /aug/17/3-more-charter-schools-denied-20180817/

Howland, L. (2016, December 01). *Students humiliated after dress code violations at James Irwin Charter High School.* KOAA. http://www.koaa.com /story/33849552/students-humiliated-after-dress-code-violations-at-james -irwin-charter-high-school

Hoxby, C. M. (Ed.). (2019). *The economics of school choice.* University of Chicago Press.

Hsieh, C., & Urquiola, M. (2002). *When schools compete, how do they compete?* National Center for the Study of Privatization in Education.

Hu, W. (2011, July 16). In Millburn, N.J., a revolt against charter schools. *The New York Times.* http://www.nytimes.com/2011/07/17/education/17charters.html

Hubbard, D. (2016, October 8). *ACLU files lawsuit, claims Bergen School District discriminates against undocumented immigrants.* Mahwah Patch. http://patch.com/new-jersey/mahwah/aclu-files-lawsuit-claims-bergen -school-district-discriminates-against

Huffington Post. (2013, January 27). *Marsha Godard, Chicago mother, fined over $3,000 for son's behavior at Noble Network charter school.* http://www.huffingtonpost .com/2013/01/27/marsha-godard-chicago-mother-fined_n_2562353.html

Hughes, J. N., Cao, Q., West, S. G., Smith, P. A., & Cerda, C. (2017). Effect of retention in elementary grades on dropping out of school early. *Journal of School Psychology, 65*, 11–27.

Huguley, J., Wang, M., Monahan, K., Keane, G., & Koury, A. (2018). *Just discipline and the school-to-prison pipeline in greater Pittsburgh.* Center on Race on Social Problems at the University of Pittsburgh. https://www.heinz.org/UserFiles /Library/Just_Discipline_and_the_School_to_Prison_Pipeline_in_Pittsburgh.pdf

Idaho Public Charter School Commission. (2015). *2015 annual report.* https://web .archive.org/web/20160429183953/https://chartercommission.idaho.gov /documents/PCSC%202015%20Annual%20Report.pdf

Imberman, S. A. (2011). The effect of charter schools on achievement and behavior of public school students. *Journal of Public Economics, 95*(7–8), 850–863.

Institute for Innovation in Public School Choice. (2014). *A current state assessment of public school enrollment and choice in Detroit.* http://www.glep.org/wp -content/uploads/2014/11/Detroit-Common-Enrollment.Feasibility_Report _Nov2014.pdf

Institute for Innovation in Public School Choice. (2015). *A current state assessment of public school enrollment in Indianapolis.* https://teachplus.org/sites/default /files/publication/pdf/2015_0514_iipsc_csa_-_indianapolis_.pdf

Institute for Innovation in Public School Choice. (2017). *Parents discuss their challenges with public school choice in Chicago.* https://static1.squarespace.com /static/5b212dce5417fcd9ddec5349/t/5cf1467b1999120001d941a3/15593160 92190/20170218+School+Choice+in+Chicago-FINAL.pdf

Jabbar, H. (2015). Competitive networks and school leaders' perceptions: The formation of an education marketplace in post-Katrina New Orleans. *American Educational Research Journal, 52*(6), 1093–1131.

Jabbar, H. (2016). Selling schools: Marketing and recruitment strategies in New Orleans. *Peabody Journal of Education, 91*(1), 4–23.

Jabbar, H., & Wilson, T. S. (2018). What Is Diverse Enough? How "Intentionally Diverse" Charter Schools Recruit and Retain Students. *Education Policy Analysis Archives, 26*(165), n165.

Jacobs, N. (2011). Understanding school choice: Location as a determinant of charter school racial, economic, and linguistic segregation. *Education and Urban Society, 45*(4), 459–482.

James Irwin Charter Schools. (2015). *Admissions procedures.* https:// jamesirwincharterschools.files.wordpress.com/2015/11/detailed-admissions -procedures2.pdf

Jarvie, D. (2021, forthcoming). *Growing charter school segregation in largest states* [Policy brief]. Civil Rights Project.

Jasis, P. M., & Ordoñez-Jasis, R. (2012). Latino parent involvement: Examining commitment and empowerment in schools. *Urban Education, 47*(1), 65–89.

Javier, C. (2020, February 26). *Facing the music: The uncertain future of the Orange County School of the Arts.* LAist. https://laist.com/projects/2020/oc-arts -charter-school/

Jennings, J. L. (2010). School choice or schools' choice? Managing in an era of accountability. *Sociology of Education, 83*(3), 227–247.

Jersey City Global Charter School. (2021a). *Home page.* http://www.jcgcs.org/

Jersey City Global Charter School. (2021b). *Enrollment package.* https://www .jcgcs.org/ourpages/auto/2020/10/5/44782922/Enrollent%20Package%20 2021-2022.pdf?rnd=1601923696000

Jessen, S. B. (2013). Special education & school choice: The complex effects of small schools, school choice and public high school policy in New York City. *Educational Policy, 27*(3), 427–466.

Jewson, M. (2015, July 17). When a top NOLA charter won't reveal its admission test—for kindergarten. *Hechinger Report.* http://hechingerreport.org /when-a-top-nola-charter-wont-reveal-its-admission-test-for-kindergarten/

Jewson, M. (2017, July 10). Sophie B. Wright's refusal to admit homeless students lacking uniforms not its 1st violation. *The Advocate.* http://www .theadvocate.com/new_orleans/news/education/article_e3807a94-64f8-11e7 -8cd5-9365c82b0a5c.html

Jewson, M. (2018, January 3). School district reprimands Einstein Charter Schools for enrolling students outside OneApp. *The Lens NoLa.* https://thelensnola .org/2018/01/03/school-district-reprimands-einstein-charter-schools-for-enrolling -students-outside-oneapp/

Jewson, M. (2019, November 7). Parent says Bricolage Academy's new aftercare policies exclude special education students. *The Lens NoLa*. https://thelensnola .org/2019/03/28/parent-says-bricolage-academys-new-aftercare-policies -exclude-special-education-students/

Jeynes, W. H. (2003). A meta-analysis: The effects of parental involvement on minority children's academic achievement. *Education and Urban Society*, *35*(2), 202–218.

Jeynes, W. H. (2007). The relationship between parental involvement and urban secondary school student academic achievement: A meta-analysis. *Urban Education*, *42*(1), 82–110.

Jimerson, S. R. (2001). Meta-analysis of grade retention research: Implications for practice in the 21st century. *School Psychology Review*, *30*(3), 420–437.

Jimerson, S. R., Anderson, G. E., & Whipple, A. D. (2002). Winning the battle and losing the war: Examining the relation between grade retention and dropping out of high school. *Psychology in the Schools*, *39*(4), 441–457.

Jimerson, S. R., & Ferguson, P. (2007). A longitudinal study of grade retention: Academic and behavioral outcomes of retained students through adolescence. *School Psychology Quarterly*, *22*(3), 314–339.

Johnson, H. B., & Shapiro, T. M. (2003). Good neighborhoods, good schools: Race and the "good choices" of White families. In A. W. Doane & E. Bonilla-Silva (Eds.), *White out: The continuing significance of racism* (pp. 173–87). Routledge.

Jones, K. (2014, August 18). *Mother says charter school denied admission to son over volunteer hours*. NBC News Miami. https://www.nbcmiami.com/news /local/Mother-Says-Charter-School-Denied-Admission-to-Son-Over-Volunteer -Hours-271772871.html

Jones, L. (2016, November 21). Classical conflict. *World Magazine*. https://wng.org /articles/classical-conflict-1620600333

Joseph, G. (2016, September 15). *Do charter schools with extreme disciplinary measures cluster in Black communities?* City Lab. https://www.citylab.com /equity/2016/09/mapping-the-extreme-discipline-of-charter-schools-in-black -communities-suspensions/499559/

Juhasz, A. (2020, February 19). New Orleans public school enrollment can be confusing. This guide should help. *WWNO New Orleans Public Radio*. https://www.wwno.org/education/2020-11-19/new-orleans-public-school -enrollment-can-be-confusing-this-guide-should-help

Justice, B., & MacLeod, C., (2017, February 7). Does religion have a place in public schools. *The Atlantic*. https://www.theatlantic.com/education/archive/2017/02 /does-religion-have-a-place-in-public-schools/516189/

Karp, S. (2021, March 15). *Top Chicago charter school network admits a racist past*. WBEZ Chicago. https://www.wbez.org/stories/top-chicago-charter-school-admits -a-racist-past/ebd3c82c-af3b-4320-befc-d7f565acc453

Kebede, L. (2018, January 30). *What needs to happen for a group of Memphis Catholic schools to become charters*. Chalkbeat. https://www.chalkbeat.org /posts/tn/2018/01/30/what-needs-to-happen-for-a-group-of-memphis-catholic -schools-to-become-charters/

Kelley, D. (2014, April 14). Colorado charter schools encounter dress code friction. *The Gazette*. http://gazette.com/colorado-charter-schools-encounter -dress-code-friction/article/1517779

Kern, N. (2016). *Intentionally diverse charter schools: A toolkit for charter school leaders.* National Charter School Resource Center. https://charterschoolcenter.ed.gov/sites/default/files/files/field_publication_attachment/NCSRC%20Intentionally%20Diverse%20Charter%20School%20Toolkit.pdf

Keys Gate Charter School. (2019). *Parent and student handbook.* https://www.keyscharter.org/pdfs/2019-2020_K-12_Student_and_Parent_Handbook.pdf

Khan, S. R. (2010). *Privilege: The making of an adolescent elite at St. Paul's School.* Princeton University Press.

Kho, A., & Zimmer, R. (2017, November). Comprehensive examination of the performance levels and churn of students served by charter schools [Paper presentation]. Fourth meeting of the Association for Education Finance and Policy, Washington, DC.

Kho, A., Zimmer, R., & McEachin, A. (2019). A descriptive analysis of cream skimming and pushout in choice versus traditional public schools. *Education Finance and Policy,* 1–65.

Khrais, R. (2016, January 21). *Exploring the racial imbalance of NC's charter schools.* WUNC. http://wunc.org/post/exploring-racial-imbalance-ncs-charter-schools#stream/0

Kim, C. Y., Losen, D. J., & Hewitt, D. T. (2010). *The school-to-prison pipeline: Structuring legal reform.* New York University Press.

KIPP. (2020, July 1). *Retiring "Work hard. Be nice." as KIPP's national slogan.* https://www.kipp.org/retiring-work-hard-be-nice/

Kiracofe, C. (2010). Isn't school supposed to be free?: An analysis of state constitutional language and school fees. *West's Education Law Reporter, 253,* 1–16.

Kleitz, B., Weiher, G. R., Tedin, K., & Matland, R. (2000). Choice, charter schools, and household preferences. *Social Science Quarterly, 81*(3), 846–855.

Klinger, A., & McGrath, K. (2021, March 12). *Success Academy charter school network ordered to pay over $2.4 million in a disability discrimination case brought by families of five former students.* JDSupra. https://www.jdsupra.com/legalnews/success-academy-charter-school-network-3311378/

Kolderie, T. (1990). *The states will have to withdraw the exclusive.* St. Paul, MN: Center for Policy Studies.

Koran, M. (2017). *District admits pushing struggling students towards charters.* Voice of San Diego. https://www.voiceofsandiego.org/topics/education/district-admits-pushing-struggling-students-toward-charters/

Kotok, S., Frankenberg, E., Schafft, K. A., Mann, B. A., & Fuller, E. J. (2017). School choice, racial segregation, and poverty concentration: Evidence from Pennsylvania charter school transfers. *Educational Policy, 31*(4), 415–447.

Kritz, F. (2018, February 15). *A lawmaker's crusade to require public charter schools to provide free lunch.* Cal Health Report. https://www.calhealthreport.org/2018/02/15/lawmakers-crusade-require-public-charter-schools-provide-free-lunch/

Lacireno-Paquet, N. (2006). Charter school enrollments in context: An exploration of organization and policy influences. *Peabody Journal of Education, 81*(1), 79–102.

Lacireno-Paquet, N., Holyoke, T. T., Moser, M., & Henig, J. (2002). Creaming versus cropping: Charter school enrolment practices in response to market incentives. *Educational Evaluation and Policy Analysis, 24*(2), 145–158.

Ladd, H. F., Clotfelter, C. T., & Holbein, J. B. (2017). The growing segmentation of the charter school sector in North Carolina. *Education Finance and Policy*, *12*(4), 536–563.

Ladd, H. F., & Fiske, E. B. (2021). *Equity-oriented accountability for charter schools: Lessons from Massachusetts. Annenberg Institute at Brown University.* https://doi.org/10.26300/ekh3-we64

Ladd, H. F., & Singleton, J. D. (2019). The fiscal externalities of charter schools: Evidence from North Carolina. *Education Finance and Policy*, *15*(1), 191–208.

Lafer, G. (2018, May). *Breaking point: The cost of charter schools for public school districts*. In The Public Interest. Retrieved from https://www.inthepublicinterest .org/wp-content/uploads/ITPI_Breaking_Point_May2018FINAL.pdf

LaFleur, J. C. (2016). Locating Chicago's charter schools: A socio-spatial analysis. *Education Policy Analysis Archives*, *24*(4), 451–457.

Lancet, S., Rhim, L. M., & O'Neill, P. (2020, June). Enrollment of students with disabilities in charter schools and traditional public schools. *National Center for Special Education in Charter Schools.* https://files.eric.ed.gov/fulltext /ED608543.pdf

Landsburg, S. E. (1995). *The armchair economist: Economics and everyday experiences.* Simon and Schuster.

Lareau, A. (1987). Social class differences in family-school relationships: The importance of cultural capital. *Sociology of Education*, *60*(2), 73–85.

Lareau, A. (2011). *Unequal childhoods: Class, race, and family life.* University of California Press.

Lattimore, K. (2017, July 17). *When Black hair violates the dress code.* NPR. https://www.npr.org/sections/ed/2017/07/17/534448313/when-black-hair -violates-the-dress-code

Lazar, K. (2017, May 12). Black Malden charter students punished for braided hair. *The Boston Globe.* https://www.bostonglobe.com/metro/2017/05/11/black -students-malden-school-who-wear-braids-face-punishment-parents-say /stWDlBSCJhw1zocUWR1QMP/story.html

Lee, J.-S., & Bowen, N. K. (2006). Parent involvement, cultural capital, and the achievement gap among elementary school children. *American Educational Research Journal*, *43*, 193–218.

Lee, J., & Lubienski, C. A. (2021). A spatial analysis on charter school access in the New York metropolitan area. *Teachers College Record*, *123*(2), 1–30.

Lehrer, B. (2015, March 25). *Eva Moskowitz;* The Nation *magazine; instability in Yemen; science of hedonism* [Radio broadcast episode]. WNYC, Brian Lehrer Show. https://www.wnyc.org/story/the-brian-lehrer-show-2015-03-24/

Leung, V., Alejandre, R., & Jongco, A. (2016). *Unequal access: How some California charter schools illegally restrict enrollment.* ACLU Southern California & Public Impact. https://www.aclusocal.org/sites/default/files/field_documents /report-unequal-access-080116.pdf

Lewis, A. E., & Diamond, J. B. (2015). *Despite the best intentions: How racial inequality thrives in good schools.* Oxford University Press.

Loew, M. (2015, August 7). *BASIS schools fight criticism, work to increase student retention.* AZ Family. http://www.azfamily.com/story/29731806/basis-schools -fight-criticism-work-to-increase-student-retention#ixzz3i9Zxh3tm

Losen, D., Keith, M., Hodson, C., & Martinez, T. (2016). *Charter schools, civil rights and school discipline: A comprehensive review*. The Center for Civil Rights and Remedies. https://www.civilrightsproject.ucla.edu/resources/projects /center-for-civil-rights-remedies/school-to-prison-folder/federal-reports/charter -schools-civil-rights-and-school-discipline-a-comprehensive-review/losen-et-al -charter-school-discipline-review-2016.pdf

Losen, D. J., & Gillespie, J. (2012). *Opportunities suspended: The disparate impact of disciplinary exclusion from school*. Civil Rights Project/ Proyecto Derechos Civiles.

Lubienski, C. (2001). Redefining "public" education: Charter schools, common schools, and the rhetoric of reform. *Teachers College Record, 103*(4), 634–666.

Lubienski, C. (2003). Innovation in education markets: Theory and evidence on the impact of competition and choice in charter schools. *American Educational Research Journal, 40*(2), 395–443.

Lubienski, C. (2005). Public schools in marketized environments: Shifting incentives and unintended consequences of competition-based educational reforms. *American Journal of Education, 111*(4), 464–486.

Lubienski, C. (2007). Marketing schools: Consumer goods and competitive incentives for consumer information. *Education and Urban Society, 40*(1), 118–141.

Lubienski, C., & Gulosino, C. (2007). *Choice, competition, and organizational orientation: A geo-spatial analysis of charter schools and the distribution of educational opportunities*. National Center for the Study of Privatization in Education. https://ncspe.tc.columbia.edu/working-papers/OP148.pdf

Lubienski, C., Gulosino, C., & Weitzel, P. (2009). School choice and competitive incentives: Mapping the distribution of educational opportunities across local education markets. *American Journal of Education, 115*(4), 601–647.

Lubienski, C., & Lee, J. (2016). Competitive incentives and the education market: How charter schools define themselves in metropolitan Detroit. *Peabody Journal of Education, 91*(1), 64–80.

Lubienski, C. A., & Weitzel, P. C. (2010). *The charter school experiment: Expectations, evidence, and implications*. Harvard Education Press.

Lucas, S. R. (1999). *Tracking inequality: Stratification and mobility in American high schools*. Teachers College Press.

Lucas, S. R. (2001). Effectively maintained inequality: Education transitions, track mobility, and social background effects. *American Journal of Sociology, 106*(6), 1642–1690.

Lusher Charter School. (n.d.). *Forms and downloads*. http://www.lusherschool.org /forms-downloads/

Maass, B. (2018, November 13). *Parents, students file first amendment lawsuit against charter school*. CBS Denver. https://denver.cbslocal.com/2018/11/13 /victory-prep-commerce-city-first-amendment-lawsuit

Madhaus. (2012, August 5). *How to destroy a top notch school district: Open a charter school!* Daily Kos. http://www.dailykos.com/story/2012/8/5/1117114 /-How-to-Destroy-a-Top-Notch-School-District-Open-a-Charter-School

Malik, A. (2015, July 25). Top charter schools in town teach very different groups of students. *San Antonio Express-News*. http://www.expressnews.com/news/education /article/Top-charter-schools-in-town-teach-very-different-6405598.php

Malkus, N. (2016). Differences on balance: National comparisons of charter and traditional public schools. *AEI Paper & Studies*. https://charterschoolcenter .ed.gov/sites/default/files/files/field_event_attachments/AEI%20Report%20 -%20Differences%20on%20Balance.pdf

Mann, H. (1848). *Twelfth annual report of Horace Mann as secretary of Massachusetts state board of education*. Commonwealth of Massachusetts Board of Education. http://www.tncrimlaw.com/civil_bible/horace_mann.htm

Marbella, J. (2019, July 16). Study: Maryland charter students' gains outpace those at traditional schools; black, Hispanic pupils benefit most. *The Baltimore Sun*. https:// www.baltimoresun.com/education/bs-md-charter-school-study-20190716 -o2kv752kx5aolb3222ejgrokxm-story.html

Marchbanks, M. P., III, Blake, J. J., Booth, E. A., Carmichael, D., Seibert, A. L., & Fabelo, T. (2015). The economic effects of exclusionary discipline on grade retention and high school dropout. In D. Losen (Ed.), *Closing the school discipline gap: Equitable remedies for excessive exclusion* (pp. 59–74). Teachers College Press.

Marcotte, D. E., & Dalane, K. (2019) Socioeconomic segregation and school choice in American public schools. *Educational Researcher*, *48*(8), 493–503.

Marra, A. (2017, January 17). PBC charter school threatens to expel student over dad's Facebook post. *Palm Beach Post*. https://www.palmbeachpost.com/2017/01/17 /pbc-charter-school-threatens-to-expel-student-over-dads-facebook-post/

Marshall, D. T. (2017). Equity and access in charter schools: Identifying issues and solutions. *Education Policy Analysis Archives*, *25*, 1–15.

Mathews, J. (2019, August 2). "No-excuses schools" make no excuse for updating their approach. *Washington Post*. https://www.washingtonpost.com/local /education/no-excuses-schools-make-no-excuse-for-updating-their-approach /2019/08/01/7a3e9052-b31b-11e9-8f6c-7828e68cb15f_story.html

Mathews, J. (2020, January 2). How much pressure is too much pressure for middle school students? *Washington Post*. https://www.washingtonpost.com /local/education/how-much-pressure-is-too-much-pressure-for-middle-school -students/2019/12/28/ff8559be-284e-11ea-ad73-2fd294520e97_story.html

Matos, A., & Brown, E. (2017, July 17). Some D.C. high schools are reporting only a fraction of suspensions. *Washington Post*. https://www.washingtonpost .com/local/education/some-dc-high-schools-reported-only-a-small-fraction-of -suspensions/2017/07/17/045c387e-5762-11e7-ba90-f5875b7d1876_story.html

Maul, A. (2015, April 27). *Review of "Urban charter school study report on 41 regions 2015."* National Education Policy Center. https://nepc.colorado .edu/%20thinktank/review-urban-charter-school

Maxwell, J. A. (2012). *Qualitative research design: An interactive approach* (Vol. 41). SAGE.

McCorry, K. (2015, April 9). Debate over "backfilling" at charters raises questions of fairness. *The Notebook*. https://thenotebook.org/articles/2015/04/09 /debate-over-backfilling-at-charters-raises-questions-of-fairness/

McCoy, D. (2018, January 18). *One system to apply for IPS and charter schools? Nearly 4,000 students gave it a shot*. Chalkbeat. https://chalkbeat.org/posts /in/2018/01/18/one-system-to-apply-for-ips-and-charter-schools-nearly-4000 -students-gave-it-a-shot/

McNeel, B. (2014, March 27). *At BASIS San Antonio, intellectual engagement is the norm*. The Rivard Report. https://therivardreport.com/basis-san-antonio/

McShane, M., & Kelly, A. (2014, April 29). *Sector switchers: Why Catholic schools convert to charters and what happens next.* EdChoice. https://www.edchoice .org/research/sector-switchers/

Mead, J. (2008). *Charter schools designed for children with disabilities: An initial examination of issues and questions raised.* https://www.charterschoolcenter .ed.gov/sites/default/files/files/field_publication_attachment/Charters%20De signed%20for%20CWDs%20Issues%20and%20Questions%20Raised%20 2008_0.pdf

Mead, J., & Green, P. C. (2012). *Chartering Equity: Using Charter School Legislation and Policy to Advance Equal Educational Opportunity.* National Education Policy Center. http://nepc.colorado.edu/publication/chartering-equity

Mead, J., & Green, P. C. (2019). *Advancing intentional equity in charter schools.* The Century Foundation. https://tcf.org/content/report/advancing -intentional-equity-charter-schools/

Medina, J. (2010, June 25). Success and scrutiny at Hebrew charter school. *The New York Times.* http://www.nytimes.com/2010/06/25/nyregion/25hebrew.html

Mellon, E. (2013, April 10). Charter school's entry fee is illegal. *Houston Chronicle.* http://www.chron.com/news/houston-texas/houston/article/Charter-agrees-to -halt-fees-tied-to-admission-4425199.php

Mercurio, R. (2016, May 5). Charter schools cater to parental "choice" of pre- dominantly White, Christian families. *Alianza North County.* http://www .escondidoalliance.com/uncategorized/charter-schools-cater-parental-choice -predominantly-white-christian-families/

Mervosh, S. (2019, March 31). Girls at North Carolina school don't have to wear skirts, judge rules. *The New York Times.* https://www.nytimes.com/2019/03/31 /us/school-uniform-unconstitutional.html

Meyer, A. (2019, September 19). Savannah-Chatham school board questions charter's empty seats. *Savannah Now.* https://www.savannahnow.com/news/20190918 /savannah-chatham-school-board-questions-charters-empty-seats

Mickelson, R., Bottia, M., & Southworth, S. (2008). *School choice and segregation by race, class, and achievement.* Education Policy Research Unit. http://nepc .colorado.edu/files/CHOICE-08-Mickelson-FINAL-EG043008.pdf

Minow, M. (2010). Confronting the seduction of choice: Law, education, and Amer- ican pluralism. *Yale Law Journal, 120,* 814.

Miron, G. (2008). The shifting notion of "publicness" in public education. In B. Cooper, J. Cibulka, & L. Fusarelli (Eds.), *Handbook of education politics and policy* (pp. 338–349). Routledge.

Miron, G. (2014). Charters should be expected to serve all kinds of students. *Education Next.* http://educationnext.org/charters-expected-serve-kinds-students/

Miron, G., Mathis, W. J., & Welner, K. G. (2015). *Review of separating fact & fiction: What you need to know about charter schools.* National Education Policy Center. https://nepc.colorado.edu/thinktank/review-separating-fact-and-fiction

Miron, G., & Nelson, C. (2002). *What's public about charter schools?: Lessons learned about choice and accountability.* Corwin.

Miron, G., Urschel, J. L., Mathis, W, J., & Tornquist, E. (2010, February 5). *Schools without diversity: Education management organizations, charter schools and the demographic stratification of the American school system.* National Education Policy Center. https://nepc.colorado.edu/publication/schools-without-diversity

Miron, G., Urschel, J. L., & Saxton, N. (2011). What makes KIPP work? A study of student characteristics, attrition, and school finance. *National Center for the Study of Privatization in Education.* https://ncspe.tc.columbia.edu/working-papers/OP195_3.pdf

Mitchum, P., & Moodie-Mills, A. C. (2014). *Beyond bullying: How hostile school climate perpetuates the school-to-prison pipeline for LGBT youth.* Center for American Progress. https://www.americanprogress.org/issues/lgbtq-rights/reports/2014/02/27/84179/beyond-bullying/

Mock, B. (2010, October 6). New Orleans accused of failing disabled students. *Newsweek.* http://www.newsweek.com/new-orleans-accused-failing-disabled-students-73991

Molnar, A., Miron, G., Elgeberi, N., Barbour, M. K., Huerta, L., Shafer, S. R., & Rice, J. K. (2019). *Virtual schools in the U.S. 2019.* National Education Policy Center. http://nepc.colorado.edu/publication/virtual-schools-annual-2019

Molnar, A., Miron, G., Gulosino, C., Shank, C., Davidson, C., Barbour, M. K., Huerta, L., Shafter, S. R., Rice, J. K., & Nitkin, D. (2017). *Virtual Schools Report 2017.* National Education Policy Center. https://nepc.colorado.edu/publication/virtual-schools-annual-2017

Mommandi, W., & Welner, K. (2018). Shaping charter enrollment and access. In I. Rothberg, & J. Glazer (Eds.), *Choosing charters: Better schools or more segregation?* (pp. 61–81). Teachers College Press.

Monument Academy. (n.d.). *Home.* http://www.monumentacademy.org/

Mooney, J. (2014, September 29). *Explainer: Getting inside the Urban Hope Act—and "renaissance schools."* NJ Spotlight. https://www.njspotlight.com/stories/14/09/29/explainer-getting-inside-the-urban-hope-act-and-renaissance-schools/

Moore, L. (2015, February 12). Should some students repeat grades? Academic State Champs' Three Oaks Academy says yes. *Muskegon News.* https://www.mlive.com/news/muskegon/index.ssf/2015/02/should_some_students_repeat_gr.html

Morgan, Z. (2019, June 26). *BCS' Bullis-Purissima enrollment preference set to return.* Los Altos Online. https://www.losaltosonline.com/news/sections/schools/209-school-news/60343-bcs-bullis-purissima-enrollment-preference-set-to-return

Morris, R. (2011, November 19). *French-immersion charter schools dispute allegation that their admissions favor the wealthy.* Uptown Messenger. http://uptownmessenger.com/2011/11/audubon-charter-school-november-board-meeting/

Morton, N. (2019, June 7). More charters to close in Western Washington, citing dwindling enrollment. *Seattle Times.* https://www.seattletimes.com/education-lab/two-more-washington-state-charter-schools-to-close-citing-dwindling-enrollment/

Murphy, J. (2015, November 19). *Audit faults Infinity Charter School for preferential enrollment policy.* Penn Live. http://www.pennlive.com/politics/index.ssf/2015/11/audit_faults_infinity_charter.html

My School DC. (n.d.). *DC residency requirements.* http://www.myschooldc.org/enroll/dc-residency-requirements

Nathan, J. (1996a). *Charter schools: Creating hope and opportunity for American education.* Jossey-Bass.

Nathan, J. (1996b). Possibilities, problems, and progress: Early lessons from the charter movement. *Phi Delta Kappan, 78*(1), 18–23.

National Alliance for Public Charter Schools. (2014a). *What is a public charter school?* https://www.publiccharters.org/sites/default/files/migrated/wp-content/uploads/2014/04/What-is-a-Charter-School.pdf

National Alliance for Public Charter Schools. (2014b). *Charter schools work for families.* https://www.publiccharters.org/sites/default/files/migrated/wp-content/uploads/2014/04/Charter-Schools-Work-for-Families.pdf

National Alliance for Public Charter Schools. (2016). *Backfilling in charter schools.* http://www.publiccharters.org/publications/backfilling-in-charter-schools/

National Alliance for Public Charter Schools. (2017). *Estimated charter public school enrollment, 2016–17.* https://www.publiccharters.org/sites/default/files/migrated/wp-content/uploads/2017/01/EER_Report_V5.pdf

National Alliance for Public Charter Schools. (2018). *Clear student enrollment and lottery procedures.* https://www.publiccharters.org/our-work/charter-law-database/components/12

National Alliance for Public Charter Schools. (2020, March 10). *2019 annual report.* https://www.publiccharters.org/our-work/publications/2019-annual-report

National Association for the Advancement of Colored People. (2017). *Task force on quality education hearing report.* https://www.naacp.org/wp-content/uploads/2017/07/Task_ForceReport_final2.pdf

National Association of Charter School Authorizers. (2018). *Principles and standards for quality charter school authorizing.* https://files.eric.ed.gov/fulltext/ED595188.pdf

National Charter School Resource Center. (n.d.). *What is a charter school?* https://charterschoolcenter.ed.gov/what-is-a-charter-school

National Council on Disability. (2018, November 15). *Charter schools—Implications for students with disabilities.* https://ncd.gov/sites/default/files/NCD_Charter-Schools-Report_508_0.pdf

National Women's Law Center. (2018, April). *Dress coded: Black girls, bodies, and bias in D.C. schools.* https://nwlc-ciw49tixgw5lbab.stackpathdns.com/wp-content/uploads/2018/04/Final_nwlc_DressCodeReport.pdf

Network for Public Education. (2017). *Charters and consequences: An investigative series.* https://networkforpubliceducation.org/wp-content/uploads/2017/11/NPE-Report-Charters-and-Consequences.pdf

New Jersey State Auditor. (2018). *City of Camden school district.* https://www.njleg.state.nj.us/legislativepub/Auditor/341017.pdf

New Vision K–8 Charter School. (2021). *Enrollment.* https://www.newvisioncharterschool.org/page/enrollment

New York City Charter School Center. (2014, October 9). *NYC Charter School Center kicks off multilingual campaign focusing on English language learners* [Press release]. https://web.archive.org/web/20141108190217/http://www.nyccharterschools.org/content/public-awareness-campaign-ells

Nichols-Barrer, I., Gleason, P., Gill, B., & Tuttle, C. C. (2016). Student selection, attrition, and replacement in KIPP middle schools. *Educational Evaluation and Policy Analysis, 38*(1), 5–20.

Nobles, W., III. (2018a, December 19). Months after Einstein bus dispute, parents still fighting for transit refunds. *Nola.* https://www.nola.com/news/article_7204ca03-2eae-55da-9f14-c12bf3a042c6.html

Nobles, W. P., III. (2018b, March 02). Charter schools battle OPSB over buses as students struggle to get to class. *The Times-Picayune*. http://www.nola.com /education/index.ssf/2018/03/einstein_student_transportatio.html

Noguera, P. (2015, June 29). Why don't we have real data on charter schools? *The Nation*. https://www.thenation.com/article/why-dont-we-have-real-data -charter-schools/

NOLA Public Schools. (2020). *Common enrollment*. https://enrollnola.org/about /enrollnola-oneapp/

Noltemeyer, A. L., Ward, R. M., & Mcloughlin, C. (2015). Relationship between school suspension and student outcomes: A meta-analysis. *School Psychology Review*, 44(2), 224–240.

Northwestern Lehigh School District. (2016). *Notice of intent not to renew*. http:// www.boarddocs.com/pa/nwlsd/Board.nsf/files/A9854307C17B/%24file /NOTICE%20OF%20INTENT%20TO%20NOT%20RENEW-1.pdf

Oakes, J. (2005). *Keeping track: How schools structure inequality* (2nd ed.). Yale University Press.

Of the Morning Call. (2016, June 16). *Circle of Seasons charter school will stay open, school board decides*. http://www.mcall.com/news/local/northwestern /mc-northwestern-lehigh-school-board-meeting-20160615-story.html

Offenhartz, J. (2019, February 27). *State finds Success Academy violated civil rights of disabled students*. Gothamist. https://gothamist.com/news /state-finds-success-academy-violated-civil-rights-of-disabled-students

Office of the State Superintendent of Education. (2017). *State of discipline: 2016– 17 school year*. https://osse.dc.gov/sites/default/files/dc/sites/osse/page_content /attachments/2016-17%20School%20Year%20Discipline%20Report.pdf

Olabi, N. (2018, March 23). *Thornton charter school faces sexual harassment, discrimination complaints*. Westword. http://www.westword.com/news /stargate-charter-school-settles-federal-sexual-harassment-and-disability -discrimination-complaints-10104305

Orfield, G. (2018). Great schools perpetuating inequality. In G. Orfield & J. B. Ayscue (Eds.), *Discrimination in elite public schools: Investigating Buffalo* (pp. 9–35). Teachers College Press.

Orfield, M., & Luce, T. (2013). *Charter schools in the Twin Cities: 2013 update*. Institute on Metropolitan Opportunity. http://www.law.umn.edu/sites/law.umn .edu/files/newsfiles/579fd7a6/Charter-School-Update-2013-final.pdf

Ortiz, A. (2018, February 1). *Parents upset over Las Vegas charter school changes*. KTNV. https://www.ktnv.com/news/parents-upset-over-charter-school-changes

Ou, S., & Reynolds, A. J. (2010). Grade retention, postsecondary education, and public aid receipt. *Educational Evaluation and Policy Analysis*, 32, 118–139.

Pacific Collegiate School. (n.d.). *Home*. http://www.pacificcollegiate.com

Palm Beach Post. (2013, October 8). *Is the principal right to force parents to Saturday School?* https://web.archive.org/web/20150929030024 /http://opinionzone.blog.palmbeachpost.com/2013/10/08/is-principal-right -to-force-parents-to-saturday-school/

Palmer, J. (2019, June 26). Former Epic teachers describe pressure to manipulate enrollment. *Oklahoma Watch*. https://oklahomawatch.org/2019/06/26 /former-epic-teachers-describe-pressure-to-manipulate-enrollment/

Parcel, T. L., & Dufur, M. J. (2001). Capital at home and at school: Effects on student achievement. *Social Forces, 79*(3), 881–912.

Patrick Henry School of Science and Arts. (n.d.) *Admissions.* http://www.patrickhenrycharter.org/admissions.html

Patriot Preparatory Academy. (2020). *Annual Report.* https://www.patriotprep.com/Downloads/Annual%20Report%20for%20PPA%20(2019-2020)3.pdf

Pattison-Gordon, J. (2016, March 09). State calls out 5 Boston schools for disparate & excessive suspensions. *The Bay State Banner.* https://www.baystatebanner.com/2016/06/29/state-calls-out-5-boston-schools-for-disparate-excessive-suspensions/

Pedroni, T. C. (2007). *Market movements: African American involvement in school voucher reform.* Routledge.

Pelto, J. (2015, January 5). How the corporate education reform industry buys elections. *The Progressive.* http://progressive.org/magazine/corporate-education-reform-industry-buys-elections/

Pembroke Pines Charter Schools. (2018). *2017–2018 orientation.* http://academicvillage.pinescharter.net/DocumentCenter/View/519/Orientation-Packet-17-18?bidId=

Pennington, M. (2014). *Three things to know about Philadelphia's school budget: Debt, pensions, and safety.* https://www.sayanythingblog.com/entry/three-things-to-know-about-philadelphias-school-budget-debt-pensions-and-safety/

Pennsylvania Department of Education. (2009). *Enrollment of students (circular).* https://www.education.pa.gov/Policy-Funding/BECS/Purdons/Pages/Enrollment Students.aspx

Performance Academies. (2021a). *About us.* https://www.performanceacademies.com/about-us/

Performance Academies. (2021b). *Application for enrollment.* https://www.performanceacademies.com/wp-content/uploads/2021/04/21-22-CPA-APP.pdf

Petrilli, M. (2014, December 11). Charters can do what's best for students who care. *The New York Times.* https://www.nytimes.com/roomfordebate/2014/12/10/are-charter-schools-cherry-picking-students/charters-can-do-whats-best-for-students-who-care

Petrimoulx, D. (2016, May 11). *Charter school apologizes for recruiting mailer.* Arkansas Matters. https://www.kark.com/news/charter-school-apologizes-for-recruiting-mailer/

Phenice, C. (2016, November 2). *No longer the schools of Trump's youth, military academies focus on college prep, character.* The 74. https://www.the74million.org/article/no-longer-the-schools-of-trumps-youth-military-academies-focus-on-college-prep-character/

Phillippo, K. (2019). *A contest without winners: How students experience competitive school choice.* University of Minnesota Press.

Phillips, A. (2019a, March 27). How a couple worked charter school regulations to make millions. *Los Angeles Times.* https://www.latimes.com/local/education/la-me-edu-charter-schools-20190327-htmlstory.html

Phillips, A. (2019b, March 28). Small districts reap big profits by approving charter schools with little oversight. *Los Angeles Times.* https://www.latimes.com/local education/la-me-edu-charter-school-fees-20190328-story.html

Pondiscio, R. (2019a, September 9). *Success Academy does "screen" students, but not the way you might think. Chalkbeat.* http://www.chalkbeat .com/posts/ny/2019/09/10/success-academy-does-screen-its-students-its-not -in-the-way-you-might-think/

Pondisco, R. (2019b). *How the other half learns: Equality, excellence, and the battle over school choice.* Random House.

Popadin, S. (2016, October 6). *Success specializes in empty seats.* United Federation of Teachers. http://www.uft.org/news-stories/success-specializes-empty-seats

Potter, D., & Roksa, J. (2013). Accumulating advantages over time: Family experiences and social class inequality in academic achievement. *Social science research, 42*(4), 1018–1032.

Potter, H., & Nunberg, M. (2019). *Scoring states on charter school integration.* Century Foundation. https://tcf.org/content/report/scoring-states-charter-school -integration/

Potter, H., & Tegeler P. (2016, February 4). *Charter schools, gentrification, and weighted lotteries.* Shelterforce. http://www.shelterforce.org/article/4288 /charter_schools_gentrification_and_weighted_lotteries/

Preston, C., Goldring, E., Berends, M., & Cannata, M. (2012). School innovation in district context: Comparing traditional public schools and charter schools. *Economics of Education Review, 31*(2), 318–330.

Prothero, A. (2014, December 5). "Mystery parents" test charters' enrollment of Spec. Ed., ELL students. *Education Week.* https://www.edweek.org/ew /articles/2014/12/05/mystery-parents-test-charters-enrollment-of-spec.html

Prothero, A. (2017, December 13). Charter schools that charge illegal fees. How pervasive is the problem? *Education Week.* http://blogs.edweek.org/edweek /charterschoice/2017/07/charter_schools_charging_illegal_fees.html

Quick, K. (2018). *Denver School of Science and Technology: Students of all backgrounds are preparing for one bright future.* The Century Foundation. https:// tcf.org/content/report/denver-school-science-technology/

Raghavendran, B. (2016, September 6). Diversity of languages among Minnesota's school children is growing. *Star Tribune.* http://www.startribune.com /hola-look-up-your-school-district-s-student-language-diversity/392194281/

Rau, A. B. (2017, Nov. 5). Richest schools get richer in Arizona's results-based funding program. *Arizona Republic.* https://www.azcentral.com/story/news/politics /arizona-education/2017/11/05/arizona-doug-ducey-performance-based-funding -boosts-higher-income-schools/782439001/

Rausch, M. K., Conlan, S., Brooks-Uy, V., & Smith, N. (2018). *A look at Massachusetts Board of Elementary and Secondary Education: Case study analysis for the Quality Practice Project.* National Association of Charter School Authorizers (NACSA). http://www.quality charters.org/research /qualitypractice-project/

Reardon, S. F. (2011). The widening academic achievement gap between the rich and the poor: New evidence and possible explanations. In G. Duncan & R. Murnane (Eds.), *Whither opportunity? Rising inequality, schools, and children's life chances* (pp. 91–117). Russell Sage Foundation.

Research for Action. (2019, November). *Equity focused charter school authorizing toolkit.* https://www.researchforaction.org/publications/equity-focused-charter -school-authorizing-toolkit/

Rhim, L. M., & Lancet, S. (2018). *How personalized learning models can meet the needs of students with disabilities: Thrive Public Schools case study.* Center for Reinventing Public Education. https://www.crpe.org/sites/default/files/crpe-case-study-thrive.pdf

Rhim, L. M., & McLaughlin, M. J. (2001). Special Education in American Charter Schools: State level policy, practices and tensions. *Cambridge Journal of Education, 31*(3), 373–383.

Rhodes, D. (2018a, April 3). Culture shock: Teachers call Noble charters "dehumanizing." NPR Illinois. http://nprillinois.org/post/culture-shock-teachers-call-noble-charters-dehumanizing

Rhodes, D. (2018b, April 30). *Feedback: Noble charter schools story hit a nerve.* NPR Illinois. http://nprillinois.org/post/feedback-noble-charter-schools-story-hit-nerve#stream/0

Rice, L. (2017, August 24). *UNO charter network rebrands as Acero schools, asks to rename 5 campuses.* DNA Info. https://www.dnainfo.com/chicago/20170824/rogers-park/uno-name-change-acero-what-does-it-mean-steel-charter-school-network/

Rich, M. (2016, March 16). Charter schools suspend Black and disabled students more, study says. *The New York Times.* http://www.nytimes.com/2016/03/17/us/charter-schools-suspend-black-and-disabled-students-more-study-says.html

Richards, J. S. (2010, November, 8). Charter's ties to Christian school draw state scrutiny. *The Columbus Dispatch.* https://www.dispatch.com/article/20101108/news/311089682

ROADS Charter High Schools. (n.d.). *Home.* http://roadsschools.org/

Robles, Y. (2019, February 7). Aurora seeks to close charter school, saying it is failing special needs students. Chalkbeat. https://www.chalkbeat.org/posts/co/2019/02/06/aurora-seeks-to-close-charter-school-saying-it-is-failing-special-needs-students/

Rocco, D. (2016, February 6). *Mast charter school holds competitive lottery to determine admission.* CBS Philly. http://philadelphia.cbslocal.com/2016/02/16/mast-charter-school-holds-competitive-lottery-to-determine-admission/

Roda, A., & Wells, A. S. (2012). School choice policies and racial segregation: Where White parents' good intentions, anxiety, and privilege collide. *American Journal of Education, 119*(2), 261–293.

Roderick, M. (1994). Grade retention and school dropout: Investigating the association. *American Educational Research Journal, 31*(4), 729–759.

Rogers, J., Mirra, N., Seltzer, M., & Jun, J. (2014). *It's about time: Learning time and educational opportunity in California high schools.* UCLA IDEA.

Roksa, J., & Potter, D. (2011). Parenting and academic achievement: Intergenerational transmission of educational advantage. *Sociology of Education, 84*(4), 299–321.

Romero, F. (2018, October 1). *LA's first common application system launches for independent charter schools.* LA School Report. http://laschoolreport.com/las-first-common-application-system-launches-for-independent-charter-schools/

Rowe, E. E., & Lubienski, C. (2017). Shopping for schools or shopping for peers: Public schools and catchment area segregation. *Journal of Education Policy, 32*(3), 340–356.

Rubenstein, G. (2018, July 5). *Success Academy left back (at least) 1/6 of their first cohort.* https://garyrubinstein.wordpress.com/2018/07/05/success-academy-left-back-at-least-1-6-of-their-first-cohort/

Rubenstein, G. (2020, August 16). *Success Academy quietly settles discrimina-tion lawsuit and pays families $1.1 million.* https://garyrubinstein.wordpress.com/2020/08/16/success-academy-quietly-settles-discrimination-lawsuit-and-pays-families-1-1-million-plus-lawyers-fees/

Ruggiero, A. (2016, August 2). Livermore: Pricey private academy, charter school to share same site. *San Jose Mercury News.* http://www.mercurynews.com/2016/08/02/livermore-pricey-private-academy-charter-school-to-share-same-site/

Russell, B. (2015, May 22). Idaho public charter schools discriminate against students of color, complaint says. *The Spokesman Review.* http://www.spokesman.com/stories/2015/may/22/idaho-public-charter-schools-discriminate-against/

Sattin-Bajaj, C. (2018, October). *It's hard to separate choice from transportation.* Urban Institute. https://www.urban.org/sites/default/files/publication/99246/school_transportation_policy_in_practice_0.pdf

Sattin-Bajaj, C., & Roda, A. (2018). Opportunity hoarding in school choice contexts: The role of policy design in promoting middle-class parents' exclusionary behaviors. *Educational Policy*, 1–44.

Schlemmer, L. (n.d.). *Controversial town-run charter schools may spread, with access to state pensions.* WUNC. https://www.wunc.org/post/controversial-town-run-charter-schools-may-spread-access-state-pensions

Schneider, M., & Buckley, J. (2002). What do parents want from schools? Evidence from the Internet. *Educational Evaluation and Policy Analysis*, 24(2), 133–144.

Schneider, M., Teske, P., & Marschall, M. (2000). *Choosing schools: Consumer choice and the quality of American schools.* Princeton University Press.

Schneider, M., Teske, P., Roch, C., & Marschall, M. (1997). Networks to nowhere: Segregation and stratification in networks of information about schools. *American Journal of Political Science*, 41(4), 1201–1223.

Schoenberg, S. (2019, January 7). Charter schools enrolling more English language learners, students with disabilities, state says. MassLive. www.masslive.com/politics/index.ssf/2015/10/charter_schools_enrolling_more.html

School District of Philadelphia. (2021). *Fast facts.* http://www.philasd.org/fast-facts/

School District of Philadelphia. (2017). *2017–2018 charter school applications.* https://web.archive.org/web/20170601165729/http://webgui.phila.k12.pa.us/offices/c/charter_schools/charter-school-applications-for-sy-2017-18

School District of Philadelphia. (2017). *Renaissance schools.* https://www.philasd.org/charterschools/portal/renaissance/

School District of Philadelphia, Charter Schools Office. (2018). *Current notices.* https://web.archive.org/web/20190505144216/https://www.philasd.org/charterschools/current-notices-2017-ace/

Schott Foundation. (n.d.). *Welcome Chartlerland.* http://schottfoundation.org/infographic/welcome-charterland

Scott, J. (2008). Managers of choice: Race, gender, and the political ideology of the "new" urban school leadership. In W. Feinberg & C. Lubienski (Eds.), *School choice policies and outcomes: Philosophical and empirical perspectives on limits to choice in liberal democracies* (pp. 149–176). State University of New York Press.

Sernoffsky, E. (2017, June 20). District yanks Oakland K-8 school's charter. *SF Gate.* https://www.sfgate.com/news/article/District-yanks-Oakland-K-8-school-s-charter-11233521.php

Shapiro, B., & Wysong, C. (2015). *Charter school enrollment in Illinois: Ensuring that admissions practices welcome all students.* Equip for Equality. http://www.equipforequality.org/wp-content/uploads/2015/08/Enrollment-Practice-Across-Illinois.pdf

Shaw-Amoah, A., & Lapp, D. (2018, December). *Students experiencing homelessness in Pennsylvania: Under-identification and inequitable enrollment.* Research for Action. https://www.researchforaction.org/publications/students-experiencing-homelessness-in-pennsylvania-under-identification-and-inequitable-enrollment/

Shibata, K. (2017, September 12). *Noble charter school community demands respect for students and teachers.* Illinois Federation of Teachers.

Shollenberger, T. (2015). Racial disparities in school suspension and subsequent outcomes. In D. Losen (Ed.), *Closing the school discipline gap: Equitable remedies for excessive exclusion* (pp. 31–42). Teachers College Press.

Siegel-Hawley, G., & Frankenberg, E. (2016, January 5). *Review of "The integration anomaly: Comparing the effect of K-12 education delivery models on segregation in schools."* National Education Policy Center. http://nepc.colorado.edu/thinktank/review-integration

Simon, S. (2013, February 15). Special report: Class struggle how charter school get students they want. *Reuters.* http://www.reuters.com/article/us-usa-charters-admissions idUSBRE91E0HF20130215

Simpson, K. (2012, March 8). Colorado legislature, school districts debate effectiveness of having struggling students repeat a grade. *Denver Post.* https://www.denverpost.com/2012/03/08/colorado-legislature-school-districts-debate-effectiveness-of-having-struggling-students-repeat-a-grade

Sinkkink, D., & Emerson, M. (2007). School choice and racial segregation in US schools: The role of parents' education." *Ethnic and Racial Studies, 31*(2), 267–293.

Smith, J., Wohlstetter, P., Kuzin, C. A., & De Pedro, K. (2011). Parent involvement in urban charter schools: New strategies for increasing participation. *School Community Journal, 21*(1), 71.

Smith, M. (2013, November 3). Debating new charter schools, their policies and their effects. *The New York Times.* https://www.nytimes.com/2013/11/08/us/debating-new-charter-schools-their-policies-and-their-effects.html

Southern Poverty Law Center. (2010, October 25). *P.B., et al. v. Pastorek.* https://www.splcenter.org/seeking-justice/case-docket/pb-et-al-v-pastorek

Southern Poverty Law Center. (2014, December 19). *SPLC negotiates landmark settlement to help New Orleans students with disabilities* [Press release]. https://www.splcenter.org/news/2014/12/19/splc-negotiates-landmark-settlement-help-new-orleans-students-disabilities

Spectrum News Staff. (2018, January 17). *New website for applying to Rochester charter schools.* Spectrum News. http://spectrumlocalnews.com/nys/rochester/education/2018/01/17/new-website-for-applying-to-rochester-charter-schools

Spillane, N. K., Kaminsky, S. E., Lynch, S. J., Ross, K. M., Means, B. M., & Han, E. M. (2013). *Denver School of Science and Technology, Stapleton High School: A case study of an inclusive STEM-focused high school in Denver, Colorado.* https://ospri.research.gwu.edu/sites/g/files/zaxdzs2456/f/downloads/OSPrI_Report_2013-03.pdf

SRI International. (1997). *Evaluation of charter school effectiveness.* Author.

Stearns, E., Moller, S., Blau, J., & Potochnick, S. (2007). Staying back and dropping out: The relationship between grade retention and school dropout. *Sociology of Education, 80*(3), 210–240.

Stein, P. (2018, February 07). D.C. charter school enrollment has slight bump, while public schools show slight drop. *Washington Post.* https://www.washingtonpost .com/local/education/dc-charter-school-enrollment-has-slight-enrollment -bump-while-public-schools-show-slight-drop/2018/02/07/deec4f28-0c12 -11e8-8b0d-891602206fb7_story.html?utm_term=.442e2c1c9c24

Stroud, J. (2016, October 26). Carbondale charter school aims to increase minority enrollment. *Post Independent.* http://www.postindependent.com/news/local /carbondale-charter-school-aims-to-increase-minority-enrollment/

Sullivan, M. (2016, May 23). What are BASIS charter schools and how are they rewriting the education rules? *Forbes.* https://www.forbes.com/sites/maureensullivan /2016/05/23/what-are-basis-charter-schools-and-how-did-they-rewrite-the -education-rules/#158e5bfcf9ca

Sylvanie Williams College Prep. (2018). *Family handbook.* https://drive.google.com /file/d/0By9vH_0ZnTf6aXkycmFiZEVBZ3M/view

Tan, S. (2015, May 10). High number of expulsions at Western New York Maritime charter school draw questions. *Buffalo News.* http://buffalonews .com/2015/05/10/high-number-of-expulsions-at-western-new-york-maritime -charter-school-draw-questions/

Tanimura, J. (2011). Still separate and still unequal: The need for stronger civil rights protections in charter-enabling legislation. *Southern California Review of Law and Social Justice, 21,* 399–429.

Taylor, K. (2015, October 15). At a Success Academy charter school, singling out pupils who have "got to go." *The New York Times.* http://www.nytimes.com/2015/10/30 /nyregion/at-a-success-academy-charter-school-singling-out-pupils-who-have -got-to-go.html

Tedesco, J., & Webb, S. (2019, November 19). Denied again: Charter schools lag in special education. *Houston Chronicle.* https://www.houstonchronicle.com /news/houston-texas/houston/article/Texas-Charter-schools-denied-special -education-14837752.php#container

Texas Education Agency. (n.d.). *Grade level retention.* https://tea.texas.gov/acctres /retention_index.html

The City School. (2017). *Annual giving campaign.* https://citycharterschools.org/tcs/support/

Thernstrom, A., & Thernstrom, S. (2003). *No excuses: Closing the racial gap in learning.* Simon & Schuster.

Tilly, C. (1998). *Durable inequality.* University of California Press.

Times Editorial Board. (2016, August 10). Editorial: The bias inherent in some charter schools' admissions process. *Los Angeles Times.* http://www.latimes.com /opinion/editorials/la-ed-charter-application-20160808-snap-story.html

Trillhaase, M. (2015, May). Charter schools leaving many Idaho kids behind. *Lewiston Tribune.* http://media.spokesman.com/documents/2015/05/Charter _schools_leaving_many_Idaho_kids_behind.pdf

Tuchman, S., Campbell, C., & Heyward, G. (2018). *Are Washington charter public schools serving students with disabilities?* Center for Reinventing Public Education. https://www.crpe.org/publications/washington-charter-public-schools -serving-students-disabilities

Tuttle, C. C., Gleason, P., & Clark, M. (2012). Using lotteries to evaluate schools of choice: Evidence from a national study of charter schools. *Economics of Education Review, 31,* 237–253.

Tuttle, C. C., Teh, B. R., Nichols-Barrer, I., Gill, B. P., & Gleason, P. (2010). *Student characteristics and achievement in 22 KIPP middle schools.* Mathematica Policy Research.

Twin Peaks Charter Academy. (2020). *TCPA fee schedule.* https://www .twinpeakscharter.org/newpagefc543054

Uncommon Schools. (2020, December 17). *Update on our DEI commitments.* https://uncommonschools.org/letter-to-community/

University Schools. (n.d.). *Application for admission.* https://drive.google.com /file/d/0B6jy-_ymJ6lPOTlydHZ2N1dFWlU/view

U.S. Census Bureau. (2014). *2010–2014 ACS 5-year estimates ward 5.* https://planning .dc.gov/node/1181211

U.S. Department of Education. (2014, November 26). *Letter: Harmony public schools.* https://www2.ed.gov/documents/press-releases/harmony-public -schools-letter.pdf

U.S. Department of Education. (2016, December 28). *Know your rights: Students with disabilities in charter schools.* https://sites.ed.gov/idea/files/dcl-factsheet -201612-504-charter-school.pdf

U.S. Department of Education, Office of Civil Rights. (2014, May 8). *Dear colleague letter.* https://www2.ed.gov/about/offices/list/ocr/letters/colleague-201405.pdf

U.S. Department of Education, Office of Civil Rights. (2015, September 30). *Noah Webster basic school OCR case number 08-15-1156.* https://www2.ed.gov /about/offices/list/ocr/docs/investigations/more/08151156-a.pdf

U.S. Department of Education, Office of Civil Rights. (2016 December, 28). *Dear colleague letter.* https://www2.ed.gov/about/offices/list/ocr/letters/colleague -201612-504-charter-school.pdf

U.S. Department of Education & Office of the Inspector General. (2018). *Nationwide Audit of Oversight of Closed Charter Schools.* https://www.oversight.gov /sites/default/files/oig-reports/a02m0011.pdf

U.S. News and World Report. (2017). *Charter School of Wilmington.* https://www .usnews.com/education/best-high-schools/search?name=charter%20 school%20of%20wilmington

Up North Progressive. (2014, December 6). *Tea Party charter school.* http://www .upnorthprogressive.com/2014/11/23/tea-party-charter-school/

Valant, J., & Lincove, A. (2018, March 16). The barriers that make charters inaccessible to disadvantaged families. *Brookings.* https://www.brookings.edu/blog /brown-center-chalkboard/2018/03/16/the-barriers-that-make-charter-schools -inaccessible-to-disadvantaged-families/

Vasquez Heilig, J. (2018). *NEPC review: "Bigger bang, fewer bucks?"* National Education Policy Center. http://nepc.colorado.edu/thinktank/review-roi

Veiga, C. (2018, March 8). *Few Black and Hispanic students receive admissions offers to New York City's top high schools—again.* Chalkbeat. https://www .chalkbeat.org/posts/ny/2018/03/07/few-black-and-hispanic-students-receive -admissions-offers-to-new-york-citys-top-high-schools-again/

Villavicencio, A. (2013). "It's our best choice right now": Examining the choice options of charter school parents. *Education Policy Analysis Archives, 21*(81), 1–23.

Vogell, H. (2017, October 6). *For-profit schools reward students for referrals and Facebook endorsements.* ProPublica. https://www.propublica.org/article/for-profit-schools-reward-students-for-referrals-and-facebook-endorsements

Vogell, H., & Fresques, H. (2017, February 21). *"Alternative" education: Using charter schools to hide dropouts and game the system.* ProPublica. https://www.propublica.org/article/alternative-education-using-charter-schools-hide-dropouts-and-game-system

Waanders, C., Mendez, J. L., & Downer, J. T. (2007). Parent characteristics, economic stress, and neighborhood context as predictors of parent involvement in preschool children's education. *Journal of School Psychology, 45*(6), 619–636.

Waitoller, F. R., Maggin, D. M., & Trzaska, A. (2017). A longitudinal comparison of enrollment patterns of students receiving special education in urban neighborhood and charter schools. *Journal of Disability Policy Studies, 28*(1), 3–12.

Wall, P. (2018a, August 30). *Students with disabilities improperly suspended at Newark's largest charter school network, complaint says.* Chalkbeat. https://www.chalkbeat.org/posts/newark/2018/08/30/students-with-disabilities-improperly-suspended-at-newarks-largest-charter-school-network-complaint-says/

Wall, P. (2018b, August 31). *Newark charter school faces firestorm after kicking out students for dress code violations.* Chalkbeat. https://www.chalkbeat.org/posts/newark/2018/08/31/newark-charter-school-faces-firestorm-after-kicking-out-students-for-dress-code-violations/

Walters, C. R. (2018). The demand for effective charter schools. *Journal of Political Economy, 126*(6), 2179–2223.

Wamba, N. G., & Ascher, C. (2003). An examination of charter school equity. *Education and Urban Society, 35*(4), 462–476.

Wang, S. (2018, June 14). *Known for "no excuses" discipline, Tindley charter network loosens policies to reduce suspensions.* Chalkbeat. https://www.chalkbeat.org/posts/in/2018/06/14/known-for-no-excuses-discipline-tindley-charter-network-loosens-policies-to-reduce-suspensions/

Warner, J. (2016, September 27). *Gap co-founder Doris Fisher is bankrolling the charter school agenda—and pouring dark money into CA politics.* Capital & Main. https://capitalandmain.com/gap-co-founder-doris-fisher-is-bankrolling-the-charter-school-agenda-and-pouring-dark-money-into-ca-politics

Washington Latin Public Charter School. (n.d.). *Dress code.* https://web.archive.org/web/20141218063408/https://latinpcs.org/wp-content/uploads/2014/09/Dress-Code-v2.pdf

Watson, S., Waslander, S., & Strathdee, M. (1999). *Trading in futures: Why markets in education don't work.* McGraw-Hill Education.

Webb, S. (2017, July 5). Some KIPP Houston schools charged unallowable fees, agency finds. *Houston Chronicle.* https://www.houstonchronicle.com/news/education/article/KIPP-schools-collected-millions-in-unallowable-11257006.php

Weiher, G., & Tedin, K. (2002). Does choice lead to racially distinctive schools? Charter schools and household preferences. *Journal of Policy Analysis and Management, 21*(1), 79–92.

Weiler, S. C., & Vogel, L. R. (2015). Charter school barriers: Do enrollment requirements limit student access to charter schools? *Equity & Excellence in Education, 48*(1), 36–48.

Wells, A. S., Artiles, L., Carnochan, S., Cooper, C. W., Grutzik, C., Holme, J. J., Lopez, A., Scott, J., Slayton, J., & Vasudeva, A. (1998). *Beyond the rhetoric of charter school reform: A study of ten California school districts*. UCLA Charter School Study.

Wells, A. S., & Serna, I. (1996). The politics of culture: Understanding local political resistance to detracking in racially mixed schools. *Harvard Educational Review, 66*(1), 93–118.

Welner, K. G. (2001). *Legal rights, local wrongs: When community control collides with educational equity*. State University of New York Press.

Welner, K. G. (2008). *NeoVouchers: The emergence of tuition tax credits for private schooling*. Rowan & Littlefield.

Welner, K. G. (2013). *The dirty dozen: How charter schools influence student enrollment*. Teachers College Record. https://nepc.colorado.edu/publication/TCR-Dirty-Dozen

Welner, K. G., & Howe, K. R. (2005). Steering toward separation: The policy and legal implications of "counseling" special education students away from choice schools. In J. Scott (Ed.), *School choice and student diversity: What the evidence says* (pp. 93–111). Teachers College Press.

West Ridge Academy. (n.d.). *Enrollment*. https://wrak8.org/enrollment/

Whitaker, H. C. (2018, February 18). *Religious-affiliation prohibition on charter schools in 20 USC § 722li* [Memorandum]. Department of Justice. https://cdn.vox-cdn.com/uploads/chorus_asset/file/21998288/Religious-Affiliation_Prohibition_on_Charter_Schools_Opinion_2.18.2020.0.pdf

Whitman, D. (2008). *Sweating the small stuff: Inner-city schools and the new paternalism*. Thomas B. Fordham Institute.

Whitmire, R. (2014). *Inside successful district-charter compacts*. Education Next. https://www.educationnext.org/inside-successful-district-charter-compacts/

Whitmire, R. (2015). *More middle-class families choose charters: A political game changer for public school choice*. Education Next. http://educationnext.org/middle-class-families-choose-charters/

Wiggs, J. (2017, August 12). Mystic Valley charter school eliminates controversial hair rules. *Boston Globe*. https://www.bostonglobe.com/metro/2017/08/11/mystic-valley-charter-school-eliminates-controversial-hair-rules/iRKY5eQ0S0EedNK9rSwqEM/story.html

Williams, J. (2018a, April 16). A third of New Orleans students don't get into one of their top 3 schools of choice. *The Advocate*. https://www.theadvocate.com/new_orleans/news/article_092f220e-418f-11e8-b0ef-4b0c406355eb.html

Williams, M. (2018b, May 02). This public charter school became the whitest in the KC district. It's trying to change. *The Kansas City Star*. http://www.kansascity.com/news/local/article209874119.html

Wilson, J. Q., & Kelling, G. L. (1982). The police and neighborhood safety: Broken windows. *Atlantic Monthly, 127*(2), 29–38.

Wilson, T. S., & Carlsen, R. L. (2016). School marketing as a sorting mechanism: A critical discourse analysis of charter school websites. *Peabody Journal of Education, 91*(1), 24–46.

Windle, G. (2018, July 19). *Franklin Towne accused of discriminating against special needs student*. Chalkbeat. http://thenotebook.org/articles/2018/07/19/franklin-towne-accused-of-discriminating-against-special-needs-student/

Winters, M. A. (2012). Measuring the effect of charter schools on public school student achievement in an urban environment: Evidence from New York City. *Economics of Education review, 31*(2), 293–301.

Wixom, M. (2018, January). *Charter schools: What rules are waived for charter schools*. Education Commission of the States. http://ecs.force.com/mbdata /mbquestNB2C?rep=CS1713

Wolfman-Arent. (2014, December 15). *Delaware school entrance assessments face tough test*. WHYY. https://whyy.org/articles/delaware-school-entrance -assessments-face-tough-test/

Wood, B. (2018, March 24). Charter school administrator is 'praying for a wall' to stop illegal immigration, while her diverse student must speak English and learn Western manners. *Salt Lake Tribune*. https://www.sltrib.com/news/education /2018/03/22/former-teacher-says-utah-charter-schools-racist-policies-include -punishing-students-for-speaking-their-native-languages/

Yamamura, K., & Kalb, L. (2015, January 29). California officials: Public schools cannot require parents to volunteer. *The Sacramento Bee*. http://www.sacbee .com/news/local/education/article8574137.html

Yonezawa, S., Wells, A. S., & Serna, I. (2002). Choosing tracks: "Freedom of choice" in de-tracking schools. *American Educational Research Journal, 39*, 37–67.

Yu Ming Charter School. (2017, December 14). *Board of directors meeting*. https:// www.yumingschool.org/wp-content/uploads/2017/12/Yu-Ming-Board-Meeting -Packet-for-12.14.17-rev.-1.pdf

Zetino, G. (2017). *Schools choosing students*. ACLU Arizona. https://www.acluaz .org/sites/default/files/field_documents/schools_choosing_students_web.pdf

Zimmer, R. W., Buddin, R., Smith, S. A., & Duffy, D. (2019). *Nearly three decades into the charter school movement, what has research told us about charter schools?* Annenberg Institute at Brown University. https://www.edworkingpapers .com/ai19-156

Zimmer, R. W., & Guarino, C. M. (2013). Is there empirical evidence that charter schools "push out" low-performing students? *Educational Evaluation and Policy Analysis, 35*(4), 461–480.

Zimmerman, A. (2019, April 23). Success Academy "dumped" elementary school student a precinct, suit charges. *The City*. https://www.thecity.nyc/2019/4/23/21211103 /success-academy-dumped-elementary-school-student-at-precinct-suit-charges

Zollers, N. (2000). Schools need rules when it comes to students with disabilities. *Education Week, 19*(25), 46.

Zollers, N. J., & Ramanathan, A. K. (1998). For-profit charter schools and students with disabilities: The sordid side of the business of schooling. *Phi Delta Kappan, 80*, 297–304.

Index

About the Authors

Wagma Mommandi is a PhD candidate in education policy at the University of Colorado Boulder School of Education. She is a former public school teacher.

Kevin Welner is a professor at the University of Colorado Boulder School of Education and School of Law (by courtesy), specializing in educational policy. He's also the director of the National Education Policy Center, housed at CU Boulder. He has authored or edited more than a dozen books and more than 100 articles and book chapters, including 2013's *Closing the Opportunity Gap* (coedited with Prudence Carter), 2019's law school casebook, *Education and the Law* (coauthored with Stuart Biegel and Bob Kim), and 2020's *Potential Grizzlies: Making the Nonsense Bearable*.